P9-AFN-101

In the Eye of the Beholder

In the Eye of the Beholder:
Critical Perspectives
in Popular Film and Television

edited by

**Gary R. Edgerton, Michael T. Marsden,
and Jack Nachbar**

Bowling Green State University Popular Press
Bowling Green, OH 43403

Permission is gratefully acknowledged for use of the following copy-righted material previously published and reprinted with permission of the Helen Dwight Reid Educational Foundation. Published by Heldref Publications, 1319 18th St. N.W., Washington, D.C. 20036-1802.

Chapter 4: "Flow, Genre, and the Television Text," by Gregory A. Waller, *Journal of Popular Film and Television* 16.1 (1988): 6-11.

Chapter 8: "Midnight S/excess: Cult Configurations of 'Feminity' and the Perverse," by Gaylyn Studlar, *Journal of Popular Film and Television* 17.1 (1989): 2-14.

Copyright © 1997 Bowling Green State University Popular Press

Library of Congress Cataloging-in-Publication Data
In the eye of the beholder : critical perspectives in popular film and
    television / edited by Gary R. Edgerton, Michael T. Marsden, and
    Jack Nachbar.
          p.   cm.
    Includes bibliographical references.
    ISBN 0-87972-753-5 (cloth). -- ISBN 0-87972-754-3 (pbk.)
    1. Motion pictures--Social aspects. 2. Television broadcsting--
Social aspects. I. Edgerton, Gary R. (Gary Richard), 1952-
II. Marsden, Michael T. III. Nachbar, John G.
PN1995.I565 1997
302.23'43--dc 21   97-14881
                                                          CIP

Cover design by Dumm Art

Contents

Introduction:
Film and Television Criticism in Cultural Context

Gary R. Edgerton, Michael T. Marsden, and Jack Nachbar

Film and television are subjects of intense study throughout higher education today. Popular culture has undergone a revolution during the last generation, progressing from a discipline at the margins that was reflexively treated with contempt to one of the most widespread and productive topic areas in the arts, humanities, and social sciences. The increased attention on film and television is clearly part of this overall acceptance and growing cachet now accorded popular culture in the academy.

Those of us specializing in sociocultural criticism, however, know the process of legitimation is not yet complete. Some scholarly traditionalists still stubbornly divide the world into high-, middle-, and lowbrow clusters, although challenges to an elitist view of culture have long ago liberated the way this seminal concept is used and understood. During the past twenty-five years, especially, sociocultural analysts have developed a wide array of critical views, ushering in more productive ways of thinking about and studying the popular tradition. Many of these critics are well represented in the selective bibliographies that compose the final two chapters of this volume.

The primary purpose of *In the Eye of the Beholder: Critical Perspectives in Popular Film and Television* is to provide a representative cross section of these outlooks, highlighting their heterogeneity, their critical strategies, and their main areas of interest. All of the scholarship included here is related in one way or another to the agenda that was established at the *Journal of Popular Film and Television* in 1971 to counterbalance the then current preoccupation with auteurism and film aesthetics. The intention of the editors was to broaden the literature to include the "public visions" of popular filmmakers, "box-office" and industrial factors, and the idea that a movie says as much about its audience as it contributes to the development of its art form. This critical view was developed to study motion pictures because of their vast popularity and widespread social influence, not despite these characteristics.

1

2 In the Eye of the Beholder

A sociocultural orientation to film and now television (beginning at the journal in 1978) has understandably matured and advanced in many diverse directions during the intervening years, but one elemental assumption remains: *The first allegiance of this genre of criticism is to the cultural context and not to the medium.* As basic as this premise is, it powerfully asserts that film and television are cultural products and forms of social knowledge. They are never neutral technologies, but only meaningful within their relationships to broader contexts, institutions, and discourses.

Also the *Journal of Popular Film and Television,* and the *Journal of Popular Culture* before it, have always been resolutely committed to the widest possible range of analytical views and techniques. These journals have consciously promoted a posture of *cultural pluralism,* resulting in an intricate web of often interconnected though diverse critical voices. Adhering to pluralism is far from unstructured and unsystematic, however; it is a frame of reference for understanding how film and television is studied from a popular cultural perspective: *This tradition holds that any cultural phenomena, including media, are far too complex to be adequately explained by any one all-encompassing theory. No theory or resulting methodology is sacrosanct, no matter how popular it may be at a given time.*

All theories are considered fluid, framing devices that are always subject to change and further refinement. Methodologies, the techniques for applying theories and conducting criticism, are likewise regarded as processes to be used, adapted, revised, or combined as is warranted by each new research question. Some theories and methods have, of course, been preferred over others in the development of popular film and television scholarship; variants of genre, sociocultural, institutional, feminist, and political criticism are all commonplace. Still the key is that the specific research question should determine the approach, not the other way around. An overfastidiousness in utilizing methods, moreover, usually signals a breakdown in critical thinking, thus placing more emphasis on the tools of enacting research than the goal of discovering something new and worthwhile to say.

Probably the most distinguishing assumption that actuates the study of movies and TV from a popular cultural orientation is the ardent belief that *popular film and television criticism should be as democratized and accessible as the media it strives to define, describe, analyze, and evaluate.* No motion picture, television, or video subject is off limits for the word processor of the popular culturalist; from the viewer-friendly high-tech extravaganzas of Hollywood or the networks, to independent film productions or public television, to pornography, documentaries, or computer-based multimedia works, no arbitrary or tacit boundaries should ever restrict a research topic.

Most popular film and television critics similarly view themselves not as detached experts but as representative members of the very audiences that watch these electronic media offerings. The subsequent criticism is intended to be read, discussed, debated, and—it is hoped—appreciated by fellow viewers, not just professional colleagues. Popular film and television analysts accordingly feel an obligation to decipher and demystify any conceptual models and wordings that are markedly arcane. They are schooled in many theories and methodologies, some of which are more easily understood in lay terms than others. The basic rule of thumb is to avoid specialized language, as much as possible, if the same speculative frameworks and methodologies can be presented in simpler terms. The discourse in popular film and television is not aimed at only a few specialists but will ideally have meaning for a broad audience of readers.

The sixteen chapters in this book are exercises in critical thinking about the media that are founded on three guiding and highly functional propositions: First, *all criticism begins with the art of question asking.* A quick review of the contents page will provide immediate cues to an assortment of research questions exploring the parameters and workings of authorship, audiences, media systems and institutions, and various textual portrayals. The title itself, *In the Eye of the Beholder*, underscores the selective nature of every critical perspective. In other words, critics can only know their subjects by the kinds of questions they ask; furthermore, the way they ask these questions, usually influences the answers they get.

For example, when George Plasketes inquires in chapter 2, "What was Lorne Michaels's role in the rise and fall of *Saturday Night Live?*" —his question comes with a point of view. He apparently expects to find a mixture of strengths and weaknesses in a production process that prompts a "rise" and then a "fall." In this case, his question turns out to be astute, relevant, and effective. It ultimately contributes to our knowledge about the possibilities and limits of creative innovation within the organizational structures of American television. Every critical insight, therefore, stems from a well-formed research question. As a result, the art of question-asking should be a main concern for all of us as students of popular film and television.

Second, *all forms of criticism are based on metaphors that organize and direct the way we think.* In chapter 16, for instance, Robert Thompson provides a valuable survey of television criticism over the last generation. He catalogues a wide assortment of books that employ both com-

4 In the Eye of the Beholder

plimentary and pejorative metaphors about TV, such as "tube of plenty," "window on the world," "groove tube," "cultural forum," "most popular art," "glass teat," "vast wasteland," "plug-in drug," "white noise," and "boob tube," to name a few. These metaphors are the lenses through which the respective authors view television, thus shaping their responses. Every critic in this compilation also uses metaphors to similarly organize their perceptions and frame their arguments. Even the title *In the Eye of the Beholder* is a metaphor, suggesting the integrity of each individual outlook, the collection's plurality of viewpoints, and the ascendancy of seeing as the preeminent means of gathering information and knowledge in the current image culture.

Third, *all communication modes and media have their own codes and conventions, which structure the way we experience and come to know our subjects.* Marshall McLuhan expressed this proposition in his eminently useful and often misunderstood metaphor, "the medium is the message." His point (and Harold Innis's before him) was that speech, writing, printing, and the various electronic media, all have their own biases that inspire certain kinds of learning and activities over others.

A major goal of this book is to focus the critical thinking process onto popular film and television, which are routinely consumed in great quantities without much reflection at all. Every author in this anthology is a practicing critic who has identified a subject; observed it long enough to ask a relevant research question; employed past experiences and knowledge to make sense of the subject's characteristics and qualities; reserved judgment in order to absorb as much new information as possible; reevaluated the original question in light of what's been learned so far (modifying as needed); utilized conceptual tools, such as creating metaphors, thesis statements, and outlines, as organizing strategies; and mapped out and analyzed the subject thoroughly before drawing final conclusions according to a well-reasoned critical perspective. This step-by-step overview is merely a blueprint on how to think critically; being a critic is far more imaginative in practice and often exhilarating.

Today we remain fully immersed in a media environment that ostensibly is invisible to us even as we busily operate inside it, habitually communicating and consuming electronic information in an often wide-eyed present tense. We are, nevertheless, captaining our own cultural juggernaut, whether we choose to acknowledge responsibility or not. We therefore need to consider where we have been and where we are going. Engaging in critical discourse may not enable us to explain all of the intricacies and excesses of the popular media, but it surely equips us with an ever clearer view of who we are, what we value, and where we might be heading in the future.

Movies and television are still taken for granted by most people. We routinely summon into our homes with a touch of a button the most extensive, albeit mediated rendering of a national heritage and culture ever available to humankind and, frankly, pay scant attention to the many lessons it has to teach us. We should do more than escape into this pool of imagery; we should investigate more closely the countless socio-cultural and psychological clues about ourselves that are suggested on a continuous basis over the nation's motion picture and TV screens. *In the Eye of the Beholder* is designed to encourage such critical practice, providing an assortment of models on which to assess the often complex and intimate relationships that most of us form with the popular films and television programs we love (or love to hate).

As we finish this collection, we would like to acknowledge our debt to Ray B. Browne for his encouragement and friendship over the years. We want to thank Pat Browne for her many kindnesses as well, including her help in preparing this manuscript for publication. We are also grateful to the editorial staff at Heldref, the nonprofit foundation in Washington, D.C., which publishes the *Journal of Popular Film and Television,* for their continuing support, especially Managing Editor Lisa Culp-Neikirk, and her two predecessors, Page Minshew and Zell Rosenfelt. Our deepest thanks go to our families for their love and understanding, and for sharing innumerable hours with us watching, enjoying, and discussing movies and television.

Part 1

The Popular Tradition

Courtesy of the Museum of Modern Art/Film Stills Archive

The most fundamental difference between the first generation of popular culture scholars, the World War II generation who made their most indelible mark during the 1960s and 1970s, and the second and third generation of popular culturalists, who are still influenced and inspired by the democratic passions of their predecessors, is the shift away from analyzing taste cultures (high versus popular versus folk art) to a preoccupation with who wields power in which contexts, over whom, and to what effect. Sociocultural analysts spend little time today questioning the validity of the "popular" anymore, or justifying its fitness as a topic; that battle is over, having been fought and won by those who went before.

During the last twenty-five years, especially, sociocultural scholars have devised a variety of critical views and ethically reasoned positions, examining the making of meaning and the privileging of some values over others, thus ushering in a more productive way of thinking about and studying the popular tradition. This process will likely take another generation before becoming the "common sense" way of appreciating that the notion of "culture" always contains liberating as well as inhumane (i.e., sexist, racist, nativist) aspects, all intertwined and deeply rooted in every society on earth. The resulting perceptions that accrue while working through this transition to a more complex understanding of culture is clearly one of the main reasons why popular film and television studies are as rich and compelling as they are right now.

Part 1 of *In the Eye of the Beholder* focuses on perennial subject areas in popular film and television criticism, such as *authorship* or creative production personnel in institutional context; *the popular text* or the conceptual parameters of movie and television content; and *reception* or the social construction of audiences in their respective viewing environments. In chapter 1 Gary Edgerton describes and analyzes the public vision of Ken Burns. He views Burns as displaying a special aptitude for bridging conventional boundaries, such as the codes of the visual media, print, writing, and speech; separate generational perspectives; and the stories of the past with the concerns of the present. George Plasketes in chapter 2 addresses the producer-writer Lorne Michaels. His is an instrumentalist approach, which examines issues and questions associated with individual creators functioning within the collaborative process of a television series and the organizational demands of a network.

Michael Marsden changes the critical focus in chapter 3 by tracing the evolution of one popular narrative from a *Gunsmoke* episode to a TV movie script, *Jedidiah*, before finally becoming the Academy Award–winning screenplay for *Witness*. He illustrates how the storytelling process is creative, dynamic, and cumulative, underscoring cross-media interactions throughout. Gregory Waller likewise grapples with the complex problem of identifying the most appropriate television text for analysis in chapter 4. His piece scrutinizes the differing theoretical appraisals about what is the most valid text for TV criticism, concluding with a call for a genre approach "from a transmedia perspective." John Cawelti then traces in chapter 5 the history of genre criticism from Aristotle through the rising interest in popular genres in the 1920s to more recent developments involving reader-response and feminist criticism, deconstructionism, and multiculturalism. All told, he outlines the specific characteristics of genre theory, the metatheoretical assumptions that underlie this approach, and its strengths and weaknesses as a critical view.

Bruce Austin surveys the existing literature concerning motion picture and television audiences from a social science perspective in Chapter 6. He succinctly describes what has been studied, the motives driving this research, what has been ignored, and how these imbalances can best be corrected. Kathryn Fuller completes part 1 by chronicling in chapter 7 the gendered construction of the silent movie fan. Her historical-critical methods disclose how a female-dominated movie audience was cultivated between 1910 and 1920 through the stories and imagery in *Motion Picture Story Magazine* and similar publications. Fuller's essay, like the previous six, indicates that the popular tradition in film and television criticism emphasizes the relationship among producers, texts, and audiences above all else. These seven authors assume that their subjects are only meaningful within the broader context of this continuing and systemic cultural interaction, never in isolation.

1

"Mystic Chords of Memory": The Cultural Voice of Ken Burns

Gary R. Edgerton

Variations on a Theme

I must admit that I have, in many ways, made the same film over and over again. Each production asks one deceptively simple question: who are we? That is to say, who are we Americans as a people? What does an investigation of the past tell us about who we were and what we have become? Each film offers an opportunity to pursue this question, and while never answering it fully, nevertheless deepens the question with each project.

—Ken Burns
"Sharing the American Experience"

Ken Burns readily attests to "feel[ing] a tremendous sympathy for this country." He recently explained how his frequent lecturing complements his many documentaries, providing him with "another means of proclaiming our many attachments to the stories and voices and moments of history . . . while forgetting is the opposite of all that . . . the worst kind of human detachment."[1] He averages "one to two talks a week," regularly evoking Lincoln's metaphor—"the mystic chords of memory"—which aptly expresses Burns's poetic intentions and his deep personal commitment to our nation's past.[2] He uses both the podium and television to summon those "chords," bringing his version of American history to life for literally tens of millions of people, a feat few have been able to accomplish before him.

At 43, Burns has already amassed a record of eleven major PBS (Public Broadcasting System) specials, addressing a wide range of American history topics such as *The Brooklyn Bridge* (PBS, 1982), *The Shakers: Hands to Work, Hearts to God* (1985), *The Statue of Liberty* (1985), *Huey Long* (1986), *Thomas Hart Benton* (1989), *The Congress* (1989), *The Civil War* (1990), *Empire of the Air* (1992), *Baseball* (1994),

11

The West (1996), and *Thomas Jefferson* (1997)—all of which have won various awards and honors from both professional and scholarly organizations and at international film festivals.

Ken Burns has indeed made the historical documentary a popular and gripping form for large segments of the American viewing public. He has successfully seized the attention of the mass audience through the subjects he chooses and the way he presents them. An examination of his background reveals several key influences in the formative years of his professional development. The form and content of Burns's productions also address many of the fundamental changes now reshaping America's social fabric. Focusing on these issues, therefore, I will provide an introduction to Burns's work, analyzing his style and perspective, and identifying those characteristics that make him one of the most significant cultural voices working in film and television today.

Personal Influences and Developing a Style

I am particularly fortunate because I [went] to Hampshire [College] which stressed the sort of self-initiated route of designing one's curriculum, a kind of mode of inquiry that I brought out into the real world, so that instead of apprenticing myself, I started my own company.

—Ken Burns, 1993[3]

Ken Burns was born in Brooklyn, New York, on July 29, 1953, and grew up in Ann Arbor, where his father, Robert, taught cultural anthropology at the University of Michigan. He is a 1975 graduate of Hampshire College in Amherst, Massachusetts, where he studied under photographers Jerome Liebling and Elaine Mayes, and received a degree in film studies and design. Upon graduation, he and two of his college friends started their own independent production company, Florentine Films, and struggled for a number of years doing freelance assignments and finishing a few short documentaries before beginning work in 1977 on a film based on historian David McCullough's book, *The Great Bridge* (1972). Four years later, they completed *The Brooklyn Bridge*, which won several important commendations including an Academy Award nomination, thus ushering Burns into the ambit of public television, where he has remained ever since.

In those early years, Ken Burns cites the films of John Ford, along with Liebling and McCullough, as being seminal influences on his development as a documentarian. In the fall of 1971, he enrolled at Hampshire College, an experimental liberal arts college founded just two years earlier, with the expressed purpose of becoming a Hollywood

Filmmaker and television producer Ken Burns. (Courtesy of General Motors/ Lisa Berg)

director. Like many of the so-called film generation, Burns became acquainted with the work of John Ford on late-night television, remembering especially *Young Mr. Lincoln* (1939), *My Darling Clementine* (1946), and *Fort Apache* (1948). Ford animated these specific pictures with a deep commitment to the frontier spirit of rugged individualism, nation-building, and traditional Christian virtues. Throughout all his films, Ford proved himself to be a visual poet of the first order; he was also a sentimentalist and a populist, stressing a sense of nostalgia and a firm commitment to the ways of the past. Many of these conventional elements still inform Ken Burns's documentaries as well.

I had always wanted to be a Hollywood director. I looked up to Hitchcock and Hawks and Ford as sort of beacons of how I'd want to do, but I think as I look back now in retrospect, I realize how influential Ford was in that if you look at sort of my whole body of work, it's a kind of documentary version of Ford that is a real love for biography, a real love for American mythology, a real love for the music of the period, a real love for ordinary characters who coexist not just on the fringes of our main characters's actions, but who are actually central to the drama and remind us that the best history is not just from the top down, but from the bottom up.

Burns likewise acknowledges that he was "fortunate to have a true mentor in college, and that was Jerome Liebling." Liebling, a celebrated still photographer whose work has been well known since the 1940s, is a social documentarian who exhibits a tough awareness of the teeming dislocations and pervasive artifice in contemporary American life. His subjects range from the stockyards of St. Paul to the streets of the South Bronx, populated by ordinary people, politicians on the stump, and even the haunting remains of unadorned cadavers. One distinctive aspect of Liebling's technique is its almost cinematic quality, revealing a sense of drama and movement within the frame, often incorporating the grammar of motion pictures with his extreme close-ups and striking angles. As Ken Burns remembers,

[I]nterestingly both of these people, Jerry and Elaine [Mayes], are still photographers, primarily, their work in film has been tangential, but they made excellent film teachers, and guided me. . . . I think the amazing thing for us was that film and photography were being taught together, which seems sort of obvious, but I don't know of any other instance where they are. And so there was essentially men and women that had a healthy respect for the image influencing us documentary filmmakers, in fact, persuading us sometimes Hollywood-headed filmmakers that the documentary world could be as dramatic and as revealing as anything that Hollywood can turn out.

The curricular linkage of film and photography eventually led to one of Burns's unique and identifiable stylistic trademarks: he treats old photographs as if they were moving pictures, panning and zooming within the frame, shifting back and forth between long shots, medium shots, and close-ups; while correspondingly, handling live shots as if they were still photographs. Whether his subject happens to be the Brooklyn Bridge, or the Statue of Liberty, or a Civil War battlefield, his own live footage is characteristically formal and painterly. This emphasis on static composition is particularly effective in evoking the mood and pre-filmic visual vocabulary of the nineteenth and early twentieth centuries, thus corresponding to the historical eras and topics that he invariably chooses to explore.

I had a case of pneumonia and a friend of mine in January of 1977, that makes that about 16 years ago, gave me the paperback version of McCullough's history of *The Great Bridge*, and I suddenly was so inspired. Here was a man who brought history to life. He is our greatest narrative historian, I think. He let the past speak for itself, something I had been experimenting with in my own crude college films, that is to say, using diaries and journals. And here was a subject that seemed to be a part of the hidden history of America, the history we were never taught, as we focused on wars and presidents and Indians fighting and lawlessness, here was something going on that seemed to speak as much about who we are as anything, and it was urban and it was eastern and corrupt and dangerous. It was about the arts and the sciences that would be more influential in the twentieth century than a lot of the mythology of the nineteenth century and I sort of went at it wholeheartedly, and more than that, as I got to know McCullough, he became very helpful in refining a story and how you tell a story. And I think if you combine this great visual and sort of honorable teachings of Jerry Liebling with McCullough's sense of narrative, that's a pretty potent combination, and two influences, the shoulders of two giants on whom I stand.

David McCullough first recalls being approached by Burns at an academic conference where the filmmaker, who was 24 at the time, expressed his interest in making a documentary on *The Great Bridge*: "I didn't want to have anything to do with him, and if anybody was going to make a film based on my book, I wanted it to be somebody who had more experience and more standing" (Duncan 77). To this day, however, Burns contends that "perseverance is the single greatest element" in his success. He wrote McCullough letters, and later he and his associates contacted him by phone. "The people who work for me, we work hard, we don't give up." McCullough finally acquiesced. As Jerome Liebling explains, Ken "had direction and tenacity, but he looked about 12 years old. People scorned his youth—who is this kid?—but as soon as he began to make films, that attitude changed" (Clark 78).

David McCullough narrated six of Burns's first eight documentaries, as well as serving as cowriter on *The Congress*.[4] He also provided Burns with a model for writing and producing history as the young filmmaker honed his own storytelling skills in the late 1970s and early 1980s, quickly maturing as an accomplished documentarian and popular historian in his own right. By almost any measure, Ken Burns's now distinctive and well recognizable style is conservative in the sense that it relies entirely on techniques first introduced decades ago; however, he arranges these constituent elements in a wholly new and highly complex textual arrangement.

Beginning with *The Brooklyn Bridge* and continuing through *Thomas Jefferson*, Burns has intricately blended narration with what he calls his "chorus of voices"—readings from personal papers, diaries, and letters; interpretive commentaries from on-screen experts, usually historians; his "rephotographing" technique, which closely examines old photographs, paintings, drawings, and other artifacts with his movie camera—all backed up with a musical track that features period compositions and folk music. The effect of this collage of techniques is to create the illusion that the viewer is being transported back in time, literally finding an emotional connection with the people and events of America's past. As Ken Burns says,

> I think I'm primarily a filmmaker. That's my job. I'm an amateur historian at best, but more than anything if you wanted to find a hybridization of those two professions, then I find myself an emotional archeologist. That is to say, there is something in the process of filmmaking that I do in the excavation of these events in the past that provokes a kind of emotion and a sympathy that remind us, for example, of why we agree against all odds as a people to cohere. You know as you look at the world unravelling, it's interesting that we Americans who are not united by religion, or patriarchy, or even common language, or even a geography that's relatively similar, we have agreed because we hold a few pieces of paper and a few sacred words together, we have agreed to cohere, and for more than two hundred years it's worked and that special alchemy is something I'm interested in. It doesn't work in a Pollyannaish way. Boss Tweed had his hands in the building of the Brooklyn Bridge. We corrupt as much as we construct, but nevertheless, I think that in the aggregate the American experience is a wonderful beacon.

What Ken Burns is enunciating is the liberal pluralist perspective where social and cultural differences between Americans are kept in a comparatively stable and negotiated consensus within the body politic. A celebration of the nation, and a highlighting of its ideals and achievements, are fundamental aspects of both consensus thinking and Burns's body of work. Moreover, he suggests that "television can become a new Homeric mode," hinting at the nature of his outlook and his ultimate intentions (Milius 43). By identifying with the Homeric model, Burns is essentially drawing narrative parameters that are epic and heroic in scope. The epic form tends to celebrate a people's shared tradition in sweeping terms, while recounting the lives of national heroes is the classical way of imparting values by erecting edifying examples for present and future generations. Ken Burns, like all important cultural voices, is a moralist, recasting and revivifying the stories of our collective history through the apt though unexpected forum of prime-time TV.

The Poetry of Remembering

> We Americans still tend to ignore our past. Perhaps we fear having one, and burn it behind us like rocket fuel, always looking forward. And that's a bad thing. The consequences are not just ignorance, or stupidity, or even repeating. It represents the deepest kind of inattention, and it becomes a tear or a gap in who we are.
>
> —Ken Burns
> "Sharing the American Experience"

Historical memory is the process by which societies reconstruct their pasts in order to make sense out of the present. Increasingly today, America's collective memory is shaped through the reach and power of the nation's media culture; and Ken Burns asserts that "television has become more and more the way we are connected to the making of history" (Burns, "In Search"). In liberal societies, such as the United States, multiple renditions of the past can and do simultaneously coexist. On the other hand, not every version of history is permitted access to the country's airwaves, or embraced with the outpouring of emotion and enthusiasm as was *The Civil War*, which attracted nearly 40 million viewers during its initial telecast in September 1990, and has since been seen by an estimated 70 million Americans. As Burns reveals, "I don't really know how to put my finger on [the level of popularity] . . . I mean these are phenomena that you set in motion and then stand back and watch, and don't really claim a kind of authorship. You are as surprised as anyone at the success or the response to the film."

Few critical notions have gone through as much reconsideration over the past generation as the idea of authorship. Ken Burns's above comments, in fact, suggest a more contemporaneous understanding of how he, as a filmmaker, draws upon the mythic structures and ideologies of our shared culture to "set in motion" his version of America. At first, it may appear that he has embraced a wide assortment of subjects—a bridge, a nineteenth-century religious sect, a statue, a demagogue, a painter, the congress, the Civil War, radio, our national pastime, the West, and a founding statesman—but there are several shared characteristics that bind this medley of Americana together.

Burns's oeuvre so far demonstrates certain narrative, ideological, and historiographical imperatives that support one another; and together form an image of America that is generally romantic, liberal pluralist, and celebratory in nature. Romanticism in the arts has always displayed an emphasis on strong and vibrant feelings above all else, separating reason from emotion, and attributing great value to the role of myth in human affairs.

In his own words, Burns "emphasize[s] the story in history, avoiding the contentions of analysis" (qtd. in Hunt 19). Narrative history is not a neutral approach, of course; and the selection of the Homeric model privileges some values, ideas, and attitudes, while suppressing others. In each of his eleven documentaries, Burns foregrounds first-person stories and anecdotes, the stuff of personal heroism and tragedy, from inside the framework of larger historical currents and events. He champions the longstanding formula of the "American original" which is succinctly outlined in the three graphics that begin *Thomas Hart Benton:*

(1) Thomas Hart Benton painted America; (2) For more than seventy years he painted its cities and small towns, its farms and backwoods. He painted its people, too: faith healers and lovers, politicians and soda jerks, farmers and movie stars; (3) most of all, Benton wanted to make his art available to ordinary people. To do that, he took on the whole art world and embroiled himself in endless controversy.

Ken Burns's chronicles are populated with seemingly ordinary men and women who rise up from the ranks of the citizenry to become paragons of national (and occasionally transcendent) achievement, always persisting against great odds. Even today, an ardent and romantic allegiance to the cult of individualism remains a popular if illusory aspect of America's cultural memory. *The Brooklyn Bridge*, for example, described by the film's "chorus of voices" as "a work of art" and "the greatest feat of civil engineering in the world," is the "inspiration" of a kind of "Renaissance man," John A. Roebling, who died as the building of the bridge was beginning; and his son, Washington Roebling, who finished the monument fourteen years later through his own dogged perseverance and courage, despite being bedridden in the process. In *The Shakers: Hands to Work, Hearts to God*, Mother Ann Lee emerges as another "American original," a former factory worker and English immigrant, who comes to upper New York State on the eve of the Revolutionary War and pioneers a peculiarly American religious movement, radical in its feminism, pacificism, and communal lifestyle, and eventually reaching 100,000 members at its height in the 1840s.

Ken Burns has created a series of films as morality tales, drawing upon epic events, landmarks, and institutions of historical significance, populated by heroes and villains who allegorically personify certain virtues and vices in the national character as understood through the popular mythology of our cultural memory. At the beginning of *Empire of the Air*, for instance, Jason Robards narrates how Lee de Forest, David Sarnoff, and Edwin H. Armstrong "were driven to create [radio] by ancient qualities, idealism and imagination, greed and envy, ambition and determination, and genius," while Burns himself describes *Huey Long* as "a tragic almost Shakespearean story of a man who started off good, went bad, and got killed for it." The filmmaker describes his interest in history this way:

As a little kid from age ten, I was never reading novels. My brother was sort of digesting them constantly, but I was reading the encyclopedia. And I went through one set, and then another set. And I'd read history and things like that, and it was completely untrained. At Hampshire I think I took one history course and that was in Russian history, something I was also interested in, and no

American history outside of the eleventh-grade survey. But low and behold, I found a kind of much deeper, less-intellectual, more emotional sympathy with the story of the country. The resonances of particular lives or events seemed to really spark powerful emotions within me that sort of demanded their exploration, and I'm still doing that. I'm still surprised continually at the depth of my real love, and I think that's the word, of the American past.

The key to perceiving a linkage between the premises of romanticism and the contours of our cultural memory is to underscore Burns's description of himself as a "historian of emotions" (Kastor G10). The English and German romanticists, and the American transcendentalists, often alluded to the heroic capacity and inherent goodness in each and every human being, believing that people should rely on their feelings, instincts, and intuitions in order to realize themselves and better understand the world. Burns's perspective is certainly more multidimensional than this nineteenth-century outlook; however, he does share the conviction that "analysis kills poetry and emotion! It's the texture of emotion that [is] important to me" (qtd. in Powers 218).

The Civil War, for example, is peppered throughout with entertaining anecdotes by the writer, historian, and master raconteur, Shelby Foote. His seemingly intimate asides about the human interest aspects of this conflict appear to transcend politics, at least on the surface. As Burns suggests,

just go back to the section on the Gettysburg Address and watch Shelby's head twitch as he talks about Lincoln stepping down from the stand, and Shelby says he came back and he turned to his friend Ward and he said "Ward, that speech won't scour," and he tilted his head as if the camera pulled back, you'd see, next to Shelby, Abraham Lincoln, and on the other side of Lincoln, Ward Lamon. And to me, any man who puts you there, that's a great gift.

In fact, each one of Shelby Foote's eighty-nine appearances in the series, or "three times the sum total of everyone else," has the effect of continually shifting the thematic examinations of American society, culture, and politics into a realm where emotions are high and consensus prevails. In one of the most-often quoted anecdotes of the series, Shelby Foote appears within the first few minutes of the final episode entitled, "The Better Angels of Our Nature," emphasizing the issue of nationhood:

Before the war it was said the United States are, grammatically it was spoken that way and thought of as a collection of independent states. And after the war it was always the United States *is* [his emphasis] as we say today without being self-conscious at all—and that sums up what the war accomplished: it made us an *is* [he smiles].

This remark is then immediately followed by the bittersweet and tragic lament that serves as the series's anthem, "Ashokan Farewell," thus reinforcing the overall heroic dimensions of the narrative. Heroism, honor, and nobility are related Homeric impulses that permeate this series, shaping our reactions to the "Great Men" of the war, such as Abraham Lincoln, Frederick Douglass, Robert E. Lee, and Ulysses S. Grant, along with two common soldiers (i.e., Elisha Hunt Rhodes, a Yankee from Rhode Island, and Sam Watkins, a Confederate from Tennessee) whose firsthand accounts we follow in all nine episodes. As a result, a crest of emotion pours forth from this and every anecdote, rendering *The Civil War* less a story of sociopolitical conflict than a poignant and mythopoeic lesson in national commitment, self-sacrifice, valor, and fulfillment.

In Burns's own words, "I try to engage, on literally dozens of levels, ordinary human beings from across the country—male and female, black and white, young and old, rich and poor, inarticulate and articulate" (*"The Civil War"*). What Ken Burns is articulating again is his liberal pluralist leanings. The tenets of liberal pluralism are basically fixed on agreement and unity, despite whatever differences of race, class, ethnicity, and gender may exist within the republic. In *The Statue of Liberty*, for instance, there is a five-to-six minute scene during the last ten minutes of the film where a montage of four witnesses presents both corroborating and conflicting opinions about the lasting meaning of this national landmark and cultural symbol. David McCullough begins by pronouncing that "the Statue of Liberty is an act of faith," followed by statesman Sol Linowitz, recalling his parents' arrival "from overseas" and their viewpoint as immigrants:

They came enchanted by an idea that here they could be themselves and be the best that was in them to be. They were coming to a place where every human being could stand erect and with dignity as a child of God. That's what I think they believe in—and that's what I see in it. It reminds me of how much we yet have to do to achieve the full promise of that statue.

The next shot is a 25-second excerpt from Martin Luther King's "I Have a Dream" speech, climaxing with a critique by writer James Baldwin, which ends: "For black Americans, for black inhabitants of this country, the Statue of Liberty is simply a very bitter joke, meaning nothing to us." Then filmmaker Milos Foreman, an expatriate from Czechoslovakia, concludes with a somewhat longer commentary over a majestic long shot of the statue silhouetted against a luminous orange sky: "There is something deep down in this society which is so valuable, so strong, and so inspiring that in spite of all the difficulties, all the troubles, all of evil, all of the crime you see around yourself, all of greed, all of hypocrisy you see, that still this is the best. And that lady up there symbolizes that."

Foreman's words have little to do with the specific substance addressed in the previous statements by either King or Baldwin, although coming where it does, his testimony cannot help but soften the references to racial prejudice and injustice that preceded it. This whole sequencing of remarks establishes the liberal pluralist consensus: different speakers might clash on certain issues (such as what degree of freedom is actually symbolized by the Statue of Liberty and for whom), but disagreements ultimately take place within a broader framework of agreement on underlying principle. In this case, the larger principle is reasserted in the film's final statement, delivered by David McCullough again:

Liberty is what we Americans have always wanted first of all. It's what the country was founded for. It's what the Revolution was fought for. All the great songs and sayings and pronouncements of those Revolutionary figures were about liberty. And they knew what it meant. (Going to a close-up of McCullough.) And because the French sent the statue here, it was their way of saying implicitly—we recognize that [the Statue of Liberty] is a gateway to a new world and to the hope of the world. (Fade out to credits and closing music.)

The expert testimonies and first-person reports that Burns employs throughout the body of his work do provide a shifting angle of vision whose multiple voices sometimes agree and, at other times, differ and contrast with each other. These multiple voices, however, form a broad cultural consensus because of the filmmaker's liberal pluralist orientation, and in Burns's words, "the power of film to digest and synthesize" (qtd. in Weisberger 99).

In many ways, Ken Burns is the ideal filmmaker for this period of transition between generations, bridging the sensibilities of the people who came of age during World War II along with his own frame of reference as a baby boomer. He claims the reason he chooses the topics he does has a great deal to do with both the fifties and sixties: "I think that maybe all of that stimulus from the centennial celebration of the Civil War, to the mythology that still pertained, not only got fixed, but then got challenged in the sixties. And I think that those two things going in opposite directions, probably accounts for why we're all drawn to [these subjects] right now."

Burns's work is very much of the moment. His historical documentaries are generally liberal on social issues, as is evident by his abiding concern for civil rights, while concomitantly traditional in respect to core American values and the nation's institutions. In *Baseball*, for instance, the country's legacy of racism and segregation is underscored, climaxing in the self-sacrifice and "mission" of Jackie Robinson. *The Congress* is similarly celebrated in its opening narration as "the place . . . our government works. It's the engine of democracy . . . the real story of our country takes place . . . [on] the hill. All the voices are there."

Scholar Barbara Fields tells us during one of her commentaries in the last episode of *The Civil War* that William Faulkner once said "History *is* as well as *was*." In this one sense, at least, all history is contemporary. We can never escape our own set of ideological predispositions; and within this context, Ken Burns articulates a version of the country's past that conveys his own distinctive voice intermingled with many widespread assumptions about the essential character of America and the challenges it faces today.

Choosing an Auspicious Alternative

> I am constantly being flirted with by studios or asked to get involved with projects, and they're very interesting. I grew up thinking that I would be a Hollywood film director but found in the dramatic life of this country, particularly its past, more truths and more opportunities to tell stories and to communicate a drama than anything they've ever done in that industry . . . and it's interesting for so long documentary filmmaking has been seen as a lower rung on a career ladder but I remember interviewing Robert Penn Warren for the *Huey Long* film and we became friends. And afterwards I said the word "career" and he said to me "careerism is death!" And later I realized that I am absolutely, particularly pleased with the drama that is more dramatic than anything the imagination can think of . . . there are too many stories in American history. I could do ten lifetimes of these stories and if I started doing them all, it would take me a thousand years just to cover the last hundred and fifty in American history.
>
> —Ken Burns, 1996[5]

So much about Ken Burns's career defies conventional wisdom. He is public television's busiest and most celebrated producer in an era when the historical documentary generally holds little interest for most Americans. He operates his own independent company, Florentine

Films, in the small New England village of Walpole, New Hampshire, more than four hours north of New York City, hardly a crossroads in the highly competitive and often insular world of corporately funded, PBS-sponsored productions. His eleven major PBS specials so far are also strikingly out of step with the visual pyrotechnics and frenetic pacing of most nonfiction television, relying mainly on documentary techniques that were introduced decades ago.

Burns recently explained how his filmmaking has almost become an approach to living. He maintains that it has trained him "how to see, how to create, how to write, how to shoot, how to interview, how to criticize, to raise money, speak in public, and how to research . . . it's a total education" (qtd. in Jackson 42). He also appears more comfortable than ever with the professional choices he has made—as well he should be. Ken Burns is among the most important filmmakers and television producers of his generation. His significance, indeed, stems from his being a documentarian who reaches his largest audiences through television, not despite this fact.

Burns is resolutely historical at a time when most Americans eschew the past, resulting in a "tear or gap in who we are." His preoccupation with the elemental question—"Who are we as Americans?"—could not be more relevant in an era when multiculturalism has become the source of sweeping and often painful reappraisals of almost every aspect of American life.

All of Burns's work is devoted to such a reexamination. He refers to his explorations into the nation's racial and ethnic heritage as the "connecting thread" in his films. For example, Burns evokes John Adams's description of *Thomas Jefferson* as a shadow man . . . he distilled a century of Enlightenment thinking into one remarkable sentence which began "we hold these truths to be self-evident, that all men are created equal." Yet he owned more than 200 human beings and never saw fit in his lifetime to free them (Burns "Sharing the American Experience"). *The West* likewise investigates this region's long-standing experience with cultural diversity, culminating in the bitter nineteenth-century "collision of native peoples and the country's newcomers."[6]

Burns's primary goal is to pursue the "profound connection between remembering and freedom and human attachment. That is what history is to me." Probing the past is his way of reassembling the future from a fragmented present. "Few things survive in these cynical days to remind us of the union from which so many of our personal as well as collective blessings flow" (Burns "Sharing"). "I know I've said it before but I see myself as an emotional archaeologist, trying to excavate what there is in our past that speaks to the unum and not the pluribus."[7]

Another tacit question that Ken Burns's work suggests is "How should we best use the medium of television?" His preoccupation with history and the extended lengths of his productions implicitly challenge the very "idea" of television programming that most Americans take for granted.[8]

Television is one of the worst features of our daily life; that it promotes disunion at a psychological, emotional, and personal level more insidiously than practically anything else in our culture. But it may also be, paradoxically, the instrument of our deliverance, a way in which we might find a common language and a common purpose. (qtd. in Hackney 48-49)

Burns's formal approach deliberately augments what is considered an inherent characteristic of the medium—TV's *immediacy*. In fact, he functions as a kind of mediating presence between a print-based and televisual way of communicating.

The historic transformations from orality to writing to printing to televising are generally understood today as producing concurrent shifts in the way in which societies privilege certain forms of expression and knowledge over others. For example, some historians have admonished Burns for emphasizing the empathetic and experiential aspects of history in *The Civil War* more than detailed analysis (Edgerton). What such critics overlook, however, is that the visual media's codes of historical representation are far different, albeit complementary to those of print. The present image culture features the tendency to engulf its participants in a simulated *immediacy* or "being there," in contrast to the printed word's propensity toward logic, detachment, and reasoned discourse.

Ken Burns's documentaries noticeably demonstrate a balance between both traditions. On one hand, film and television are incapable of rendering temporal dimensions with much precision. They have no grammatical analogues for the past and future tenses of written languages. Instead, the visual media amplify the present sense of *immediacy* out of all proportion. As a result, Burns fully understands and capitalizes on this dynamic throughout his work. For instance, he explains in respect to *The Civil War* that

we wanted you to believe you were there . . . we wanted you to live inside those photographs . . . once you've taken the poetry of words and added to it the poetry of imagery and a poetry of music and a poetry of sound, I think you begin to approximate the notion that the real war could actually get someplace, that you could bring it back alive.

He therefore supplements images with words by fusing them together during his "left-hand, right-hand process" of simultaneously shooting and writing his scripts.[9] Preparing each of his productions includes the disciplined and well-reasoned rigors of researching his subject, writing grant proposals, collaborating and debating with an assortment of scholarly advisors; composing at least a dozen drafts of the off-screen narration, as well as selecting the historical readings and expert commentaries. Film, television, print, and speech, all share a metaphoric relationship to history, each offering different ways to reconstruct the past; and Burns's most distinctive stylistic achievement so far is his skill and versatility in integrating these diverse communication forms into a "poetic" whole.

Overall, then, Ken Burns displays a special aptitude for bridging various traditional parameters, such as the codes of the visual media, print, writing, and speech; separate generational perspectives; and the stories of the past with the concerns of the present. His description of *Jazz*, his next major PBS special, is another case in point.[10]

Jazz was born out of a million *American* [his emphasis] negotiations; between having and not having; between happy and sad, country and city, North and South; between men and women and black and white; between the Old Europe and the Old Africa—that could only have happened in an entirely New World. (Burns "Sharing")

Burns's importance as a cultural voice resides in this singular ability to create a detailed, complex, and compelling vision of America, eventually pulling together despite its chronic differences, even as many of his professional contemporaries portray the same society coming apart at the seams.

Notes

1. Personal interview with the author on 27 February 1996.

2. Lincoln employed "the mystic chords of memory" in his first inaugural address of 1861 to invoke the bond "from every battlefield and patriot grave" of the Revolution "to every living heart and hearthstone all over this broad land." Lincoln ended this passage by declaring that the "mystic chords" will "swell the chorus of the Union," thus touching "the better angels of our nature," another of Burns's favorite metaphors.

3. This quotation by Ken Burns and those without parenthetical attribution that follow are from an extended telephone interview with the author on 18 February 1993.

4. David McCullough narrated the *Brooklyn Bridge, The Shakers: Hands to Work, Hearts to God, The Statue of Liberty, Huey Long, The Congress*, and *The Civil War.*

5. Personal interview with the author on 27 February 1996.

6. Ibid.

7. Ibid.

8. All of his documentaries are, of course, designed and presented without commercial interruption. In addition, *The Civil War* is 11 hours long; *Baseball* 18 1/2; *The West* 12; and *Jazz* is set to be 12.

9. Personal interview with the author on 27 February 1996.

10. *Jazz* is scheduled to debut on public television in the fall of 2000.

Works Cited

Burns, Ken. "In Search of the Painful, Essential Images of War." *New York Times* 27 Jan. 1991: sec. 2, 1.

——. "Sharing the American Experience." Speech delivered at the Norfolk Forum, Norfolk, Virginia, 27 Feb. 1996.

"*The Civil War*: Ken Burns charts a nation's birth." *American Film* 15.12 (1990): 58.

Clark, Tim. "The Man Who Had to Kill Abraham Lincoln." *Yankee* Oct. 1990: 79-83, 162-65.

Duncan, Dayton. "A Cinematic Storyteller." *The Boston Globe Magazine* 19 Mar. 1989: 19, 72, 77-83.

Edgerton, Gary. "Ken Burns's Rebirth of a Nation: Television, Narrative, and Popular History." *Film & History* 22.4 (1992): 118-33.

Hackney, Sheldon. "A Conversation With Ken Burns on *Baseball*." *Humanities* 15.4 (1994): 4-7, 48-53.

Hunt, Robert. "WarStorie: Ken Burns' epic-length *Civil War* moves from the home front to the front lines in its exhaustive coverage." *The (St. Louis) Riverfront Times* 11-17 July 1990: 18-19.

Jackson, Donald. "Ken Burns puts his special spin on the old ball game." *Smithsonian* July 1994: 38-50.

Kastor, Elizabeth. "For Filmmaker Ken Burns, The Culmination of a Five-Year Crusade." *Washington Post* 23 Sept. 1990: G1, G10-G11.

Liebling, Jerome. *Jerome Liebling Photographs* with essays by Anne Halley and Alan Trachtenberg. Amherst: U of Massachusetts P, 1982.

McCullough, David. *The Great Bridge.* New York: Simon & Schuster, 1972.

Milius, John. "Reliving the War Between Brothers." *New York Times* 16 Sept. 1990: sec. 2, 1, 43.

Powers, Ron. "Glory, Glory." *GQ* Sept. 1990: 216, 218, 222.

Weisberger, Bernard. "The Great Arrogance of the Present Is to Forget the Intelligence of the Past." *American Heritage* 41.6 (1990): 96-101.

2

The Rise and Fall of *Saturday Night Live:* Lorne Michaels as a Television Writer-Producer

George Plasketes

The romantic image of the artist commonly pictures a solitary individual working on a piece from conception to completion. Individual creators in the popular arts, however, must work within the context of organizational structures and processes, which in turn operate within the broader scope of economic, legal, sociocultural, political, ideological, and other institutional arrangements.

In television's collaborative expression, performers in their various dramatic or comic roles commonly overshadow the efforts of the writers. Dating back to the medium's infancy, *Your Show of Shows* (1950-1954) offers a prime example. While Sid Caesar and Imogene Coca were courting laughs from viewers, often overlooked were the architects of their sketches—a writing staff comprised of Mel Brooks, Woody Allen, Larry Gelbart, Carl Reiner, and Neil Simon. From the characters in a dramatic ensemble or the dialogue between a sitcom family, to a Johnny Carson or David Letterman late-night monologue, television programs begin with words on a page.

But how does the writer function within television's creative processes? And how do the assembly line demands and various production environments ultimately shape material written for programs? Lorne Michaels's development as a creator of television programming not only offers insight into the evolution and functions of the writer but illustrates how different production environments affect the writer and his or her material. While Michaels is but one example and has worked primarily in the comedy genre, the stages of development in his career parallel those of many television writers. The familiar path includes "paying dues" writing for different shows, struggling for creative autonomy, and gaining some degree of control of one's material by becoming a writer-producer.

27

Everything Is Beautiful: From Phyllis Diller to Downtown Burbank

Before working in American television, Lorne Michaels, a Toronto native, wrote and performed for various Canadian Broadcast Corporation (CBC) radio and television productions and as the "straight man" in a comedy team. After outgrowing Toronto's spawning ground, Michaels left for New York City's big pond in the late 1960s with "very young messianic feelings about comedy, that it should be of some use." While performing comic routines at The Improvisation, Michaels and his partner, Hart Pomerantz, attracted the attention of Woody Allen's manager, Jack Rollins. Rollins offered the duo a writing stewardship under Allen, who was still doing stand-up comedy at the time. Michaels recalls the experience and his impressions as a young writer:

My first monologue for Woody was something like an eye doctor who only treats Cyclopes. We sat there in a room with Woody, the best comedy writer in the world, talked ideas, and I thought, "Wow, this is what show business will always be like." He explained something I still remember vividly. Woody said he is his premise. The premises don't have to be silly—he did the same jokes as Bob Hope. This was a great leap for me.[1]

The brief stint under Allen's wing led to another writing arrangement, this time with Joan Rivers. Her style, a considerable contrast to Allen's cerebral comedy, made for an easier writing task. Rivers bought three monologues, parts of which she used, from Michaels and Pomerantz "for about $150," hardly enough to make significant headway in New York. Following a brief return to Toronto to work in Canadian television, Michaels was lured back to the states, only this time Los Angeles, where he joined the writing staff of *The Beautiful Phyllis Diller Show* (Sept. 1968-Dec. 1968) and later *Rowan and Martin's Laugh-In.* (1968-1973).

Michaels's initiation into American television proved to be an eye-opening experience for the young writer. The writing itself and the variety formats were not new to Michaels. He had always been drawn to writing, particularly comedy, and expected to further develop his craft by working in Hollywood. However, show business turned out to be much different from what Michaels naively believed it was always like: he was no longer sitting around talking ideas with Woody Allen. The apprentice soon discovered aspects of television's creative process that were less than fulfilling. It was a combination of these factors and Michaels's dissatisfaction with them that contributed significantly to the shaping and refining of Michaels's personal approach to television as a writer and eventually as a producer.

The Beautiful Phyllis Diller Show, a comedy-variety hour that aired Sunday nights on NBC, featured the fright-wigged, cackling comedienne, Phyllis Diller, and a supporting cast including Norm Crosby, and the song-and-dance troupe, the Curtain Calls. Michaels was one of the show's ten writers. "Our fares were paid to Hollywood, I was given an office there, and we wrote like crazy," said Michaels. "It was big-time TV and a valuable experience for all of us as writers. You learned structure, there were certain expectations, and we wrote blackout sketches."

The staff was also exposed to that part of show business known as hype. "It was the first time I'd encountered hype," said Michaels. "Everyday, network people came in the office; I'd ask, 'How's the show look?' All they'd say is, 'It's great!'" (qtd. in Burke 33). A common practice before shows is to do a warm-up. A performer, perhaps the host or guest star, comes out and tells a few jokes or does whatever it takes to "loosen up" or put the audience in the right frame of mind before the actual production. There may even be more than one warm-up, delivered by different performers; it was all part of the hype. Diller's crude jokes were particularly effective preparing audiences for the tapings, which lasted until the early morning hours. Champagne was served in the congratulatory atmosphere of the studio afterward. Later, a fellow writer said to Michaels, "You know it's garbage, don't you?" Michaels didn't:

I still thought I'd really written something. This was a profound lesson, my first—how easily, in television, you can be seduced. That was the beginning of the realization that I had to pay very close attention. When you wrote more than anything you wanted to be good. And if the audience laughed, you felt it was good. They were the user and you had to make the material accessible to them. I realized that didn't necessarily mean it was good.

Michaels's next stop was *Rowan and Martin's Laugh-In,* an experience that proved equally unsatisfying for him. On the surface, *Laugh-In* appeared to be an ideal environment for a young writer. George Schlatter's kaleidoscopic creation was the No. 1 rated program on television and the comic style was familiar territory to Michaels. As a native Canadian in America during the 1960s unrest, Michaels also found *Laugh-In*'s satirical and sociopolitical humor appealing. However, it was while writing for *Laugh-In* that Michaels began to resist traditional television and its formulas. It was not so much the actual show or its appearance but the production process behind the show that left Michaels rather disillusioned.

The sheer mechanics of a *Laugh-In* production were staggering compared to most technical preparations for other programs. While one show was being edited, another was being taped, another was in rehearsal, and a fourth was in the mechanical stages of having sets built and wardrobes fitted. In addition, a script for a fifth show was being written and a sixth show was in the conceptual stage.

The process of putting together *Laugh-In*'s asides started with the show's thirteen writers who spent a week writing each script. The script, usually 250 pages long, was 100 pages longer than that of any other one-hour show. Each joke got its own page in the script, and many pages had less than half a dozen words on them. "If you wrote a bank teller blackout, you had to write fifteen of them," said Michaels. "Then they would tape fifteen of them in a row." Revolutionary editing techniques were the cornerstone of the show's rapid-fire comic philosophy. Since the show was taped, the writers worked six to eight weeks in advance; most of the writing was done in hotel rooms where the staff usually wrote separately. The script was then polished during a two-week period by head writer Paul Keyes, who eventually became a speech writer for Richard Nixon, and by members of the cast. From Michaels' point of view:

The process was, and still is, that of any TV variety show: You handed in what you'd done to the head writer who then wrote it to fit the star's style. That's a very valid form of TV production—but zero interest to me. The tradition I went back to was more "New York"—Kauffman and Hart, theatrical, with Ed Sullivan sort of in the background. And it was about putting on a show in front of the audience and letting the audience be the judge of it.

Within the process, the *Laugh-In* writers had difficulty recognizing the remaining fragments of their material by the time it was filtered through the rewrite stages. "It was very confusing to me because at the end of it, I didn't know what I'd done," said Michaels. "Everyone was sitting around, congratulating the writers, saying what a great script it was." Even getting an Emmy nomination as a writer for *Laugh-In* was less than gratifying to Michaels, who said he felt like he "was standing next to the guy who gets shot and you both get the Purple Heart" (qtd. in Burke 35).

Michaels was certainly not the first writer to be left discouraged by television's production process. In her interviews with those individuals involved in television's production chain—writers, producers, directors, actors—Muriel Cantor characterized writers as "the closest to the stereotype of the lone artist of any of the creative people in Hollywood." According to Cantor, most writers say they would prefer to write drama or other fiction that is generally considered more "highbrow" than material generally written for television (89).[2]

Thus, a significant issue emerges for the writer: control. Joan Moore also describes the television writer as having little or no control over any aspect of his/her writing; work is rewritten as a matter of routine and may be changed without a writer's consent by a story editor, producer, director, or actor. Cantor's research in Los Angeles and New York reinforces Moore's contention. Producers have to worry about changes from the networks, program suppliers and advertisers; likewise writers must cope with continuous creative meddling. While some writers welcome the tension, arguing that setting limits increased creativity and gives them something to "push against," others tend to view creative meddling as a constraint that is counterproductive (Ettema 104).

Michaels's *Laugh-In* experience further reinforced what he learned earlier about "paying attention." During the Diller show, Michaels had to determine how much of the audience laughter was due to hype and how much could be attributed to well-written material. *Laugh-In*'s process was slightly different. Because the show was taped out of sequence, there was no studio audience. Twenty unrelated bits were sometimes done against one background, the recurring cocktail party set being one example. If there had been an audience for the taping, they would have had to sit in the studio for eight to ten hours at a time. It became even more difficult to judge the "success" of material. As a result, the only remaining criterion was the laughter that came from crew members or casual drifters moving in and out of the studio. *Laugh-In*'s approach was to get off ten jokes in thirty seconds, each from a different face and place. The show depended on laughs being produced by the sheer pace and energy, thus making the jokes that worked funnier than they actually were and the "duds" harder to notice.

To Michaels, television seduction was at work again. The laughs were fabricated and controlled by the person working the laughtrack, a device that always tittered, roared, or howled on cue. Thus, by air time, virtually all the spontaneity had been drained out of the material. Having been exposed to production elements, such as hype and the artificial sweetening that laughtracks and editing provide, Michaels became interested in a style that was more direct with the audience.

You've got to be close to the audience and be a good listener as a producer. I think the more you edit, mix, add music, laughs—all those things without the audience—you're getting further away from your ear. Although everybody says it's a visual medium, I listen to it more than I watch it. I trust my ear and that becomes transient for me—the sound, the rhythm. But television is too small a screen for spectacle. That's not what impressed people; people watch people.

Despite the show's production process, Michaels benefited from the experience. He summarized his *Laugh-In* tenure:

It was nice because the credit was great and because people had enormous respect for you simply because you were on a "hit." I've learned that nobody questions what anybody does if they are associated with a hit. But I didn't learn anything on *Laugh-In*. What I did learn from there was the structure and sort of industrial way in which television shows were produced. The show's producer, George Schlatter, was brilliant, as were the editors. They were the real "stars" of that show. The writers were only a part of it and the audience even less a part of it. It was all electronics, but very innovative in its day.

Michaels's training in the Canadian television system also offered a different perspective on the production process. According to Michaels,

You couldn't be a producer at CBC without knowing how TV shows are made from the beginning to end, and also knowing things that least affect the quality of the show. And you were rewarded with high quality. There, you conceived the idea, wrote it, directed, produced, and even sometimes acted it. You did everything.

In either system, Canadian or American, the most common route to becoming a producer is to work one's way through the writing ranks. According to Cantor, most producers start as writers and their career patterns progress from there to associate producer and finally to producer. This development is rather logical as writers and producers have similar functions. Since the role of the producer is closely tied to story writing, script selection, and idea formation, most producers continue to function as writers on their own productions.

Most writers are drawn to producing for two reasons: one is to protect their material; and second, producing is somewhat an extension of writing.[3] Producing essentially translates into control and creative autonomy. As Michaels's early experiences illustrate, perhaps nothing is more disturbing to a writer than to have his material altered and rewritten beyond recognition by the time it is filtered through the stages of the production process. The writer created the character, setting, situation, mood, and other elements, and therefore knows better than anyone what he or she is trying to achieve. By producing one's own written material the writer-producer can control the atmosphere, set design, clothes, actors, and other elements that best express the original ideas and artistic intention as television. However, this is not to imply that actors, directors, or others in the creative chain do not contribute to the overall shape of the work.

There is a potential problem in this development from writer to producer, a point Michaels addressed concerning the CBC. In their determined haste to become producers, many writers may have the tendency to overlook both major and minor details of the production process. They may have a limited understanding of those factors from beginning to end that contribute to and least affect the quality of a production. Although the writer-producers can control their material, they may not be aware of alternatives or possibilities that might make for a better presentation.

Following *Laugh-In* and a brief return to CBC-TV, Michaels returned to write for *The Burns and Schreiber Comedy Hour* (June 1973-Sept. 1973). He finally began to gain a greater degree of control over the material he was writing when he was given the opportunity to co-produce three Lily Tomlin specials and a Flip Wilson special in the early 1970s. Michaels's collaboration with Tomlin resulted in two Emmys as a writer and several nominations for producing. Experience taught Michaels that perseverance was a significant trait of the writer in his struggle for creative autonomy. "There's a morality that takes over in process. And process, structure, and determinism are the things that began to obsess me," said Michaels. "I became a producer to protect my writing, which was being fucked over by producers. What I learned from experience is that if you're wrong at point A, it will never get any better."

On April 1, 1975, Michaels signed a contract with NBC to develop and produce a late-night comedy program. The show became a television "institution" in the mid-to-late 1970s and had a significant impact on both comedy and television. That show was *Saturday Night Live* (1975-present) and it marked Michaels's first opportunity in American television to apply what he had learned to his own production environment and those individuals working with him.

The Producer: Finding Enough Colors to Make a Rainbow

Although Michaels controlled almost every aspect of the *Saturday Night Live (SNL)* production, he was most closely associated with, and excited about, the writing. This can be attributed in part to his own background as a writer as well as to his conviction that things had to be done right at conception. Michaels viewed the writing as the backbone of *SNL*:

I envisioned this show in which all these individual styles were gotten across as clearly as possible with me clearing the network and technological barricades. What distinguished the show from anything else were the writers. They are what the show was about. In magazines like *The New Yorker* and even *Rolling Stone*, you could always tell who wrote what. Or you could look forward to a piece by so and so. I hoped it would be that way with us.

Michaels felt his writers distinguished themselves to the point that the more discerning *SNL* viewer could spot a piece by Al Franken and Tom Davis, Rosie Shuster, Alan Zweibel, or any of the writers. To Michaels, the writers behind the collective comic mask of the show were *SNL*'s "stars."

Michaels intended for *SNL* to be a workshop where writers were trained to be television comedy writers. It was no surprise that *SNL* was more or less their lives because for three consecutive weeks a month, ninety minutes of comedy had to be written, rehearsed, and performed live on the air. The demands made for a very hectic work week. "When I was first putting the schedule together, it came out to nine work days. That was the luxurious schedule," said Michaels. "I cut it down to seven days and then we had six."

In those six days, everything happened simultaneously. As scripts were being written, sets were being designed, and films were shot. For producer Michaels, it was problem solving at a rate that bordered on being out-of-control. The creative process and virtual nocturnal existence for the writers began inconspicuously on Monday and built to a state of frenzy six days later, right up until air time on Saturday night.[4] On Monday afternoon they met as a group with the week's guest host to begin to develop ideas for the upcoming show. Michaels felt that the guest hosts forced the writers to tailor their material to a new performer each week and provided a thread to keep the show's uneven formula together.

On Monday evenings, the writers met with Michaels to present their fragments, ideas, and concepts for sketches. They mentioned what they were thinking about or wanted to work on. It was not uncommon for writers who initiated an idea to suggest another writer to develop the concept. Together they selected ideas to be developed and Michaels began to get the barest sense of the shape of the show. Michaels allowed the writers freedom to present any idea they wanted and also to write it if they believed in the piece. As a producer, he had to listen on "about five to ten different levels," and in his words, "tried to find enough colors to make a rainbow" (qtd. in White 49).

Once Michaels decided who was to develop which ideas, the writers moved into high gear. Some ideas were shelved for rewrites for future shows, but for the most part they were not stockpiled weeks in advance. The writers spent most of the week in the office, getting sleep when they could on beds and couch space. Mondays they worked through midnight, while Tuesdays were all-nighters in an attempt to prepare the script for Wednesday's read-throughs. On Wednesday afternoons the full cast and crew saw the scripts for the first time. Michaels discussed his role in the writing process:

While I was very involved creatively with all the pieces, my writing suffered a little as it was absorbed in editing, memos, or notes to myself in the studio. I did most of my writing at the talking stage. I talked down the idea with the writer until I felt it was sort of satisfactory. We'd talk through "the beats" of the piece—first this move, then this, then that, and this is the ending. When I felt it could be told to me or I could tell it back, then we were in agreement and that was the final draft. From that point on, it would be edited, rewritten, changed . . . but that idea had been "approved." So my function was an editor and to be involved in rewrites.

As is to be expected, some cast members spent more time working with specific writers because of their particular style. Michaels acknowledged the collaboration:

The actor might say, "This whole section isn't working." And since they had the experience of being up there on stage during dress rehearsal with it, that was a consideration for me. There is a certain sensitivity the writer must have to the actor. Actually, the writer in a situation can possibly be the actor or even a director. I try to get as much information as possible from everyone before completing a piece.

Thursdays and Fridays were spent rehearsing and polishing other technical preparations. Saturday afternoon was an entire run-through, although the cast and crew seldom were able to rehearse the entire show. Following the evening dress rehearsal, there remained anywhere from ninety minutes to an hour before 11:30 air time to make changes and adjustments in costumes, camera movements, cue cards, and even scripts. Despite being a live presentation, *SNL* was rigidly scripted. Shows were also deliberately written long so that sketches could be cut more conveniently after dress rehearsal. While the tension between everyone involved with the show mounted, Michaels had to make decisions on which sketches played well, which should be cut, and the best possible running order for them all. Some of the editing occurred during the course of the live show, a practice consistent with Michaels's philosophy that "comedy minds don't work ahead, they work under the gun."

Even though scripts were handed in on Wednesdays, the writers remained involved with their sketches up to and during air time. Partial or complete rewrites were a normal part of even *SNL*'s process. During the run-through, the writer of a particular sketch was usually there watching, seeing what played well, and thinking of new lines and ideas. For the most part, each writer took care of his or her own piece and its revisions. Michaels allowed them the freedom to have a say about their sketch, whether with him, the performers, art director, set designers, costumers, or other crew members. The writers were even responsible for seeing that the proper cue card changes were made and in order. Michaels's workshop was an ideal situation for the writers as each was essentially an assistant producer for his or her sketch. Michaels commented on the freedom he allowed his writers:

It was freedom with a lot of responsibility. So, if the graphics fucked up on a piece, I didn't yell at the graphics people, but the writers. They were in charge of their piece. It wasn't so much they were responsible for anything in a kind of "grand sense," but they were following it through from conception to execution. When I was on *Laugh-In,* writers weren't even allowed to come into the studio, whereas on *SNL,* the writers would be there for the camera blocking and dealt with the director and set changes.

The amount of control and involvement Michaels allowed the writers on *SNL* was unique compared to standard West Coast productions where, in many cases, scripts are written months in advance and writers get to see what is done with their script when the show is performed for the studio audience. Michaels's experience taught him that there was little satisfaction for a writer creating under this rewrite-beyond-recognition terms. "In order to get a writer to work very hard and all night if necessary, it always has to be referred to as 'his or her piece,'" said Michaels.

Another aspect of the production process that directly affected the writers was the censors. Since the earliest days of the variety show with Milton Berle, to *Laugh-In, The Smothers Brothers,* and up to and including *SNL,* censorship has checkered the history of the genre. As *SNL*'s producer, Michaels's task was to be the negotiator between his writers and the network. He viewed the relationship this way:

When I was on *Laugh-In,* the battles with the censors involved getting four-letter words on the air, or stronger sexual inferences, and I did not want to play that way. The tone of the discussions between me and the network was relatively high. I wasn't interested in getting four-letter words on the air. If you want to write in a certain way, there are plenty of other outlets. I was more interested in the intelligence of what we did.

Scripts for each show were submitted to the Broadcast Standards Department (BSD) during the week as they were completed. There were often requests by the BSD for editing, ranging from minor revisions and deletions to total rejection. When there were disagreements, Michaels normally did the negotiating. There were cases, due to the pressure of time, when the writers themselves had to argue their cases. It was a difficult position for Michaels because of the production schedule. His selection of which pieces to fight for was often dictated by factors other than the kind of material being censored. The senior and most productive writers often got preference and pieces also were considered within the context of each particular show.

Michaels and his writers did not censor themselves. There were, however, tricks of the writing trade that became valuable pawns in the negotiating game. The writers purposely sent pieces that were so outrageous they were assured of not getting past the censors. Michaels wanted the censors to have their victories; the harder he fought and the more he appeared to compromise on the clearly inappropriate material, the more likely the censors were to let the borderline cases slide by. Usually the borderline cases were actually the pieces Michaels and the writers believed in and felt were necessary for the show. Even though the censors claimed their share of victories, *SNL*'s writers felt they had a pretty free hand in the material and often stretched the bounds of acceptability on television. Most of the changes in the scripts came from Michaels, the writers, and performers—not the censors. Although much of the freedom can be attributed to the late-night weekend time slot, Michaels's understanding of television's system and his abilities as a producer to successfully operate and negotiate within those layers also contributed to the show's creative license.

In comparison to his training in what he called "the other TV system," Michaels characterized his *SNL* experience as "exhilarating because the show existed, miraculous because they didn't slip back into being television." Michaels related what he learned in his evolution from writing to being a successful producer:

It's a collaborative medium and who-does-what tends to blur in practice. There is a credit in television called "created by," which I don't take because I always think that no one person does. As a producer, I think you can learn to hold back at times. If somebody else is doing a piece, you don't necessarily need to jump in. Producing is an invisible art; if you're good at it, you leave no fingerprints.

And, after the set designer designed the sets, the director directed, the writer wrote it, and you didn't do anything, that's when you're great at producing. When you divide up the pie, you realize at the end that you are the pie. And so each time you do a show, it's like the phoenix—you rise up from the ashes and fly out of it.

Within the various stages of the production process, Michaels strived to sustain his personal vision and *SNL*'s artistic intentions without compromising the integrity of the show's writers and performers. Michaels developed an environment where his writers could express themselves without the usual restraints of television production. Certainly, Michaels's method of handling an ensemble of television's artists is not the only prescribed way in television's production universe. There is no formula; what worked for *SNL* might not be the most effective approach with other individuals or shows. While *SNL*'s success cannot be attributed exclusively to the show's production process, the workshop atmosphere that Michaels fostered contributed significantly to the levels of productivity and creativity achieved by the Not Ready for Prime Time Players.

If It Ain't on the Page . . .

Lorne Michaels's evolution from writer to producer and his experience in contrasting production environments provides a perspective on issues relevant to individual creators working in television. In the complex web of interrelationships within mass media organizations, creativity must be viewed as a process that includes, among other variables, collaboration, constraint, and compromise. Individual artists encounter these variables at various stages of the production process—from paying dues, developing their craft, and learning the system, to struggling for creative autonomy, controlling their material, and responding to both success and failure.

In the organizational framework and collaborative expression of television, it is difficult to single out one individual as being more vital than another in the creative chain. Much depends on the successful interaction and compromise within and between both the creative and executive levels of the organizational structure. During the initial stages of a production, the one individual who takes on special significance is the writer. The value of the writer's role extends beyond an image or stereotype of the lone artist because the writing itself can be viewed as the conception point in television's production stages. Although the writer may be perceived as having the least power in the production hierarchy, programs depend on his/her ability to develop ideas for scripts. Thus, writers do have power and it is reasonable to consider them the backbone of a production. Everything begins with words on a page. As television's law of supply and demand goes, anyone wanting to provide any number of programming hours must begin with a comparable number of hours in scripts.

The writer's significance is also manifest beyond program scripts. In the progression and ranks of the television industry, the writer-producer can protect and control his or her material as it is funneled through the production chain. A writer's "lowly" position on television's totem pole can be viewed in favorable terms. Individuals can take advantage of their apprenticeships by using the time to learn the various operations, structures, and rules of television's system. Within this process, a writer can shape a personal philosophy and approach to the medium that can be applied once given the opportunity as a producer. The challenge remains for the writer to view "paying dues" in positive terms. The greater temptation is to rush through the initial career stage in order to gain more control of the material. Michaels is an example of one individual who chose to view his dues-paying stage positively as he used the time to develop his writing craft, as well as an awareness of the details, styles, limitations, and potential for quality in television's system.

Individuals in other segments of television's industry—network programmers, studio executives, producers—can also shape the development and productivity at the creative levels. Network executives share some responsibility with writers in not rushing individuals through the initial stages of training. Because of economic imperatives and other pressures, networks and studios frequently take writers who should spend years as writers and make them producers before they are ready. In Michaels's case, he benefited from training in both the Canadian and American television systems. The CBC is less prone to rush writers through the ranks. Individuals learn how television shows are made from beginning to end and are able to recognize elements that affect the show's quality. Thus, when writers become producers, they know not only about writing but about directing, casting, and virtually all the technical, formal, and executive procedures.

Central to the relationship between creative executive levels are the issues of meddling and autonomy: To what degree should a network be involved in a production? Writers often become frustrated with the many channels their work must pass through before it is aired. They complain that their "good" material is left behind, rewritten, or censored. As a result, television loses many good writers, who leave discouraged and seeking other outlets where they can write under less restrictive conditions. In addition, by choosing people they consider, in some sense, "safer" producers of entertainment, the networks impose a rather severe limit on the range of experimentation and originality.

The present generation of television writers provides a final consideration relevant to creators—writing from personal experience. While many of the programming architects such as Normal Lear, Gary Marshall, Alan Burns, James Brooks, and others have moved on from the small screen to work in other areas, a new group of writers is in the ranks. The younger generation of writers is sometimes prone to write or recycle from a television frame of reference rather than from personal experience. This is not to imply that a piece of work must always be personal in order to be considered valid. As a producer, Michaels encouraged his writers to write "from their own lives." In doing so, *SNL* provides a sense of social history and a record of both a generation as well as the lives of the people doing the show. Perhaps the most important contribution that Lorne Michaels made to *SNL* was to foster a working environment that was relatively free of extensive interference and constraint, where the writers were able to focus on their creative tasks and do what they could do best—write.

Myth and Mogul: Becoming an Institution

The *Saturday Night Live*-generated myth surrounding Lorne Michaels has followed a familiar course along the spectrum of success, one that frequently evolves toward some level of demystification. By 1996, as *SNL* celebrated its twenty-first season—sixteen of those years under Michaels's guidance—his creation had become a television institution, something Michaels had always feared, resisted, and perhaps in his heart knew was inevitable.

Scathing critical reviews of Michaels's creation are now widespread. National publications such as *Newsweek* (October 17, 1994: 82) urged, "Please Die." Manhattan locals from *New Yorker* to the *New York Post* were likewise merciless—"Saturday Night' Dive—Oh No! It's Even Worse Than Before."

Granted, the accessibility of early episodes, whether through video or cable outlets such as Comedy Central, make classic comparisons convenient for critics and consumers. Yet, the commitment to creativity and the cutting edge that drove *SNL* for so many years appears to be absorbed into the mainstream market of the familiar and the formulaic. Michaels's defense is that his show has mined so much territory comically over the years, there remain few fresh resources for it to explore.

What is more disappointing than the lack of new or funny material is that as a producer, Michaels has become "safe." The lack of willingness to take risks or probe new boundaries has been missing for years.

Critics point out that when the show was in its defiant prime, Michaels and his staff would have automatically chosen the chain-smoking, bad girl Tonya Harding over the ratings-friendly ice princess Nancy Kerrigan to host the show. When Sinead O'Connor ripped up a picture of the Pope during her musical performance in October 1992, Michaels avoided the controversy, claiming he or his production crew were unaware of the papal picture sitting on the table in front of O'Connor on stage. To no one's surprise, the entire O'Connor performance was eliminated when the episode repeated.

The Michaels mystique and working environment were further tarnished in a *US* magazine article (December 1994) in which Tom O'Neill probed *SNL*'s sexist standards and its anachronistic treatment of its female writers and performers over the years. Among those expressing disappointment at the working conditions and circumstances were original Not Ready for Prime Time Player, Jane Curtin, Julie Louis-Dreyfus, Nora Dunn, Victoria Jackson, and other former cast members.

"[Michaels] is a mogul now, spreading himself thin over a comedy conglomerate," appropriately characterizes *Newsweek*'s Rick Marin. The Lorne Michaels empire clearly rests upon its *SNL* laurels; comic vision has become commodity. Michaels's multimedia marketing machine includes feature film versions of late-night characters and sketches (e.g., *Wayne's World* and *WW II, The Coneheads*, and *It's Pat*), Broadway reproductions (*Gilda Radner Live from New York*), *Best of SNL* video compilations, syndicated reruns, CD-ROMS, and slickly packaged merchandise, the most notable being a $25 coffee-table book commemorating the show's first twenty years. (The only non-*SNL* project Michaels has been involved in is also a remake, *Lassie,* which he produced for Paramount.) Even *SNL* could not escape its own legacy. In April 1995, the show may have reached a nostalgic low as Michaels recruited original cast member Dan Aykroyd to appear. Resurrecting mid-1970s characters Irwin Mainway, and the worn Blues Brothers routine with host John Goodman replacing John Belushi, the episode was a desperate attempt to rescue *SNL*'s plummeting ratings and image. Michaels has clearly violated one of his own artistic rules with *SNL* by "staying on too long." Still his early work with *SNL* will continue to have a significant influence on television comedy for many years to come.

Notes

1. Unless otherwise indicated, quotes in the text from Lorne Michaels are from personal interviews conducted by the author with Michaels in New York

City on November 20, 1984, and April 11, 1985. The author wishes to thank Lorne Michaels; and Christina McGinness at Broadway Video and John Fortenberry for their assistance in arranging the interview sessions.

2. Muriel Cantor focuses on the relationship between writers and producers in greater depth in her earlier work, *The Hollywood Producer: His Work and Audience* (New York: Basic Books, 1971).

3. In *The Producer's Medium*, Horace Newcomb and Robert Alley interview various television producers, including Quinn Martin, Gary Marshall, James Brooks, Grant Tinker, and others who discuss the development from writer to producer.

4. For participant-observation accounts of *SNL*'s production process, see Steve Ryan's "Behind the Scenes at *Saturday Night Live*," in *Broadcast Programming and Production*, March 1979: 8-13; Robert Pekurney, "The Production Process and Environment of NBC's *Saturday Night Live*," *Journal of Broadcasting*, 24.1 (1980): 91-99; and Doug Hill and Jeff Weingrad, *Saturday Night: A Backstage History of Saturday Night Live* (New York: Beech Tree, 1986).

Works Cited

Burke, Tom. "NBC's *Saturday Night*." *Rolling Stone* 15 July 1976.

Cantor, Muriel. *Prime-Time Television: Content and Control*. Beverly Hills: Sage, 1980.

Ettema, James S. "The Organizational Context of Creativity: A Case Study from Public Television." *Individuals in Mass Media Organizations: Creativity and Constraint*. Ed. James S. Ettema and D. Charles Whitney. Beverly Hills: Sage, 1982.

Newcomb, Horace, and Robert S. Alley. *The Producer's Medium*. New York: Oxford, 1983.

White, Timothy. "Saturday Night Quarterback, Lorne Michaels: The Man Who Put the Vision Back in TV?" *Rolling Stone* 27 Dec. 1979-10 Jan. 1980.

3

Evolution of the Academy Award–Winning Script for *Witness*

Michael T. Marsden

On March 15, 1985, I and fellow researcher, Kristine Fredriksson, went to the Los Angeles home of writer William Kelley to interview him about his role as a script writer for the television series, *Gunsmoke*. His coauthored film, *Witness*, had just been released and the sound track from the film filled the air as we entered his home. A chance remark of his about the origin of the script for *Witness* sent me on a seven-year search for its evolution into an Academy Award–winning script.

At the beginning of our interview that March afternoon, William Kelley remarked that it had begun as an unproduced *Gunsmoke* script. He said:

Back in the last year of *Gunsmoke* we came up with a story, you know, as we usually did sitting around with (John) Mantley in his office. About a group of people who were, I call them Simonites, but they were actually based like Simon Peter, you know . . . We called them Simonites and the story basically was that a young gunfighter . . . who was one of several sons of David Huddleston, would provoke a girl, a member of this plain sect and rip her bonnet off and say, *"Let me look at your hair."* And along came a young man, I forgot who it was supposed to be in *Gunsmoke* and I think it was supposed to be Buck Taylor, and get into the middle of it and get himself shot while defending himself against four or five other people. And . . . when he got shot, they took him back to the bruderhof and in the course of mending himself, he fell in love with the girl. But then the bad guys, David Huddleston and his sons, found them out and came looking for him. . . .

Well, then *Gunsmoke* got cancelled and so we carried it over to *How The West Was Won*, and I did it for *How The West Was Won*. During the last strike four years ago Earl called me from Fresno. "Earl Wallace," he says "Bill, remember that story you did for Gunsmoke that was transferred over?" He was then a story editor, had been on *How The West Was Won,* and we did do the Simonite story.

43

Well he said, "Remember that?" I said yes, and he said, "Well, I find myself ten pages into a script all about the whole situation, only now it's modern, it's a Philadelphia cop and an Irish woman in Lancaster County. They're plagiarizing you." Or words to that effect. He said, "Would you be interested in collaborating?" And I said to him, "You know, you and I are about the most unlikely collaborators in America. But sure, I'll think about it." And he said, "Why don't you read these papers?"

And so I did and I said, "Let's collaborate." So we did the script together, and Earl's wife, Pamela, was slightly involved. . . . They had lived in Philadelphia and Earl became the Philadelphia police expert and I was the Amish expert. In a way, then, *Witness* came out of a *Gunsmoke* story if that is of any interest.

Of course, it was of considerable interest and I made an initial attempt to collect the necessary manuscript materials in 1985-86, which was only partially successful. In the fall of 1991, I visited the John Hay Library at Brown University in Providence, Rhode Island, which contains William Kelley's papers. It was only then that I really began to piece together the story of the remarkable transformation of the unproduced script for a made-for-television movie entitled *Jedidiah* in 1973, to the unproduced *Gunsmoke* script in 1975, to the "Pig Man" segments of *How The West Was Won* (1978-1979) in 1976, to finally the award-winning, coauthored *Witness* script in 1984.

While this bit of literary detective work has been satisfying, the process has also revealed an essential truth about popular storytelling: it is dynamic and cumulative, not static and singular. Research into popular storytelling benefits not only from traditional literary analysis, including the study of manuscripts, but also from the interaction with the authors through interviews, correspondence, and telephone conversations. After my return from the John Hay Library, I wrote to William Kelley with some questions I could not answer from the manuscript materials. The response came in the form of a long telephone call that clarified much and intrigued me even more about this thing we call the creative process. But to the story of the story.

In the beginning there was the writer. As his biographical sketch in the John Hay Library notes, William Patrick Kelley was born in 1929 in Staten Island, New York. After spending some time in a Catholic seminary and working on the family farm, Kelley served in the Air Force from 1947 to 1950. He then studied at Villanova College and transferred to Brown University where he earned his B.A. in 1955. He was awarded a tuition scholarship to study law at the Harvard Law School but switched courses of study and graduated with an M.A. in literature in 1957.

Witness illustrates the culmination of a complex storytelling process which began in series television, developed into a made-for-TV script, and eventually resulted in a theatrical film. (Courtesy of the Museum of Modern Art/Film Stills Archive)

At various times he has been "a writer of novels, an editor, a reviewer, and a television and screenwriter." In 1957 and 1958, he was an editor at Doubleday. From 1958 to 1961, he was their West Coast editor, and from 1961 to 1962, he was an editor with McGraw Hill. He is the author of three novels, *Gemini* (1959), *The God Hunters* (1964) and *The Tyree Legend* (1979) as well as a biography, *Miracle in the Evening* (1961). Unable to make a living as a novelist, Kelley turned to more lucrative screenwriting at which he became commercially and artistically successful, winning major recognition for his work, including the Spur Award and Western Writers of America Awards.

The first version of the *Witness* script emerged in 1973 when Kelley was hired to write a script for a made-for-television movie, *Jedidiah*, which would deal with the Amish. Since he knew little about the Amish,

NBC sent him out to study these rural people in Lancaster County, Pennsylvania. His main informant became Bishop Miller. But according to Kelley, neither the Bishop nor other Amish he met were forthcoming about details of Amish life and culture, until he struck a deal with Bishop Miller, a carriage maker, to buy ten of his carriages for the film and agree to sell them back to the Bishop after the filming for 25 percent of the original purchase price of $10,000 to $12,000 each (Telephone conversation Feb. 24, 1992).

Due to the tragedy of a plane crash involving several of the key people for the network production, the film was never made. The script is a powerful story of Jedidiah Kipp, an Amish Bishop, whose wife has recently died and who decides to head west. So he sells his farm and equipment, saving only his sturdy Amish carriage and his horse, Titus, as he begins his 3,000 mile westward trek. Kelley's rich opening descriptions of Jedidiah Kipp and his Amish world are worth quoting to establish the man and his vision of the world:

Jedidiah Kipp is a prodigy of sheer physical presence . . . So far in his adult life, no man has seen fit to try Mr. Kipp physically. One *did* manage to affront him so infuriatingly and flagrantly one afternoon in Lancaster—a Green Beret Major in uniform, and something of a hero, and quite drunk, who accosted Jedidiah's now-deceased and beautiful wife, Susannah, as she waited on a street corner for Jedidiah to pick her up . . . the Major so determined to get a look at Susannah's hair that he threatened her, offered her money, and finally grabbed her and ripped her black bonnet from her head . . . just as Jedidiah drove up—that Jedidiah made the first (and, as it turned out, the only) move: he threw the Major (without actually intending the placement) into the back of a passing pickup truck loaded with washers and dryers. The Major wasn't heard from again. Jedidiah's only comment was: *"The Lord giveth, and the Lord taketh away."* (2)

Jedidiah is pursued by an attorney who seeks to persuade him that he is the right and proper owner of a Baltimore apartment building that is about to be torn down by the city to make way for a housing project. Jedidiah is staunch in his insistence that neither he nor his deceased wife owned any such property. The attorney is equally insistent that he does because it was inherited by his deceased wife. Although Jedidiah wants no part of the sale or proceeds from the condemnation of such a building, he decides to go to Baltimore and fix up the apartment building in memory of his wife.

The site of an Amish horse and buggy in inner-city Baltimore causes insensitive comments and unfriendly gestures. Jedidiah remembers his relatives talking of the house and its two-hundred-year history. Before actually seeing the building, he decides that it must be of sturdy beam and timber construction and thus must be saved. Kipp finds himself lost at night in Baltimore. He happens upon a burlesque house and stripper by the name of Fritzi Dalton who is attracted to this strange man enough to offer him clear directions to his apartment building where, as fate would have it, she is a tenant.

Kelley's description of Fritzi is effective at establishing precisely the type of woman she is and the kind of woman Kipp could never have known:

She's had the gambling, booze, and narcotic scenes . . . has blown-it-all-in time and again, and lost . . . gone for broke and got busted . . . paid her dues at the devil's high table with interest and penalties. But that was yesterday . . . now nothing to drink between shows . . . damned few men, and no women . . . savings account . . . and nothing more narcotic than a joint (pot) with a consenting male adult before her very occasional sexual indulgences. She's a practical, hard-nosed, good natured, but thoroughly disenchanted female person who has not permitted her intense sexuality to take charge of her in almost five years— since the last bad-ass bastard of a lying, schizoid, good-looking pimp of a night-club owner turned her on to speed, prostitution (she lasted through four tricks, then attempted suicide), and—as a by-product—the deviousness and cold calculation of your average, working bisexual American son-of-a-bitch. (31)

Kipp learns quickly about his other tenants—Miss Tallulah Mulligan and her two cats (Rhett and Butler), Amy Schuster, Roy Fry, her would-be pimp, and her husband, ex-tenant Edward Schuster. Kipp arrives just as Schuster has set fire to the roof over the apartment where his wife and her pimp are sleeping. Kipp tries to stop Schuster, but gets knocked out for his troubles.

Kipp is unwilling to fight the city in court and instead spends his time and money fixing up the building as a monument to his deceased wife. In the process, he becomes more and more attracted to Fritzi and eventually comes to understand her occupation and way of life. His outrage at her moral milieu fights for control over his growing love for her.

While the building cannot be saved, it is discovered that it was, in fact, built around 1800 by Benjamin Henry Latrobe, who subsequently became the architect who rebuilt Washington after the British burned it in the War of 1812. This allows Kipp to arrange for the structure to be moved to a plot of land nearby where it can be preserved as an historic building. On the morning of the big move, trucks and busses of Simonites arrive to help in the great event, a scene which foreshadows the barn raising scene in *Witness*. But, in this version, they first dismantle a structure before reassembling it.

While Jedidiah Kipp is not a man of violence, he physically ejects the pimp from his apartment house after he finds the man taunting Fritzi. While Jedidiah Kipp is not a man of the civil law or the courts, he does find a legal and satisfying solution to his problem of owning property he does not wish to own by means of relocation and historical presentation. While he is a man of high moral values and a strong Biblical sensibility, he loves and makes love to the tainted but honest Fritzi. He leaves his monument and his loves behind as he turns his carriage west to a new beginning once he has paid his past debts.

Given that *Jedidiah* was never produced and the *Gunsmoke* version never filmed, Kelley seized the opportunity to salvage the concept in the "Simonites" episode of *How the West Was Won* (1976). Known as "The Pig Man," the episode became one of two running story lines he authored in the successful miniseries. Kelley's narrator at the beginning of the script sets the tone:

In the early days of the West, there were many unique, highly religious sects dedicated to agrarian culture and community living, but above all to an ideology that identified almost anything frivolous as sinful. Perhaps the best known of these groups were the Quakers, the Amish, the Mennonites, the Hutterites, the Mormons, and later, the Russian Dukhobors. These God fearing groups wished nothing more than to be left alone to pursue the quiet tenor of their lives, but frequently their peaceful mode of existence came into harsh and terrifying conflict with the ignorant, and often violent, forces which, unfortunately, were also a part of the birth pangs of a new nation. This is a story about such a community. (N.p.)

The script opens with the young Erika Hanks's being harassed by two cowboys, with a third looking on. Also present are Erika's father, her young brother and another Simonite man. Two of the cowboys, Billy and Charley, are the Judson brothers. Their taunting of Erika escalates, even though she does not resist and the Simonites do nothing to interfere except asking the ruffians to stop. The scene is certainly similar to the scene described but not acted out in *Jedidiah* and foreshadows the town scene in *Witness*. The arrival of gunman Seth Macahan heightens the tension, and after his departure the brutishness of the Judson brothers is revealed. Seth returns for a showdown in which he kills Billy Judson in a fair fight.

Subsequently, Seth is ambushed by the two remaining cowboys and taken to the bruderhof by Erika and her brother to recover. While the elders are disturbed at having a gunman in their community, they relent when he acknowledges his wrongdoing, expresses his sorrow, and states his intent to live "plainly" among them. His growing affection for Erika is certainly part of his new found salvation; but so is the fact that he is tired of running away from anyone who thinks he has a faster gun.

His sanctuary among the Simonites notwithstanding, Seth is pursued by the vengeful father of the brutish cowboys, Christy Judson, whom Kelley describes as "a man of Biblical proportions and passions" (13). Unaware of the pursuing danger, Seth falls in love with Erika and his affection turns to passion. Although he has difficulty coming to terms with the pacifism of the Simonites, particularly after Erika reveals her own mother was raped and killed by itinerant railroad workers and her father almost killed, yet they pressed no charges, Seth comes to the conclusion that "the more I see of you people, the more I think maybe you got the right idea about things" (32).

Seth's role in the community is clarified when it becomes known they need a man to tend to the pigs and he has had experience on the family farm. A traveling salesman spots him at the bruderhof and conveys the information to the vengeful Christy Judson. While he awaits the final showdown, he instructs Joshua, the young brother of Erika, about violence in the world. Seth says to Joshua, "I'd far rather be a good man like your daddy, and these others, than an outlaw any day" (37). Seth has given up his guns for farm tools and wishes to change his fate.

Despite the warnings of her father, Elam, who tells her, "But be on your guard, Erika, my child. Against the rise of untoward affections. He is not Plain. He is not among us" (41), Erika becomes one in spirit with Seth, even if not in flesh. But the inevitable danger and violence arrive just as Seth is making long-term commitments to the Simonite community.

Christy Judson's vengeance knows no bounds. If the Simonites will not give Seth up to him, he will kill them and then Seth. When Seth appears unarmed, Christy and his hired hands shoot at him. Young Joshua had hidden Seth's six-gun and retrieves it in time for Seth to protect himself and the Simonites against the unchecked violence they have witnessed. Seth concludes: "I wanted it . . . I really wanted to be like you: to be a Simonite, I thought I could. I know now that I can't. The road you've chosen takes more courage than I'll ever have" (63). Seth cannot live their ways and avoid his fate; he must leave, but he is infused with a new understanding of the alternative to violence, even if it doesn't work for him.

Bill Kelley met Earl Wallace when Wallace was a Fresno, California, newspaperman who had sold a couple of scripts for *Gunsmoke* and became the story editor for the series. When Wallace was looking for some new script ideas during the final years of *Gunsmoke*, Kelley discussed the unproduced *Jedidiah* with him and they agreed it could be made into a one-hour *Gunsmoke*. But the series went off the air before that happened. As was recounted earlier, during a writers' strike in the early 1980s, Bill Kelley found himself with a request from Wallace to collaborate on the script for *Witness*. Wallace penned the Philadelphia police sequences and Kelley wrote the Amish scenes. A March 9, 1981, letter from Wallace to Kelley gives clear evidence of the respective areas of responsibility of this collaboration Wallace wrote:

Here are the pages that wrap up the Philadelphia sequence. On the whole I think it works pretty well, but I think we might want to know a little more about Book, and certainly anything we can add to make Rachel's character more robust and vital will be helpful.

You may want to note some changes in the early pages. I reworked Rachel's motivation for leaving the farm.

P.S. You'll also notice I wantonly plundered *"JEDIDIAH"* in a couple of instances.

It is not a Simonite bishop nor a gunman who is the hero of *Witness*, but a Philadelphia policeman. John Book is not Jedidiah Kipp nor is he Seth Macahan; in fact, he is the best of both the traditions of contemplation and of action placed in a contemporary urban environment of the mid-1980s. Director Peter Weir's comments on *Witness* in a March1986 interview in *American Film* are revealing:

QUESTION: *Witness*, a cop thriller set in the Amish country, seems to have a very different look from your other films.

WEIR: I think it's a case of using one's talents to serve the idea rather than imposing a style overall. The challenge was really to deal with the melodrama with as much grace and style as I could, but not drift too far from it. That's where the producer and I were a good team. Ed Feldman is an old-time show-biz man, and when I started to become too Amish he would remind me that this was a Western we were making, and to get some more shotguns in there! (14)

While the exchange in this interview reveals a lack of sensitivity to the delicacy of the film's plot, it does suggest a continuity with the threads of the former lives of the *Witness* script.

Although the film was criticized by some for not being an accurate portrayal of the Amish, it spends as much if not more time and effort establishing the cultural milieu of the Amish than did either *Jedidiah* or

"The Pig Man" story line of *How The West Was Won.* The opening scene of the funeral of Jacob Lapp and the introduction of the strong character of the widow Rachel Lapp introduces the Amish setting in stark terms. Needing time to come to terms with her grief, Rachel takes her son Samuel on a trip to Philadelphia to visit her sister. It is there in a train station bathroom that young Samuel witnesses a murder which will change his and his mother's lives forever.

While Rachel and Samuel in their Amish attire are strangely out of place in the train station and in the police station, they are clear representatives of truth and morality in a society given to corruption at the very highest levels, even in the police department, as the script slowly reveals. Detective John Book's violent methods of crime-solving are not reconcilable with the God-fearing and gentler ways of Rachel Lapp. The industriousness and cleanliness of Rachel and her son, Samuel, are contrasted with the slovenliness of Book's sister, Elaine, to whom Book takes them to give them a safe place to sleep for the night.

The corruption inside the police force sends Book undercover after he is shot. He drives through the night to return Rachel and Samuel to the safety of the Amish community. As in "The Pig Man" story line of *How the West Was Won,* John Book is accepted by the elders into the care of the community until his wound heals.

In a scene reminiscent of the exchange between Seth and Joshua in "The Pig Man," Book begins to give lessons about the gun to young Samuel until he is severely reprimanded by Rachel. Book must shelve his pistol when he is with the Amish. Samuel's grandfather, Eli, gives the boy an important Amish lesson by reminding him, "What you take into your hands, you take into your heart . . . Don't you see . . .? The hand leads the arm leads the shoulder leads the head . . . leads the heart. The one goes into the other into the other into the other . . . And you have changed, and gone amongst them" (62).

Book, like Seth before him, adopts the Amish ways and learns to do his part of the chores. He has some carpentry skills which he puts to good use in repairing a birdhouse knocked over with his car upon his arrival and in helping with an Amish barn-raising in one of the most powerful scenes of the film. Unlike the house dismantling in *Jedidiah,* this is a community "mantling." And Book makes a significant contribution to the community he is adopting.

There is a visually powerful scene in the film where Book happens upon Rachel washing herself in the kitchen. It harkens back to a scene in *Jedidiah* where Jedidiah recalls II Samuel 11 in which David was aroused from his bed and walked upon the roof of the king's house and saw a beautiful woman washing herself. But Book walks away, knowing it is not right and "plain." A later scene finds Book in town with the Amish getting some supplies and being harassed by some rowdies. Book intervenes in an uncharacteristically Amish fashion, but in a manner consistent with the legend of Jedidiah, he rights the unrighteous through violence.

The final showdown is necessarily bloody as the legal forces of might come into conflict with the moral forces of right in an environment of brotherly love. But unlike the film, the screenplay resolves the dilemma with only necessary violence and without the blaring of shotguns which Peter Weir suggests producer Ed Feldman demanded for effect. Book's major antagonist, Schaeffer, is dissuaded from violence against Book through the determination of throngs of Amish. He just drives away, defeated. The film, however, climaxes in a major shotgun fight which results in the defeat and the arrest of Schaeffer, as befits a mid-1980s society obsessed with clear and definite ideas on law and order.

Book, like Seth Macahan cannot stay. He must return to his world. But the script for *Witness* through its four major versions, provides a unique look at cultural conflict in the modern world, however broadly drawn. If the picture is less than accurate in its details of Amish culture, Kelley would remind us that the Amish are living an oral culture and do not write down their history and customs. Additionally, they are slow to share their world with outsiders, particularly people from Hollywood.

As a case study, this analysis of the evolution of an Academy Award–winning script illustrates the essential complexities and yet the quintessential simplicity of the storytelling process, which is molded and shaped by the various media it is designed and redesigned to fit through its multiple retellings. In the process, the externals contract and expand to meet the needs of the various media and their audience, and the story even crosses genres from the western to the detective story to maintain audience appeal. But the core attraction remains constant in the powerful story of deep values in continuing and ongoing conflict in our world.

Note

The author would like to acknowledge the considerable assistance he was given in this research project by the following people: Alexandra Brouwer and Edward Feldman of Paramount Pictures Corporation, M. N. Brown of the John Hay Library in the Brown University Library, and, of course, William Kelley. He would also like to thank Gary Edgerton of Old Dominion University, Jack Nachbar of Bowling Green State University, and Madonna Marsden for their most helpful suggestions for strengthening the article.

References

John Hay Library of Brown University Library, *"Biographical Sketch."*

Kelley, William. *Jedidiah*, First Draft. 3 Dec. 1973.

——. Personal interview. 15 Mar. 1985.

——. *"Pig Man,"* from *How the West Was Won,* Second Draft. 4 Feb.1976.

——. Telephone conversation. 24 Feb. 1992.

Wallace, Earl W., and William Kelley. *Called Home*, Revised Draft. 8 Apr.1984.

Weir, Peter. *American Film* 11. 5 (1986): 13-15.

4

Flow, Genre, and the Television Text

Gregory A. Waller

According to John Hartley, one of the principal reasons for television's "dirtiness"—and hence for its power and significance—is that television is not only "recalcitrant when it comes to identifying where the text should stop" (120) but it is "resistant to classification into texts" (126). This view quite obviously runs counter to virtually all program guides, newspaper reviews, and popular histories, which assume that television's texts are easily identifiable and named (and by extension easily read). Juxtaposing Hartley's dirty television with the cleanliness of *TV Guide* raises basic questions about the common ways we have of speaking about television texts—in terms of schedules, programs, episodes, series, serials, and specials—and about two concepts that are particularly important in contemporary television criticism, flow and genre.

"Flow," Raymond Williams affirms in his influential 1974 study, *Television: Technology and Cultural Form*, is the "central television experience" (95). In part, Williams's seminal analysis of flow is offered as a response to mass communication studies of "effects," to McLuhan's technological determinism, and to criticism's traditional concern for the "discrete event" and the individual text. Television, he argues, presents itself as "programme"—a sequence of "timed units" marked by clear intervals (89)—yet the incorporation of commercials and trailers underscores that the "real broadcasting" is a "flow series of differently related units" (93), which is the product of both advertising and the competition for viewers among TV networks. Thus in lieu of analyzing television programming in terms of individual units, Williams proposes three objects of study, from "long-range to "close-range": the sequence of programs (TV's self-proclaimed "programme"); this sequence plus all the material that appears "within and between" programs; and the messy string of specific images and sounds that constitute the "real character of television flow" (115). The study of flow, in other words, requires what could be called close textual analysis. Williams's sample analyses suggest that approaching television in these terms will enable us to better differentiate among TV networks and to identify the relations between programs and advertising/trailers. Most important, television's flow itself "establishes a sense of the world" (116) and reveals the "flow of meanings and values of a specific culture" (118).

A good deal of the most perceptive recent criticism of television's ideological implications draws upon Williams's study. Margaret Morse, for example, discusses the privileged programming position of TV sports in terms of the concept of flow, and Tania Modleski studies "the flow of daytime television" by exploring the way "soap operas, quiz shows, and commercials interrelate" (67). Williams's formulations have also been amended, qualified, and redirected in different ways by, among others, Stephen Heath and Gillian Skirrow, John Fiske and John Hartley, John Ellis, and Horace M. Newcomb and Paul M. Hirsch.

Beginning, like Williams, with the paradox that the "television message sequence is certainly naturally continuous" and yet also broken into "discrete programmes" (166-67), Fiske and Hartley in *Reading Television* stress the importance of boundaries—the credit sequences for individual programs as well as the trailers and other elements that reinforce the continuity between programs. Such transitions operate as "boundary rituals" and thereby reinforce the fact that "the different programmes which together make up television's total output paradigm mean what they do in opposition to each other" (169). Fiske and Hartley's insistence on the continuousness and the structured oppositions of television's "message sequence" does not preclude their taking the "discrete programme" as a valid object of study. When they offer a semiotic and ideological reading of *Ironside* (1967-1975) or the British police detective series, *The Sweeney* (1974-1978), Fiske and Hartley begin with an individual episode; the most important context for this text is not flow as Williams defines it but rather other episodes of the series and other contemporary examples of the police detective genre.

John Ellis in *Visible Fictions* acknowledges that his definition of "TV's commodity as a programmed series of meaningful segments used in a domestic context" (117) is indebted to Williams's conception of flow. Ellis differs from Williams, however, in insisting on segmentation as the definitive feature of broadcast TV as cultural and narrative form. Television segments are brief, "relatively self-contained," and clearly demarcated units; each is characterized by "completion and internal coherence," though in context they participate in a continuous process of repetition and difference. Even within the individual episodes of a dramatic or action series, the movement from segment to segment is most often "a matter of succession rather than consequence" (148-49). "Broadcast TV narration," he argues, "takes place across these segments, characteristically in series or serials" (112). Rather than the individual program or what Williams calls the "actual succession of words and images" (96), the series and serial—as general modes of narration and as specific products—become for Ellis the privileged object of study if one wants to analyze "TV's process of segmentalisation of its flow" (126).

As might be expected, Ellis is not alone in according special status to the series and serial. (Network programmers and publicity departments, along with TV reviewers, often foster the idea that the quintessential television product is not flow or the individual program but the series.) Stanley Cavell, who asks much different questions about television and television viewing than does Ellis, proposes that we "locate television's aesthetic interest in a serial-episode mode of composition" (251). Intentionally leaving open the nature of the relationship between serial and series, Cavell turns his attention to specific television formats and to a more general consideration of the formulaic and the improvisatory in the serial-episode mode. One reason this mode is of aesthetic interest is because it acknowledges the continuousness of television, which for Cavell is not flow but "current," characterized by the "act of switching" (from, say, program to commercial) that is always "effected simultaneous with our watching" (253).

Newcomb and Hirsch, in their essay "Television as a Cultural Forum," offer a view of "television as a whole system" (64) that is much more closely aligned with flow as Williams defines it than with Ellis's dialectic of segmentation and continuity or Cavell's current. Newcomb and Hirsch propose that the most revealing and valid television text is not the individual episode, series, or genre, but the "viewing strip"—for example, "any given evening's televiewing"—taken in its entirety (66). The viewing strip is, like the examples Williams considers, a section of flow isolated for study by the analyst. (In this article, at least, Newcomb and Hirsch imply that the strip is, above all, a string of programs; they pay little or no attention to those elements "within and between" programs that for Williams create the flow of television broadcasting.) One justification for taking the viewing strip as text is that it is "akin" to the "actual experience" of TV viewers (66); another more significant reason is that the strip best reveals the role of television as "cultural forum." Challenging what they perceive to be reductive assessments of television's relations to ideology and the hegemonic, Newcomb and Hirsch stress television's "multiplicity of meanings," its "rhetoric of discussion," and its "raising of questions" (61-64).[1] Better than any single program or series, the "viewing strip" or "flow strip" (66) is a microcosm of the "whole system" of television, which "presents a mass audience with the range and variety of ideas and ideologies inherent in American culture" (64).

Flow is possibly the wrong word to describe the process of television as cultural forum. Flow suggests continuousness and continuity, even, perhaps, a sort of ideological leveling and smoothing out or an easy plentitude; Newcomb and Hirsch's cultural forum, in contrast, is unceasingly "complex," "contradictory," and "confused" (71). In their insistence on the *cultural*—pragmatic, referential, reflective—role and place of television and on TV's function as a *forum*, that is, as a public site for debate, discussion, and the presentation of "ideas and ideologies," of meanings, Newcomb and Hirsch are quite clearly poles apart from the sort of extreme conventionalist/textualist position argued by, for example, Mimi White, who finds that commercial television's "progressively all-encompassing self-referentiality" reveals the extent to which "the whole of television" has become a "self-defining and self-contained" fictional world ("Crossing Wavelengths" 56, 59).

Granted, Newcomb and Hirsch's essay is presented in the spirit of a proposal rather than a fully elaborated critical method, but there still seem to me some basic questions concerning the viewing strip as the most appropriate and revealing television text. For instance, does the viewing strip as cultural forum only apply to strips of major network telecasting? to strips of primetime television? Is the cultural forum best (or only) in evidence in a strip of "new" programs? Here I have in mind the common practice of reruns and the syndication of "old" programs. Interweaving the familiar or the dated or the already-shown with the new surely compounds the complexity and the contradictions of any viewing strip. This situation has always been evident in the programming of independent stations and in the netherland between daytime and primetime schedules of network affiliates. With the spread of cable systems the spectrum of available programs—both old and new—increases substantially. More important, what increases even more dramatically with cable TV is what Newcomb and Hirsch call "the range of options offered by any given evening's televiewing" (66). I realize that cable TV is not available to or affordable by all viewers and that "television" is still equated by many with primetime network programming, but consider how much broader the cultural forum of television becomes with the inclusion of superstations, MTV, the Christian Broadcasting Network, and C-SPAN—and consider also what a complex task it becomes to identify the "range of options" and analyze the viewing strips contained in an evening's worth of cable TV.

Particularly for Williams and Newcomb and Hirsch, flow is the definitive characteristic of television programming and the flow strip is the most telling and most appropriate text for analysis in part because of the way they understand what it means to watch television. Recall that Newcomb and Hirsch justify their insistence on the flow strip because,

If we are to define the television text in terms of "actual viewing experience," then the individual program as well as the viewing strip has a claim to our attention. (Courtesy of the AFI Collection)

among other reasons, this text is "akin to [the] actual experience" of the television audience (66). Going with the flow in this context does not mean that television viewers are necessarily docile, indiscriminating, interchangeable zombies. (On the contrary, Newcomb and Hirsch are at pains to insist that the viewer is active, alert, and individual.) It simply means that the television audience watches TV—not this or that program, series, or genre, but television, as in "let's watch some TV," or "turn on the TV."

Understood in this way, watching TV is surely a common "actual experience" for certain viewers in certain situations. However, whether watching TV was or is still the "normal experience of broadcasting," as Williams asserted in 1974 (89), seems to me problematic.[2] In all likelihood, viewing habits run the gamut from Newcomb and Hirsch's sense of watching TV to turning on a set and selecting a channel solely for the purpose of seeing an individual program—a "special" presentation or a specific example of a favorite series or format or genre. One noteworthy example of this latter type of viewing is the use of videocassette recorders for "time-shifting," rerunning, and in some cases even accumulating private collections (libraries? archives?) of individual programs. This act of co-opting and taking possession of a program affirms the independent status of the program, as does in a different fashion the phenomenon of the rerun and the syndicated program.[3] (Further, we should note that certain television programs—most often made-for-TV movies and miniseries—have subsequently been marketed as individual videocassettes.)

If we are to define the television text in terms of "actual viewing experience," then the individual program as well as the viewing strip has a claim to our attention. I am not suggesting that the individual program somehow be studied "in itself"—decontextualized, as it were—for as White notes, "[I]t is almost impossible to watch television without being referred to other aspects of the medium in some way" ("Crossing Wavelengths" 61). And taking the program as text does not necessarily preclude the analysis of flow. Even removed from its original broadcasting context, the program will in the great majority of cases still bear the traces of flow, segmentalization, and the cultural forum—though these characteristics of television will be more readily apparent in, depending on the critic, the flow strip, the series, or the serial.

Any reading of a television text, however defined, should take into account the specificity of broadcast television, that "central experience" (Williams 95), "distinctive aesthetic form" (Ellis 112), or set of televisual codes that the critics I have surveyed identify as, or link to, the seemingly paradoxical and dirty mix of the continuous and the discrete. In practice, what would this entail for the study of an individual program? On the one hand, one would examine how the program exemplifies television's flow or negotiates what Jane Feuer calls the "dialectic of segmentation and flow" (15). On the other hand, one would examine the program in the context of its "original" viewing strip (defined as a schedule of programs, an evening's televiewing, a week of programming, or perhaps even a television season), analyzing it in relation to the texts that surround (or, more accurately, precede and succeed) it, with an eye toward tracing, for example, ideological continuity or the diversity and contradictions of the cultural forum. These two lines of inquiry are complementary, for in both cases the study of flow underscores the significance of syntagmatic relations.

A quite different but equally important reading of the individual program would proceed horizontally rather than vertically, situating the text in terms of relations that we might say exist *across* television rather than in the consecutiveness of the flow. From this perspective, more concerned with the paradigmatic dimension of the text, the program could be discussed as a particular instance of a television format—the series, for example, or the serial, anthology, miniseries, or made-for-TV movie, each of which is characterized by a certain conception (and certain codes) of narrative structure and closure. For those programs that are examples of the series or serial format, a related but nonetheless distinct procedure would be to read the program as one episode or installment or instance of a specific series or serial, thus raising questions about the role of the viewer's memory and expectations and about the ideological and aesthetic implications of the relations between repetition and difference, the familiar and the novel.

Similar questions are raised when we (re)place the individual program in its generic context, a context that also cuts across television's flow.[4] Genre, however, is a less manageable and more dirty concept than format, and it is obviously much easier to identify the NBC program telecast last Thursday at 9:00 P.M. as an episode of *Cheers* (1982-1993) than it is to identify with any precision the genre to which this episode belongs. Should we label this episode a comedy, a sitcom, an "adult" sitcom, and/or perhaps an example of a subgenre that would include other primetime shows that prominently feature what Thomas H. Zynda calls the "workplace or professional family" as figuration of community (256)? An attention to genre must, in White's words, "involve recognition of generic overlap and mixing within individual texts" ("Television Genres" 41). Thus genre criticism, I suggest, involves both the analysis of already-named categories—what Neale calls "systems of orientations, expectations, and conventions that circulate between industry, text, and subject" (19)—and also the tracing or heuristic invention of "new" categories and lines of intertextuality. There is no reason to junk the notion of genre (and subgenre) because of the taint of subjectivity or because cultural products cannot be categorized and classified as precisely and objectively as natural flora and fauna. For one thing, we simply can't do away with genre, unless we choose to ignore that the important functional role of genre—as a marketing strategy and a means of regulating the production of and directing the reception of popular culture—is constantly reinforced by the industries that produce, distribute, and market television programs, movies, recorded music, and paperback books. For another, the very haziness of the boundaries around any specific genre, subgenre, or cycle, the continual overlapping, mixing, and realignment of one category and another, and the capacity of genres to change to accommodate diversity seem to me to be of central importance in any consideration of the aesthetic and ideological workings of contemporary American popular culture.

Fiske and Hartley's analysis of *Ironside* exemplifies one common form of genre criticism: The individual episode is read in the context of the entire series, then is differentiated from other examples of the "police series genre" (177), which are drawn from British as well as American TV and are all roughly contemporaneous with *Ironside* (1967-1975). Quite clearly, genre here cuts across individual networks and across television's flow. Fiske and Hartley's comparison of *Ironside* with *Starsky and Hutch* (1975-1979) is a particularly apt example of the way different programs "mean what they do in opposition to each other" (169), since both series are readily identified by producers and consumers alike as belonging to the police detective genre and both were at one point telecast during the same TV season. A corollary procedure might focus also on the opposition between *Ironside* and examples of adjacent genres and subgenres, including police—but not detective—shows (like *The Rookies* [1972-1976] and *Police Story* [1973-1977]) and detective—but not police—shows (like *Cannon* [1971-1976] and *The Rockford Files* [1974-1980]) whose primetime runs overlapped with *Ironside*'s. While the notion of adjacency underscores the fact that contemporary popular genres form a continuum, the many recombinant or hybrid texts that in various ways draw upon the conventions of different genres remind us that this continuum is in a continual process of transformation and realignment.

Attentiveness to the role of genre in television programming leads to a consideration of the diachronic as well as the synchronic—in other words, to the relations between an individual text and its immediate precursors and successors and, more broadly, to its generic inheritance (which may or may not be explicitly marked or self-consciously alluded to in the text). Whatever consistency and conventionality genres may demonstrate, they are not static. Particularly in popular culture, their evolution or (if the connotation of an "organic" and "natural," self-determined process makes "evolution" an unacceptable term) their historical transformation is ever present. Indeed, this strikes me as a definitive feature of television, movie, and rock music genres. Thus Todd Gitlin quite correctly observes that in analyzing what he calls the "hegemonic process in television entertainment . . . whenever possible it is illuminating to trace the transformations in a genre over a longer period of time" (257). Writing the history of a popular genre has traditionally meant surveying the genre's masterpieces and most commercially successful examples in chronological order. John Cawelti and Will Wright, among others, have offered more sophisticated models for analyzing the historical transformation of popular genres, as has Robert C. Allen in *Speaking of Soap Operas*, which focuses on both the institutional history of this genre and the "history of soap opera reception" (96-179).[5]

Furthermore, reading a television text in terms of genre not only carries us against the flow and into history, it also very often leads outside television to radio, print journalism, or most interestingly, to movies and popular fiction. There is a host of commonplace phenomena—usually disregarded or dismissed by television, film, and literary scholars—that indicate the varied, shifting interrelations among the articulations of a given genre in different media: novelizations and paperback tie-ins to film or television production; telefilms and TV series based on hit movies or on successful trends in other media; the telecasting of theatrical films; the careers of well-known actors, comedians, directors, and writers; and the adaptation of fiction and nonfiction publications for film and television.[6] Analyzing from a transmedia perspective the contemporary breadth and the historical depth of a given genre need not and should not disregard the individual text, the quite different forms of institutional pressure brought to bear on, and manifested in, any work of art, and the specificity of television or film or literature. Understood in this way, genre criticism is not a quest for a closed set of definitive features, an essential formula, or an archetypal narrative. Nor is its goal the establishment of a comprehensive catalog or a hierarchically arranged guidebook. Instead, it foregrounds the formal and ideological interplay between repetition and variation by examining the way a group of texts "mean what they do in opposition to each other."[7]

Genre removes us from the flow and the viewing strip, but nonetheless it complements what Newcomb and Hirsch call TV's role as cultural forum. At once diffuse and standardized, assimilative and inbred, topical and traditional, contemporary American popular genres stretch across media to enact, display, and create the "range and variety of ideas and ideologies inherent in American culture" (Newcomb and Hirsch 64).

Notes

1. One position in the debate over television and ideology is exemplified by E. Ann Kaplan, who assumes without question that the "signifying practices" of the television text "embody the dominant ideology" and so work to "ensure cultural hegemony" (xiv). However, as Todd Gitlin insists, "hegemony is reasserted in different ways at different times, even by different logics; if this variety is analytically messy, the messiness corresponds to a disordered ideological order, a contradictory society" (254). Fiske and Hartley make a comparable point when they examine the "mythologies" and the "bardic function" of television (85-100). See Williams (1977) for a more general study of the complex process of hegemony.

2. Granted their limitations, empirical surveys of viewing habits and preferences might be of some service here. For example, Comstock et al. cite a study of "Motives for Viewing" in which 81 percent of the adult respondents in 1970 gave as the reason they "usually" watch television "to see a specific program," while 46 percent of these respondents watched because they "felt like watching television" (131).

3. For Gitlin the growth of the home video recorder market does not so much alter the television text as it demonstrates how "the widely felt need to overcome assembly-line 'leisure' time becomes the source of a new market-to sell the means for private, commoditized solutions to the time-jam" (255).

4. For an introduction to the most familiar and traditional television genres, see the essays included in Rose.

5. For a discussion of the diachronic transformation of traditional literary genres, see Fowler.

6. In proposing that we follow the transformations of a genre and its manifestation in different media I am not implying that viewers of, say, TV detective shows are necessarily readers of detective novels or patrons of detective movies, or that they are necessarily familiar with even the recent history of this genre. One anomalous type of "informed" reader in this respect is the horror or science fiction devotee, who often follows his or her favorite genre in all of its manifestation. Thus a horror "fanzine" like *Fangoria* includes articles and interviews on horror films and made-for-TV examples of the genre, as well as reviews of horror novels, historical surveys, and autobiographical reminiscences.

7. For an application of this type of genre criticism, see Waller.

Works Cited

Allen, Robert C. *Speaking of Soap Operas*. Chapel Hill: U of North Carolina P, 1985.

Cavell, Stanley. "The Fact of Television." *Themes Out of School: Effects and Causes*. San Francisco: North Point, 1984.

Cawelti, John G. *Adventure, Mystery, and Romance: Formula Stories as Art and Popular Culture*. Chicago: U of Chicago P, 1976.

Comstock, George, Steven Chaffee, Natan Katzman, Maxwell McCombs, and Donald Roberts. *Television and Human Behavior*. New York: Columbia UP, 1978.

Ellis, John. *Visible Fictions: Cinema; Television; Video*. London: Routledge & Kegan Paul, 1982.

Feuer, Jane. "The Concept of Live Television: Ontology as Ideology." Kaplan 12-22.

Fiske, John, and John Hartley. *Reading Television*. New York: Methuen, 1978.

Fowler, Alastair. *Kinds of Literature: An Introduction to the Theory of Genres and Modes*. Cambridge: Harvard UP, 1982.

Gitlin, Todd. "Prime Time Ideology: The Hegemonic Process in Television Entertainment." *Social Problems* 26 (1979): 251-66.

Hartley, John. "Encouraging Signs: Television and the Power of Dirt, Speech, and Scandalous Categories." Rowland and Watkins 119-41.

Heath, Stephen, and Gillian Skirrow. "Television: A World in Action." *Screen* 18.2 (1977): 7-59.

Kaplan, E. Ann. Introduction. *Regarding Television: Critical Approaches*. Frederick: University Publications of America, 1983.

Modleski, Tania. "The Rhythms of Reception: Daytime Television and Women's Work." Kaplan 67-75.

Morse, Margaret. "Sport on Television: Replay and Display." Kaplan 44-66.

Neale, Stephen. *Genre*. London: British Film Institute, 1980.

Newcomb, Horace M., and Paul M. Hirsch. "Television As a Cultural Forum: Implications for Research." Rowland and Watkins 58-73.

Rowland, Willard D., Jr., and Bruce Watkins, eds. *Interpreting Television: Current Research Perspectives*. Beverly Hills: Sage, 1983

Rose, Brian, ed. *TV Genres: A Handbook and Reference Guide*. Westport: Greenwood, 1985.

Waller, Gregory A. "Re-placing *The Day After*." *Cinema Journal* 26 (Spring 1987): 3-20.

White, Mimi. "Crossing Wavelengths: The Diegetic and Referential Imaginary of American Commercial Television." *Cinema Journal* 25 (Winter 1986): 51-64.

——. "Television Genres: Intertextuality." *Journal of the Film and Video Association* 38.3 (1985): 41-47.

Williams, Raymond. *Marxism and Literature.* New York: Oxford UP, 1977.

——. *Television: Technology and Cultural Form.* New York: Schocken, 1974.

Wright, Will. *Sixguns and Society: A Structural Study of the Western.* Berkeley: U of California P, 1975.

Zynda, Thomas H. "Fantasy America: Television and the Ideal of Community." Rowland and Watkins 250-65.

5

The Question of Popular Genres Revisited

John G. Cawelti

Some Generic Observations about Genre

Aristotle started it all. His *Poetics*, the earliest recorded work of Western civilization concerned wholly with literary criticism, is also the first example of genre theory. For Aristotle, art is essentially the imitation (mimesis) of life. Genre is the result of strategies of mimesis: (1) the manner or form of representation—lyric (one voice speaking for itself), epic (one voice representing many voices), or dramatic (many voices representing themselves); or (2) types of action represented—tragic, comic, etc. These two principles of genre classification have been fundamental concepts of literary criticism since Aristotle. In recent times, discussion of the manner of representation has been complicated by the development of radio, film, television, and other means of representation beyond the spoken voice and print. In response to this, new theories of media criticism have come to exist beside the traditional literary classifications of lyric, epic, and dramatic, though the latter still persists in traditional literary criticism and teaching, albeit in a rather residual and attenuated fashion.[1] However, it is the other type of genre theory—genre based on the type of content or, as Aristotle put it, the object of imitation—that I am primarily concerned with in this discussion, since it is this conception of genre that underlies the idea of popular genres.

Genre criticism has long been a standard approach to literature and the other arts, primarily because of its advantages for the organization of criticism as a collective enterprise. For one thing, genre criticism provides a simple method for dividing up the critical work: It makes it possible to specialize in one genre, to examine subgenres of a particular type or period, and so forth. Because these different critical and historical studies can be coordinated, the concept of genre encourages more specific and complex forms of analysis. In addition, genre criticism encourages the comparison and synthesis of different analyses of the same genre—that is, of different formulations of the supertext—and thereby increases the sophistication of generic definitions. Finally, the generic approach makes possible the comparison of particular texts in different media and from different periods because they relate to the same supertext.

Genre criticism also has its limitations: It tends to lose sight of the genius of individual works and creators. It can encourage the kind of pigeonholing of the arts that Shakespeare satirized in Polonius's speech on the varieties of drama. When genre critics forget that their supertexts are critical artifacts and start treating them as prescriptions for artistic creation, the concept of genre becomes stultifying and limiting. Finally, genre criticism does not directly address those basic questions of artistic inspiration, impact, rhetoric, and ideology that Plato first defined, and which have been recurrently important in literary discussions, such as at the present time.

In constructing his theory of genre, Aristotle was reacting to Plato, whose ambiguities about art are well known. Plato raised many important questions about art, which Aristotle apparently felt he had either resolved or bypassed with his theory of mimesis and genres. Among these questions were (1) the nature and significance of the artist's creation; is it divine inspiration or human artifice? (*Ion*); (2) the question of art's impact on its audience; is it single or diverse, ennobling or corrupting? (*Republic*); (3) the relationship of art to truth; is it a copy of reality or an illusion? (*Phaedrus*); (4) is there a true (serious) art, and how is it different from false (popular) art? (*Gorgias*). Aristotle's *Poetics* did not completely resolve these basic questions and they continue to resurface in the history of criticism to challenge the validity of genre as a critical principle.

The essence of genre criticism is the construction of what, in contemporary critical jargon, might be called a macro- or supertext. The supertext (genre) claims to be an abstract of the most significant characteristics or family resemblances among many particular texts, which can accordingly be analyzed, evaluated, and otherwise related to each other by virtue of their connection with the supertext. Because it is a consolidation of many texts created at different times, the supertext is one way of conceptualizing artistic traditions. Studying developments and changes in particular texts related to a supertext is a way of tracing changes in an artistic tradition, just as studies of the way in which one supertext relates to others can be one way of tracing the history of culture. Thus, the supertext can also be treated like an individual text: Its history can be constructed; its impact and influence can be explored; it can be compared with other texts; it can be used as a source for constructing histories and theories of art and culture.

Different genre theories construct their supertexts in various ways. Some do so inductively, creating the supertext by generalizing from many individual texts. Others generate supertexts deductively from some general theory of art or human nature. Most commonly, genre theories involve a combination of deduction and induction—Aristotle proceeded from the basic assumption that art is imitation to an examination of the elements common to many different Greek tragedies.

These limitations of the genre principle have led to numerous reactions against genre in the history of Western civilization. In fact, genre is commonly associated with the ideals of classicism and their revival in such periods as the Renaissance and the eighteenth-century Neoclassical movement. The romantic and realistic movements of the nineteenth century both reacted fundamentally against the idea of genre, though for different reasons. The romantics were primarily interested in the full expression of individual artistic genius and, to them, ideas of genre seemed debilitating and restrictive. Romantic poets and dramatists rebelled against the neoclassical genres and unities and created forms of poetry and drama that expanded the boundaries of the lyric (for example, Wordsworth's *The Prelude*) and the theatre (Goethe's *Faust*). Similar rejections of the classical limits of symphonic form appeared in such composers as Beethoven and Berlioz. The realists, on the other hand, rejected generic traditions because they sought an ideological goal: the use of literature as a criticism of life. For them, the loose and flexible form of the novel seemed the most appropriate vehicle for the expression of the ideological purposes. These two extrageneric principles—the individual artistic vision and the role of art as ideological expression—have continued to exist in a dialectic with genre criticism and are, in fact, behind many recent efforts in criticism to go "beyond genre."

The most important innovation in genre criticism in the twentieth century has been the development of the idea of popular genres, a concept that has made possible the sophisticated analysis of popular culture. Popular genres, formulaic narrative types, or category literature—whatever these new supertexts are called—have made possible more complex critical, historical, and evaluative approaches to the vast output of the modern mass media.

Popular Genres and Popular Culture

The idea of popular genres developed from the assumption that such established categories of popular culture as westerns, detective stories, romances, gothic horror, situation comedies, and so forth, were comparable in some ways to traditional artistic genres like tragedy, comedy, the social novel, picaresque, pastoral, and satire. Popular genres were assumed to be analogous to these traditional supertexts in that they were authentic artistic types, which differed, however, in the kind of artistic principles that governed their construction.

The earliest use of the idea of popular genres appears to have been in the 1920s in the pioneering appreciations of movies and other popular arts in such criticism as Gilbert Seldes's *The Seven Lively Arts* (1924). During the 1930s and 1940s, when treated at all by the critical community, popular genres were mostly anathematized as examples of capitalist exploitation or of the decadence and corruption of mass culture. Only in the late 1950s did a more positive treatment of popular genres begin to appear in works like the British Stuart Hall and Paddy Whannel's *The Popular Arts* (1964) and the American Reuel Denney's *The Astonished Muse* (1957). By the mid-1960s, the Pop Art movement in art and literature and the development of popular culture studies in scholarship and criticism were well underway, giving the idea of popular genres additional significance.

The concept of popular genres has been a major basis for the development of an effective criticism of popular culture involving not only the whole range of what used to be called subliterature, but also of film, and, most recently, of television. Film criticism came of age with the development by French and English critics of the concept of auteurism, which applied a traditional technique of literary analysis—the study of a particular author's distinctive combination of style, forms, and dominant themes and ideas—to film by assuming that the director was the true "author" of works of cinema. As developed by French *cinéastes* like Bazin, Truffaut, and Godard, and in English critics like Robin Wood, auteurism has most often been combined with the concept of popular genres. In fact, much of the most effective film criticism and scholarship of the last two decades has involved a dialectic between the analysis of directors and the study of genres, the genres providing a framework for defining a director's unique achievement as in studies of westerns by John Ford, Sam Peckinpah, Budd Boetticher, Howard Hawks, and others.[2] Similarly, the history of such genres as westerns, crime films, musical comedies, silent comedy, and film noir have been organized around analysis of the contribution of significant directors to each genre. Scholars such as Stuart Kaminsky and Thomas Schatz have also made studies of the complex of supertexts that make up the system of Hollywood film genres.

Though the theories of structuralism and semiotics have suggested new ways in which to define the supertexts of film, these new critical theories have thus far been most effective when assimilated into the framework of genre criticism. Television criticism, too, has been vitally influenced by the concept of genre in its recent development. Beginning with Horace Newcomb's pioneer work of 1974, *TV: The Most Popular Art*, the concept of genre has become an increasingly important aspect of television criticism, dominating anthologies like Newcomb's *Television:*

The Critical View (1976), Adler and Cater's *Television as a Cultural Force* (1976), and Kaplan's *Regarding Television* (1983), as well as the pages of the *Journal of Popular Film and Television*, which has published much outstanding work in the study of popular genres.

Another instance of the creative way in which younger television critics have made use of the concept of popular genre is David Marc's *Demographic Vistas* (1984). Marc adapts the auteurist idea to the analysis of television genres by assuming that the producers and the major comic performers are the auteurs of television. In an excellent chapter on the work of Paul Henning, writer-producer of *The Beverly Hillbillies* (1962-1971), *Petticoat Junction* (1963-1970), and *Green Acres* (1965-1971), Marc discusses Henning's artistic accomplishments and limitations as a creator in the tradition of rural comedy, a genre not only significant in television and film but as a major American tradition going back to late eighteenth-century popular drama, to southwestern and New England humor, and to Mark Twain. Marc also analyzes the evolution of the crime genre on television through a chronological discussion of the work of several different producers: Jack Webb (*Dragnet* [1952-1970]); Quinn Martin (*The Untouchables* [1959-1963], *The Fugitive* [1963-1967]); Roy Huggins (*77 Sunset Strip* [1958-1964], *Hawaiian Eye* [1959-1963]); Aaron Spelling (*Mod Squad* [1968-1973], *Charlie's Angels* [1976-1981]); Stephen J. Cannell (*The Rockford Files* [1974-1980]); and Steven Bochco and Michael Kozell (*Hill Street Blues* [1981-1987]). Using complex comparisons between genre, auteur, and cultural background, Marc is able to construct an insightful account of the development of the crime show and the cultural significance of its changing patterns. Marc's work is only a first step toward the very large goal of a sophisticated analysis of the supertext system of commercial television, but it shows how effectively the concept of genre can be combined with other critical approaches to develop the historical, artistic, and cultural analysis of television.

Thus, the concept of popular genres seems firmly established in the criticism of popular film and television. In the last few years, however, some important new critical theories have challenged the primacy of genre as a basic critical concept. The next important task of genre theory is to examine these objections in order to discover to what extent they require revision of the theory of popular genres and to what extent they may require us to go "beyond genre."

Beyond Genre?

This is a time of great ferment in critical theory. The influence of new European philosophies of analysis and interpretation such as the poststructuralist "deconstructionism" launched by Jacques Derrida, the "hermeneutics" of Hans-Georg Gadamer and others, the neo-Freudianism of Jacques Lacan, and the neo-Marxian "cultural studies" of Fredric Jameson and others have challenged many traditional critical approaches and made critical theory an important new academic discipline. In the criticism of popular film and television, structuralism and semiotics, particularly as developed in the critical theories of Christian Metz, have played a significant role.[3] The concept of "reader-response" criticism has become increasingly important in analyses of popular culture,[4] and last, but not least, there have developed important new schools of feminist gender theory as well as concepts of multicultural criticism.

From the standpoint of genre criticism, these new theories restate in contemporary terms those fundamental Platonic questions that have always pointed to the limits of genre criticism: How do we treat the artist's inspiration? (Deconstructionists believe that it is fundamentally self-contradictory, for example); How do we understand art's impact on an audience? (Reader-response criticism is deeply concerned with this issue; so, in another way, are the neo-Freudians and neo-Marxians); What is the relationship of art to truth? (Structuralists and semioticians think that because it depends on the structures of language, art can be best understood not as mimesis but as a wholly artificial construction; thus, insofar as traditional theories of genre assume mimesis, they are misguided.)

While I doubt that these new approaches to analysis and interpretation will ultimately render the conception of popular genres obsolete, there is clearly much room for expansion and sophistication of our generic categories and of the method by which we relate generic conceptions to the study of popular culture. I would like to make a tentative contribution to this reexamination of genre criticism by considering how some of these newer critical approaches can contribute to our understanding of popular genres.

Deconstructionism seems to be the new theoretic approach least relevant to the idea of genre. Since genres are abstracted conceptions of structure and the basic premise of deconstruction holds that structures are inherently self-contradictory, the two approaches would seem to be in conflict. Not surprisingly, most deconstructionists have ignored or bypassed the question of genre, preferring instead to deal with individual texts as their primary means of exploring shifting and ambiguous meanings, which they assume to be the inevitable result of any attempt to construct a complex linguistic structure. Perhaps, there is no way to reconcile the basic assumptions of deconstructionism and genre analysis.

The most important innovation in genre criticism in the twentieth century has been the development of the idea of popular genres, a concept that has made possible the sophisticated analysis of story forms such as the western. (Courtesy of the Museum of Modern Art/Film Stills Archive)

However, the practice of deconstructive analysis may yet have something to offer the study of popular genres if we consider that a genre is a sort of text and that genres as texts may be as susceptible to deconstructive analysis as any other sort of text. Certainly, criticism of popular genres has often noted elements of contradiction and ambiguity as central characteristics of such genres as the romance and the detective story. For example, it seems clear that there is a great deal of ambiguity about the sequence of "solutions," which seems to be one primary structural aspect of the detective genre. By presenting the reader with a parade of misleading clues, false suspects and other red herrings, the writer sets up a series of false "solutions" that both deceive the reader and prepare for the "real solution" which the detective offers at the end of the story. The latter, by convention, is supposed to give satisfying closure to the whole process. Yet there are inherent problems and built-in ambiguities about this sort of structure, which deconstructive analysis may help sort out more clearly than we have done thus far.

Cultural studies with its assorted blends of Marx and Freud clearly offers many ideas that have great potential for enriching our understanding of popular genres, particularly in relationship to their social and historical contexts. While the currently dominant concepts of cultural studies—ideology and hegemony—tend to erase generic differences in their attempts to understand how literary or cinematic structures reinforce (or resist) the ideological perspective of the ruling hegemony of a particular society, there is no reason that popular genres cannot also be seen as significant means for producing cultural values. A number of critical studies have already undertaken to begin this kind of analysis of popular genres such as crime, detective, and spy stories. As Frederic Jameson, one of the leading American exponents of cultural studies, puts it,

[G]enres are essentially contracts between a writer and his readers; or rather, to use the term which Claudio Guillen has so carefully revived, they are literary *institutions*, which like other institutions of social life are based on tacit agreements or contracts. The thinking behind such a view of genres is based on the presupposition that all speech needs to be marked with certain indications and signals as to how it is properly to be used. (Jameson 135)

Possibly the analysis of the various tacit agreements implied by the "indications and signals" characteristic of different genres can help us understand why a particular genre has been shaped in the way it has by the society that produces and uses it.

Reader-response criticism can be broadened to include the study of audience responses to nonliterary media like film and television as well.

This is a rather complex movement, which has developed out of some dissatisfaction with the way in which critics have traditionally made assertions about responses to literary works. In particular, reader-response critics have felt uncomfortable with the assumption that everyone reacts or ought to react in approximately the same way to literary works, and that this reaction can be defined as a fairly straightforward understanding by the reader of such aspects of texts as character, plot, and theme. According to the conventional critical approach, the reader identifies these primary elements and then reacts accordingly. The role of the critic and interpreter is to help the reader recognize what the important elements of the text are.

The first reader-response idea was that texts often (or always) structure not only the actions they represent, but the way in which readers encounter and experience the work. Developed particularly by Stanley Fish and his followers, this kind of reader-response criticism tried to evolve a new approach to the analysis of texts by focusing attention on the act of reading. In structuralist terminology, these critics tried to attend not so much to such paradigmatic aspects of a text as character and plot but to the syntagmatic or diachronic dimension of the text's structuring of the way a reader experiences the process of reading. This involves the analysis of the developing perception and understanding the reader has from moment to moment as he or she goes through the text. Because this approach is an open invitation to the elaboration of purely personal, subjective responses—"at this moment the text made me feel gay, then I encountered this image, which made me unhappy, etc."—it has inspired some of the most dubious analysis in the history of criticism. However, when used by intelligent and well-trained minds, the analysis of the reader-response structure of a text can lead to new and important insights, such as Stanley Fish's famous reinterpretation of many seventeenth-century poetic texts as "self-destructing artifacts"— poems whose experiential structure tried to make the reader turn his thoughts away from the delusions of the world to a new realization of God's grace, a feeling that, in turn, made the poem no longer necessary. Whether or not one ultimately agrees with such reinterpretations, they give new insights into the richness of major works like Milton's *Paradise Lost*, just as Lévi-Strauss's structuralist reinterpretation of the Oedipus myth gave us a new understanding of the power of Sophocles' play.[5]

In the analysis of popular genres, this idea of reading as an act or process has become an important new approach. As Janice Radway points out in her study of the romance, the reading of a popular book or the viewing of a television program is part of a larger process of experience. When Radway began talking to a group of women who regularly read romances, she soon discovered that

I would have to give up my obsession with textual features and narrative details if I wanted to understand their view of romance reading. Once I recognized this it became clear that romance reading was important to the Smithton women because the simple event of picking up a book enabled them to deal with the particular pressures and tensions encountered in their daily round of activities. Although I learned later that certain aspects of the romance's story do help to make this event especially meaningful, the early interviews were interesting because they focused so resolutely on *the act of romance reading* rather than on the meaning of the romance. (86)

As Radway's work illustrates, the reader-response idea of analyzing the process of reading a text can also be applied effectively to the super-texts of popular genre. Here, however, the act of reading is not only shaped by the way in which the elements of a text are presented syntag-matically but by the part that the act of reading plays in the whole social and psychological life of the reader. This consideration brings us to the second major idea associated with reader-response criticism—the insistence that different readers make very different interpretations of the same text or supertext and that these various readings have an equal or nearly equal validity. Norman Holland's theoretical approach to the "dynamics of literary response" and his careful studies of the variant interpretations of individual readers have been particularly important in developing this approach to the study of individual readers, but a similar approach to the study of audiences has become an important part of new research and theory in England and Australia where the political philoso-phy of democratic socialism makes the idea of many different, equally valid audience responses particularly congenial.[6]

This new variety of audience research is refreshingly different from the major tradition of audience research in American sociology with its massive offshoot in advertising, marketing, and mass communications, such as the Nielsen ratings of television. Because its context is primarily that of finding out whether audiences will approve certain candidates or policies in politics, consume certain products, or watch certain movies or television programs, this tradition of audience research defines the public as a monolithic statistical aggregate capable of only three kinds of response: yes, no, or no opinion. More sophisticated forms of such research may offer a scale from positive to negative with five or more positions on it, but the basic assumption remains that audience response is best understood as an abstract generalization based on a one-dimensional range of responses from positive to negative. The new kind of research assumes, on the contrary, a very diversified audience capable of creating a multitude of different interpretations of a particular book, show, or film:

This new audience research does not ask what effect television has on its audience, nor what use does the audience make of television; rather it asks how a particular television work, seen as a polysemic potential of meanings connects with the social life of a viewer or group of viewers. It is concerned then with how a television text is created out of a work (or program) by the active reading of an audience, and how this activity of reading can be explained in terms of a theory of culture. (Fiske, "Television" 6)

Moreover, these multiple readings are not simply variants of a general line of interpretation defined by the intended meaning of the text. Audience interpretations can actually run counter to the obvious intentions of the text's producers, and these opposite readings are just as significant as the intended interpretations. This phenomenon has long been apparent to mass communications researchers, appearing in such studies as those of the portrayal of bigoted characters like Archie Bunker where the creators intended to satirize bigotry but found that large numbers of viewers thought bigotry was being portrayed in a positive fashion. This kind of response was usually dismissed as a result of the audience's ignorance or prejudice making it unable to correctly interpret the message. The new audience research denies this kind of conclusion by insisting that variant responses are an appropriate aspect of the communication process.

Hall argued that the most a television text could do was to prefer a reading, but that it could not impose one on its viewers. Members of the audience, his argument ran, can oppose this reading by rejecting the dominant ideology of the text, and thus produce a reading that serves their interests rather than those whose interests are structured into the form of the text. Alternatively they can negotiate meanings that accept the dominant ideological frame, but that find the space within it to negotiate inflections that suit their own class positions (Fiske, "Television" 3).

Certain problems still remain with the concept of multiple meanings of texts, particularly when we encounter some of the wilder flights of reader-response criticism. The basic issue is whether all possible readings are equally valid, and if not, what principles determine whether one reading is more valid than another. This becomes a real difficulty in connection with the deconstructionist assumption that all significant texts are inherently self-contradictory. The same concern applies to the interpretation of such supertexts as the western, the detective story, or the romance. When is an interpretation of a genre valid, and when is it not? I encountered this issue when developing my own interpretation of the Western genre in *The Six-Gun Mystique* and I resolved it in what now seems to me as a partly correct fashion, which, however, completely failed to deal with the key issue. I argued at that time that

a popular formula like the Western cannot be understood as the effect of any single factor. However simple the formula may be, the artistic, social and psychological implications it synthesizes are extremely complex. . . . The Western's capacity to accommodate many different kinds of meaning have made the formula successful as popular art and entertainment over many generations. (113)

This seems to suggest that any meaning is possible, but I would reject that idea, just as I would oppose the view that *any* interpretation a reader arrives at of a particular text is as good as any other.

Reader-response criticism has not yet clearly faced up to the implications of this issue. Insofar as the reader-response approach assumes that all reader responses are equally valid or relevant it raises serious problems. Surely there is something more than off center about the reader who laughs at Quentin's suicide in Faulkner's *The Sound and the Fury* (1959), or who is depressed when the heroine is reunited with the hero at the end of a romance. One cannot deny that there is a wide range of significant differences in the responses of both individual readers and communities of readers to the same texts and genres. The problem lies in how to determine the range of meaningful responses as differentiated from those which are ignorant or perverted.

Leaving aside the thorny question of what principles might establish the limits of meaningful individual interpretations, that is, when and how we can decide that a reader is simply wrong, it seems to me that one of the most important aspects of recent critical theory lies in the extent to which it has defined new audience communities based on gender and multiculturalism. Radway's work was particularly significant because it not only pioneered a new approach to the analysis of responses to the popular genre of romance, but because it based that analysis on interviews with a community of women and thereby gave us new insight into that genre's connection with gender and with the social and cultural situation of women. This new interest in the gendering of generic analysis and the related investigation of subcultural traditions within a multicultural society has led to much of the most challenging recent work in the study of popular genres.

It is hardly surprising that gender would turn out to be a major factor in the history of genre, for the two words have the same linguistic root. Certainly writers, publishers, producers, and critics have always been aware of the intricate connections between gender and genre. Some genres have been thought of as distinctly gender-oriented, while others seem to have shifted in their gender orientation at different historical periods.

The popular romance, for example, has always been thought of as primarily a woman's genre, just as during the height of the Hollywood studio system there was a kind of production widely known as the woman's film or "weepie." Contrarily, action-adventure genres like the hard-boiled detective story, the western, and the war adventure have been produced with the image of a male audience in mind and have often been characterized by misogynistic themes, symbolic abuse of women, and macho masculinity.

In its early phases, the novel, itself, was widely thought to be primarily reading for women, and many of the literary and cultural debates about this new genre centered around the issue of whether this was uplifting or corrupting for the "fair sex." Many of the most successful early forms of the novel, such as the sentimental romances and tragedies created by Samuel Richardson, or the gothics produced by Mrs. Radcliffe had female protagonists and a distinctly feminine point of view. This practice continued in the highly popular sentimental novels of the nineteenth century, but clearly changed in the course of the nineteenth century. By the early twentieth century men had apparently become as important an audience for novels as women. One might even argue that the rise of what we now see as the major tradition of the American novel in writers like Cooper, Melville, and Hawthorne, culminating in the modern American novel of Hemingway, Fitzgerald, Dos Passos, and others, was at least partly inspired by the attempt to take that novel away from that famous "mob of scribbling women" that irritated Hawthorne. A number of recent feminist scholars have argued as much.

Clearly, the history of genres needs to be reexamined from a gender-oriented point of view and many feminist scholars are in the process of doing just that. Similar work related to masculinist genres and to male ideologies is needed, and a few scholars, like Fred Pfeil in *White Guys* (1995) have made an excellent start on this task. Analysis is also badly needed in the case of other audience communities such as those based on ethnicity and "race." This seems particularly important in the case of the history of popular genres, where the interplay between subcultural generic traditions and the mainstream of American popular culture has been perhaps the most dynamic force in the evolution of American culture.

One of the most significant recent phenomena to emerge in connection with these developments is what might be called the regendering and reethnicizing of contemporary popular genres. What I'm referring to here is the tendency of current popular writers to take genres that used to be largely oriented to white male fantasies and to rewrite them with women, African American, and ethnic hero-heroine figures. This has been particularly notable in the area of mystery and detective fiction, where the contribution of women writers was a major factor in the generic tradition beginning with the first American detective novel, Anna Katherine Green's *The Leavenworth Case* (1878). However, even the most successful women mystery writers of the first half of the twentieth century—heavy hitters like Agatha Christie, Dorothy Sayers, Margery Allingham, Ngaio Marsh, and Josephine Tey—mainly wrote about male detectives. The rare female detectives tended to be highly eccentric amateurs like Christie's Miss Marple. Even Dorothy Sayers noted, in 1928, that "there have also been a few women detectives, but on the whole, they have not been very successful. In order to justify their choice of sex, they are obliged to be so irritatingly intuitive as to destroy that quiet enjoyment of the logical which we look for in our detective reading" (Sayers 58-59).

This has changed dramatically since the 1950s. A new type of female detective has emerged in the work of writers like Marcia Muller, Sue Grafton, Sara Paretsky, Patricia Cornwell, Margaret Maron, and Julie Smith. Moreover, the books of these writers involve for the most part a regendering not of the classical ratiocinative tale, but of that most antifeminist of mystery genres, the hard-boiled detective story. These woman writers create detectives who are highly professional, as knowing and cynical as Sam Spade and Philip Marlowe, and as physically tough as Mike Hammer. Yet, these detective heroines also manifest qualities of sensitivity and concern for the weak and helpless that are traditionally associated with women. Currently, there is much discussion among feminist critics about whether these new woman detectives actually reflect feminist ideals and values or simply reinforce traditional masculine ideologies by dressing them up in women's clothes.[7] However, whether truly feminist or not, some of these writers have been enormously successful with the contemporary reading public. Paretsky, Grafton, and Cornwell are perennial bestsellers.

What I've called the reethnicizing of popular genres has also been a very significant feature of current detective stories. This trend was pioneered by the fine African-American writer Chester Himes, who in the 1960s, created a wonderful series of detective stories describing the adventures of black Harlem police detectives Cotton Ed Smith and Grave-Digger Jones. For a time Himes's only significant competitor was a white writer Ernest Tidyman who created the elegant African-American detective Virgil Tibbs. Tibbs, however, was in most respects a traditional great detective in blackface. It was not until 1990 when Walter Mosley published his first book about Easy Rawlins, *Devil in a Blue Dress*, that a detective fully immersed in African American life again walked the mean streets of the city and this time he became a highly successful bestseller. Other ethnic groups began to find representation in the detective story genre over the last decade as well: there was, for example, Robert Campbell's Irish Jimmy Flannery, James Lee Burke's Cajun Dave Robicheaux, K. K. Constantine's Slavic Mario Balzic and Les Roberts's Slovak Milan Jackovic.

Regendering and reethnicizing have proceeded much further in the case of the detective story than in other popular genres, and this may tell us something about the detective genre or at least about its contemporary significance. However, there have also been attempts to do this to other genres. The western has been regendered in the successful television series *Dr. Quinn: Medicine Woman* (1993-   ) though other attempts along these lines have not been particularly successful. One movie, *The Ballad of Billie Jo* (1993), was an excellent treatment of gender issues in the Wild West but was not highly successful at the box office. Michael Cimino's disastrous epic *Heaven's Gate* (1980) was an attempt to ethnicize the western but was generally clumsy and unsuccessful. Reethnicizing the western has been more promising with movies treating Native American cultures in an increasingly sympathetic and complex way. Here, recent films like *Dances With Wolves* (1990) and *Geronimo* (1993) have attempted with some success to transform traditional western formulas like the clash between pioneers and savages, cavalry and Indians into a new perspective on the significance of the American frontier. But whether these new versions of the western reflect a transformation of the myth or its demise remains to be seen.[8]

Perhaps the ultimate test of the significance of regendering will reveal itself in connection with the popular genre of romance. This genre has had the strongest ties to women and has been perhaps the most traditional in holding to certain fixed formulas over the years. However, there are definite signs of new interests in romance such as a more explicit treatment of sexuality as well as a proliferation of new settings and characters. It is still hard to imagine what a regendered romance would be like, but in a culture where so many changes have been occurring in the relationships between men and women, we may even see the emergence of a type of romance catering directly to men.

The study of the regendering and reethnicizing of popular genres is obviously in its infancy; the trend itself is only beginning to spread throughout American popular culture. Thus, it is very hard to predict just what direction the analysis should take and what sort of conclusions will emerge. But it is clear that this is one of the most exciting and important areas now opening up in the study of popular genres.

Two final considerations: we need to recognize that the multiple interpretations that can be offered both of particular texts and of genres are themselves aspects of culture, gaining their significance from the particular groups, within a culture, that hold them. Thus, the meaning and consequence of genres must be understood not only in formal or structural terms but through a better understanding of the way in which particular cultural groups interpret texts and supertexts in the process of making them a part of their everyday lives.

Lastly, the construction and criticism of genres is itself an important cultural process that involves writers, publishers, producers, directors, actors, readers, and many others as well as critics. Thus, a fuller understanding of popular genres requires further investigation of the process by which genres are created and experienced. Some promising work has already begun along these lines, particularly in the analysis of the role of genre in television and film production.[9]

Our discussion of newer interpretive ideas and methods suggested by the various schools of contemporary criticism indicates that we need not abandon the concept of genre but that there are new directions in which our studies of genre should move. In particular, we need to examine more carefully the relationship between popular genres and broader social and cultural contexts by studying the actual experiences of readers and audiences with genres. This kind of reader-audience research seems to be the most important direction for future work in the study of popular genres.

Notes

1. See Paul Hernandi, *Beyond Genre: New Directions in Literary Classification* (Ithaca: Cornell UP, 1972).

2. See Jim Kitses, *Horizons West: Anthony Mann, Budd Boetticher, Sam Peckinpah: Studies of Authorship Within the Western* (Bloomington: Indiana UP, 1969) and Paul Seydor, *Peckinpah: The Western Films* .

3. See Brian Henderson, *A Critique of Film Theory;* John Fiske and John Hartley, *Reading Television* (New York: Methuen, 1978); and E. Ann Kaplan, *Regarding Television: Critical Approaches—An Anthology*.

4. See John Fiske, "Television and Popular Culture: Reflections on British and Australian Critical Practice," and Janice Radway, *Reading the Romance: Reading, Patriarchy, and Popular Literature*.

5. See Claude Lévi-Strauss, *Structural Anthropology* (New York: Basic, 1963).

6. See Fiske, "Television and Popular Culture."

7. Cf. the discussion of these issues in Sally Munt's *Murder by the Book: Feminism and the Crime Novel*, and in Glenwood Irons, ed., *Feminism in Women's Detective Fiction*.

8. The most astute and learned student of the myth of the frontier, Richard Slotkin, believes that the myth of the frontier no longer makes sense of American experience and that we will have to create a new myth of America based on the idea that "our history in the West and in the East was shaped from the beginning by the meeting, conversation, and mutual adaptation of different cultures" (655). In effect, Slotkin seems to be saying that the old myth of the frontier, which involved the white pioneer's overcoming of the savage wilderness, will have be replaced by a new myth of multiculturalism and that the traditional western genre probably cannot be successfully adapted to this new myth.

13. See Thomas Schatz, *Hollywood Genres: Formulas, Filmmaking and the Studio System* and Todd Gitlin, *Inside Prime Time*.

Works Cited

Adler, Richard, and Douglass Cater, eds. *Television as a Cultural Force.* New York: Praeger, 1976.

Cawelti, John G. *The Six-Gun Mystique.* 2nd ed. Bowling Green, OH: Bowling Green State University Popular Press, 1984.

Denney, Reuel. *The Astonished Muse.* Chicago: U of Chicago P, 1957.

Fish, Stanley. *Is There a Text in This Class? The Authority of Interpretive Communications.* Cambridge: Harvard UP, 1980.

Fiske, John. "Television and Popular Culture: Reflections on British and Australian Critical Practice." Mimeographed paper presented at the University of Iowa Conference on Television Criticism, May 1985.

Fiske, John, and John Hartley. *Reading Television.* New York: Methuen, 1978.

Gitlin, Todd. *Inside Prime Time.* New York: Pantheon, 1983.

Hall, Stuart, and Paddy Whannel. *The Popular Arts.* New York: Pantheon, 1964.

Henderson, Brian. *A Critique of Film Theory.* New York: Dutton, 1980.

Hernadi, Paul. *Beyond Genre: New Directions in Literary Classification.* Ithaca: Cornell UP, 1972.

Holland, Norman. *The Dynamics of Literary Response.* New York: Oxford UP, 1978.

——. *Five Readers Reading.* New Haven: Yale UP, 1975.

Irons, Glenwood, ed. *Feminism in Women's Detective Fiction.* Toronto: U of Toronto P, 1995.

Kaminsky, Stuart. *American Film Genres: Approaches to a Critical Theory of Popular Film.* Dayton: Pflaum, 1974.

Kaplan, E. Ann. *Regarding Television: Critical Approaches—An Anthology.* Frederick: University Publications of America, 1983.

Kitses, Jim. *Horizons West: Anthony Mann, Budd Boetticher, Sam Peckinpah: Studies of Authorship Within the Western.* Bloomington: Indiana UP, 1969.

Lévi-Strauss, Claude. *Structural Anthropology.* New York: Basic, 1963.

Marc, David. *Demographic Vistas: Television in American Culture.* Philadelphia: U of Pennsylvania P, 1984.

Munt, Sally R. *Murder By the Book: Feminism and the Crime Novel.* London: Routledge, 1994.

Newcomb, Horace. *Television: The Critical View.* New York: Oxford UP, 1976.

——. *TV: The Most Popular Art.* Garden City: Doubleday, 1974.

Pfeil, Fred. *White Guys: Studies in Postmodern Domination and Difference.* London: Verso, 1995.

Radway, Janice. *Reading the Romance: Reading, Patriarchy, and Popular Literature.* Chapel Hill: U of North Carolina P, 1984.

Sayers, Dorothy. Introduction to *The Omnibus of Crime. Detective Fiction Essays.* By Robin Winks. Woodstock: Countryman, 1993.

Schatz, Thomas. *Hollywood Genres: Formulas, Filmmaking and the Studio System.* Philadelphia: Temple UP, 1981.

Seldes, Gilbert. *The Seven Lively Arts.* New York: Harper, 1924.

Seydor, Paul. *Peckinpah: The Western Films.* Urbana: U of Illinois P, 1980.

Slotkin, Richard. *Gunfighter Nation.* New York: Atheneum, 1992.

6

Researching Film and Television Audiences

Bruce A. Austin

Among the few things about which there is little doubt is this: there is no scarcity of published writing on popular film and television audiences. Naive mass communication students who approach their professor complaining that, look though they might, they "can't find *anything*" in the library on their term paper topic are routinely met with skeptical, if gentle, responses. However, when it involves film audiences, the students' assertion has merit. This essay provides a brief, introductory overview of contemporary scientific perspectives and research on popular film and television audiences.

The importance in noting the neglect shown to theatrical motion picture audiences is underscored today, especially, as we move into an era of abundant moving-image media. The absence of data on earlier forms (such as film) necessarily deprives us of a rich, contextual base from and within which we might understand, explain, and hypothesize about these newer vehicles for manufacturing, delivering, and "consuming" moving image media. In short, we may fall prey to yet another of our graduate professors' pithy proverbs about "reinventing the wheel."

Balance and Imbalance[1]

Another truism is that research on televiewing (viewing the medium/program) and the television experience (encompassing a broader context that includes the medium, physical and social contexts) is broader and offers deeper insight than that on the audiences for motion pictures. Evidence for this imbalance is easily found among the numerous books with such titles as *Television and the Public* and *Television and the Quality of Life* and the very few similar books using "Movies" in their titles.[2] What accounts for this?

Differences in the social scientific attention paid to each medium is in part accounted for by television's obligation to be a "public trust." The medium's fiduciary responsibilities to serve the public interest and its use of a resource owned by the people not only justified but perhaps insisted on attentive research interest including but not limited to programming issues and audience effects. Ultimately, one consequence of the public trust imperative was the development of a body of research and a theoretical apparatus that help us to understand, explain, and predict the social consequences of televiewing.

Movies, on the other hand, lacked this responsibility. Always privately endowed and benefiting private interests (including those of shareholders), the owners could and did determine their own research agenda—or its omission. Arguments in support of motion picture regulation notwithstanding, and despite the absence of first amendment protection for their first half-century of existence, a policy impetus failed to materialize in terms of generating research and research attention. There is one significant exception: among the earliest forays into scientific research on motion pictures were The Payne Fund Studies, conducted by sociological and education researchers, and driven by William Short's private censorial interests.

While public policy concerns helped fund and drive TV audience research, social issues were equally potent. The medium's pervasiveness and invasiveness helped engender research interest. The perceived status and importance of the medium's messages (for example, political, public affairs, consumer issues), and that TV was an in-home medium, all helped to attract research attention. Movies, meanwhile, were denigrated in popular and academic circles as "mere" entertainment and, for the most part, remained firmly nested within that context.[3]

Commercial advertising interests, too, offered an impetus for research. TV is an advertising-driven medium where the audience is the commodity being sold. Facts and information about the audience were consequently a necessity, not an option. Hence the research interest.[4] Absent advertiser influence, the movie industry not only had no one to "report" to, but no one to push for, require, or support audience research.

Research on movie audiences more often than not can be characterized as one-shot and disconnected from theory. This is unlike TV research, where there grew a group/community of scholars investigating the medium's audience with an eye, especially, to TV's social effects and later the audience's uses and gratifications of and from the medium. For movies, not only did no such community exist, vacant property was permitted to lie fallow and undeveloped. TV-land was fertilized and nourished; tilled by scientific farmers who intentionally or not formed cooperatives (that is, theories) that served to guide and shape the forms by which the property would be developed. Even the "Hovlanders" at Yale, who investigated the effectiveness of various persuasive filmic strategies, were driven more by interest in the psychology of attitude and attitude change than in the medium; motion pictures were simply the stimulus material introduced in an experiment's methodological design (see Hovland, Lumsdaine, and Sheffield).

Once scientific research finally arrived in Hollywood in the 1950s, it lacked theoretical ambition and generally was content to remain in its role at an administrative and marketing level. Even then, when research was initiated at a meaningful (if elementary) level, it was primarily employed as an anecdotal means to understand the empirical effects of television on movies. The principal concern was the financial impact derived from diminishing audience size and the positive response sought from the Wall Street financial community. The cloak of science was donned in order to legitimize the medium's business operations with the intended result of bringing investors, bankers, and loan officers into the fold.

TV researchers inherited (or chose to take on) the psychosociological methodological heritage developed by such communication founding fathers as Berelson, Lasswell, Lazarsfeld, and Lewin (see Berelson). In contrast, the tone and thematic interest for the study of film was perhaps initiated by Vachel Lindsay with his treatise "The Art of the Moving Picture." This theme took a humanistic approach informed by literature and art and was later developed as a means for legitimizing movies both in the marketplace and in the college curriculum. Differences and squabbling within the academic community exacerbated research biases as well. Various disciplines sought ownership of film: English, literature, and art departments early on, and communication much later. A cursory review of conference programs for communication professional associations (for example, the International and the Speech Communication Associations) reveals numerous TV-related audience research papers and (to be generous) few film papers. Similarly, examination of University Film & Video Association or Society for Cinema Studies programs reveals that while discussion of the medium is profuse, analysis of the medium's audiences is scant. Indeed, the latter two organizations focus their interests primarily on what's *on* the screen rather than who's *in* the audience *watching* the screen.

A theme that does *not* account for the differential research attention is each medium's popularity or attractiveness among audiences. Arguably, movies drew a proportionally greater-sized, more loyal audience with greater attendance than did TV, at least early on.

The discussion above underscores and reintroduces Simonet's 1978 assessment of the state of film audience research: it "has been growing as a science from humble beginnings to more grandiose beginnings. But it seems always to have been making beginnings" (72). The legacy of neglect concerning the audiences for theatrical motion pictures leaves us poorer on an absolute basis and perhaps even more so on a comparative (to TV) level.

The (Ir)relevance of the Scale

In the not too distant past, if a friend told you that they "saw a good movie last night," most likely your response would have been: "What [title] was it?" Today, however, you will probably seek a context first: did your friend see the movie in a theater, on PPV television, on broadcast TV, or on a rented videotape? Likewise, the same holds true for television. In the presumably simpler world of yesteryear, comments on an enjoyable television show would have prompted questions of series title rather than source. The formerly clear distinctions between TV and motion pictures have all but disappeared. In both social practice and economic reality, movies and TV have merged in such ways that now TV is the primary venue for audience consumption of movies. Moreover, it is not simply TV as we once understood the acronym; instead, today TV *means* "monitor," a device upon which things are presented, and not necessarily received as broadcast. "Television" has become reconfigured as an appliance on which one sees (and perhaps watches) the images.

Before launching into maudlin eulogies on the "death" of the movies, the accumulated evidence thus far unambiguously assures us that audiences have not so much abandoned the medium as they have the place. And, moreover, we can probably rest assured that movie theaters will not become twentieth-century dinosaurs, though they most likely will enter an endangered species list by virtue of reduced numbers of screens and by increased levels of consolidation of ownership and geographic placement. To the extent that these events have occurred, seeking a contemporary balance between the research traditions of TV and film audiences may today seem irrelevant. Moreover, this appears to render as fundamentally irrelevant and wrong-headed the conclusions of a 1995 study by Yankelovich Partners Inc. stating that people go to the movies for reasons that are "unique and beneficial" (qtd. in Honeycutt 6). Or does it?

Since 1975, three innovations in consumer technology have resulted in a new conceptualization and understanding of the terms "television" and "motion pictures": videocassette recorders (VCRs), remote control devices (RCDs), and cable television. They stand out among the nearly numbing number of "new" technology acronyms that together form the alphabet soup of modern communications contributing to the blending of movies and television.[5] Two-thirds of all United States homes are at some level cable subscribers, three-quarters own at least one VCR, and much like the ubiquitous digital clock that accompanies virtually every household appliance, it is nearly impossible today to purchase a TV

Post-television audience behavior has shifted from going to *the* movies to going to *a* movie. (Courtesy of the Academy of Motion Picture Arts and Sciences)

without an RCD. Unquestionably, these devices and the human behaviors associated with them help account for modestly increased number of hours of televiewing, as Xiaoming found.

Without exception, VCRs, RCDs, and cable offer audiences important viewing and programming advantages over previous technologies and enhanced conveniences for how and when to view moving image media. Both cable and VCRs quantitatively increase the viewer's availability of program options; at the same time, this is not to say that any qualitative increase in diversity of viewing choices necessarily follows. VCRs allow viewers greater control over the timing of their moving image exposure: that is, where and when they view. And RCDs make it easier for viewers to quickly, and from the comfort of their easy chairs, link program preferences with program choices. Interestingly, none of these three technologies is inherently a production vehicle for moving image material; both VCRs and cable require the external assistance of some other (frequently well-established) manufacturer to fulfill consumers' software needs. As Syd Silverman, publisher of *Variety* noted in 1983: "No one ever bought a ticket to watch technology . . . The people in Hollywood who make the crucial decisions know that *content* will determine the entertainment choices of the public, regardless of the means of distribution" (13).

Given this scenario, a new stage is set for research questions. At the risk of sounding like Jerzy Kosinski's *Being There* character Chance the gardener (Chauncey Gardiner), what and how do we watch? While we can be reasonably certain of *what* we watch (box-office and ratings data offer rough estimations), we know little about other issues. What motivates our viewing? How important are these motivations? Which motivations are satisfied? Such questions inquire about where we view, what we view, how we chose our program viewing and our level of involvement in it, and how we respond to what we see.

As movies are increasingly consumed in the home, research that quite literally examines the space and place becomes important for contextualizing the viewing environment. The issue of space and place is one familiar to students of both architecture and nonverbal communication (see for instance, Sommer). A qualitative study by Pardun and Krugman examined how the architectural style of homes was related to family television viewing. The authors found that families living in traditional (or more privacy-oriented, closed-plan) homes tended to view TV individually and planned their acquisition of multiple TV sets in the home. In contrast, families living in more community-oriented, open-style homes preferred family viewing and acquired multiple TVs in a more ad hoc manner.

As the number of program choices and medium venues increases, how will these variables affect placement and viewership behaviors? To what extent does the innovation and adoption of "home entertainment centers" affect space and place as well as how, where, when, and with whom leisure is spent? The home entertainment center, too, introduces a new form of furniture as well as a sited media situation, thereby promoting research interest by scholars of both communications and material culture. Moreover, as work-at-home and electronic commuting increases, to what extent do these behaviors integrate or conflict with entertainment centers? Certainly psychologists and sociologists will find this topic of interest. In short, the issue of space and place for moving image media prompts inquiry from a broad range of disciplinary, theoretical, and research perspectives, well beyond those of traditional mass communications scholarship.

To what extent do viewers perceive differences between watching movies at the theater and viewing them on videotape? Anecdotal reports (frequently tinged with annoyance) suggest that, increasingly, theatrical moviegoers have brought with them to the theater their at-home televiewing behaviors. Hence as evidence for this, such reports say, the need for theaters to run on-screen messages reminding people not to talk while the movie is in progress.

Numerous authors have reported that video viewing has somewhat displaced attendance at films as well as viewership of TV programming. Clearly, renting movies for playback on VCRs is the most important benefit of owning a VCR. Rubin and Bantz confirmed the intuitive guess that VCR use is goal directed and reflects intentional selection; that is, VCR viewing is more selection-oriented than traditional broadcast fare.[6] The analogy for motion pictures is the shift in post-television audience behavior from going to *the* movies to going to *a* movie (see Austin, *Immediate Seating*). Lin found that VCRs enhanced the at-home viewership of movies and increased the amount of time spent with TV. Further, she identifies videotapes as performing "substitution" and "gratification" utility functions insofar as they displace time spent with other similar media: "VCR users are very utility-conscious and well aware of the available alternatives for enhancing their home entertainment experience" (Lin 840).

Krugman, Shamp, and Johnson's study inquired about consumer perceptions of videotape movies viewed at home as contrasted with broadcast TV movies. They sorted their sample into two groups: those who felt that watching a VCR movie was more like watching a movie on broadcast TV and those who felt it was more like watching a movie in a theater. Perhaps surprisingly, their results indicated that persons with higher levels of income were associated with the perception that VCR movie viewing was similar to watching a film in a theater. While this runs counter to both intuition and other available research in that higher income is also associated with more frequent and more discriminating moviegoing, the finding provides support for the notion that theatrical and at-home movie viewing has begun to merge.

A related report employed focus groups, a mail survey and in-home observations and sought to measure people's preparation for viewing of traditional TV broadcasting and viewing of VCR movie rentals (Krugman and Johnson). Here the authors found "the viewing experience for traditional television and VCR movie rentals to be different" (228). Specifically, VCR viewing was more focused than viewing of broadcast TV: there were fewer interruptions and a lower likelihood of engaging in other activities (reading, conversations) while viewing. Extrapolating from their data, the authors note that VCR movie rental viewing shows a relational link to viewing movies in theaters, perhaps because "VCR movies may have greater viewing status than television programming" (Krugman and Johnson 229).

What none of these reports indicates, however, are the specific similarities and differences between the movie and the at-home TV *experience*. Regrettably, the absence of film audience research means there is little to inform us of audience reports on the film experience, though there is no shortage of romantically-tinged anecdotes about its singularity and specialness. And asking people today to reflect on their movie experience post hoc is a little like asking contemporary children to think about and explain a train-ride experience. Most likely, the kids won't have any train ride experience and, perhaps, we will eventually find that people are largely unfamiliar with a ("traditional") theatrical film experience, too. For plainly such current playback options as fast forward/reverse and stop action will meaningfully change the moving image viewing experience.

Questions concerning how we watch are at least partially addressed by examining the literature on RCDs. With the 1974 publication of *The Uses of Mass Communications*,[7] researchers have increasingly emphasized the importance of conceptualizing media audiences as active rather than passive. Paradoxically, or at least ironically, RCDs represent perhaps the ultimate active audience device: thumb and forefinger activity as generated from a cushy armchair. An abundance of anecdotal reports attests to the concerns of network programmers regarding viewers' propensity for channel flipping or grazing. A methodological measurement study by Ferguson reveals that self-reported survey responses regarding channel flipping frequency tended to underestimate actual channel flipping. Eastman and Newton's summary of RCD studies reveals a virtual cottage industry of research on grazing, reasons for grazing, who controls the RCD, programming strategies to combat grazing, and when (part of the hour) grazing occurs (80-81). Their study of remote control use, in contrast to Ferguson, however, found rather limited use of RCDs with the most frequent use being punching in a specific channel number and that this behavior occurred at the hour and half hour. In other words, RCD use was "a direct substitute for [manual] dial turning" (77).

Two additional studies suggest other directions for research. Auter and Moore content-analyzed two teleshopping programs, The Fashion Channel and Quality Value Convenience Network, in order to compare how each utilized parasocial behavior and compliance-gaining techniques. Although this study did not directly examine audiences—and instead investigated the messages and the *forms* of messages audiences receive—it offers a necessary first step to a broader understanding of audience interactivity with a specific form of televised content. Further research, perhaps, will more broadly begin to identify not only the effectiveness of various forms of persuasive appeals and strategies but will also inquire about the "value-added" nature of this kind of televiewing experience. Priest and Dominick's study of talk shows is of interest here insofar as it indirectly exemplifies how the roles of viewer and participant are exchanged. Indeed, the study of talk shows seems inherently interesting in that viewers suspend their own conversations in order to listen, watch, and "participate" in the mediated conversation.

Conclusion

What we know about film and television audiences today is a function of what has been researched, the motives driving that research, and what has been ignored. The imbalanced body of evidence about audiences between media forms reveals an uncorrectable mistake that today results in a failure to adequately inform us about moving image audiences as changes in the media landscape emerge. More important, this insists upon research action on the "new" media environment as a way to inform scholars when the next set of changes arrives.

The moral to the preceding text is not one about hand-wringing or teeth-gnashing over the absence of research and missed opportunities. Rather, if nothing else, the lesson to be drawn from the present story is that new research opportunities have introduced themselves to us for our action. We can, one supposes, choose to turn our backs and ignore them, thereby repeating the mistakes of the past, or we can warmly embrace them and get on with the business of building knowledge.

Notes

1. This is not an insistence that some mathematical equivalency exists or ought to occur. Rather, the imbalance in number of research projects is surprising if for no other reason than given the number of years each medium has been present. The present telescopic history of imbalance informs us as to both the methods and the topics of scholarly inquiry about the audiences for these two media. Moreover, this is also not to say that all such publications are "good," "valuable" or "important." As is true for any discipline's body of knowledge, a discerning and critical lens must be used to inspect the research documentation. Extended discussion on the reasons for the absence of movie audience research may be found in my *The Film Audience* and *Immediate Seating*. A limitation of the present chapter is its focus on data-based empirical studies and not other methodological analyses of "reception" or "receivership."

2. Exceptions include Handel's *Hollywood Looks at Its Audience* and some of the Payne Fund studies, c.1930.

3. This argument, of course, ignores that most television programming (including news) can also be categorized accurately as "entertainment." In fact, and ironically, television has been regularly criticized for its focus on entertainment (at the expense of other program types) and given the policy concerns, this argument served as an insistence for audience research.

4. The nascent advertising industry at the turn of the century can accept responsibility for furthering social scientific methods as well as research interests (see Ewen).

5. "Blending" may not be the best metaphor. For an alternative take on this see Edgerton.

6. Given predictions for various direct broadcast satellite systems and pay-per-view operations, we might expect even greater selectivity to occur.

7. See Blumler and Katz. The "uses and gratifications" approach can be traced as far back as Herzog's study of radio soap opera listeners in the 1940s.

Works Cited

Austin, Bruce A. *The Film Audience: An International Bibliography of Research*. Metuchen: Scarecrow, 1983.

——. *Immediate Seating: A Look at Movie Audiences*. Belmont: Wadsworth, 1989.

Auter, Philip J., and Roy L. Moore. "Buying From a Friend: A Content Analysis of Two Teleshopping Programs." *Journalism Quarterly* 70.2 (1993): 425-36.

Berelson, Bernard. "The State of Communication Research." *Public Opinion Quarterly* 23 (1959): 1-17.

Blumler, Jay G., and Elihu Katz, eds. *The Uses of Mass Communications: Current Perspectives on Gratifications Research.* Beverly Hills: Sage, 1974.

Eastman, Susan Tyler, and Gregory D. Newton. "Delineating Grazing: Observations of Remote Control Use." *Journal of Communication* 45 (1995): 77-95.

Edgerton, Gary R., ed. *Film and the Arts in Symbiosis: A Resource Guide.* New York: Greenwood, 1988.

Ewen, Stuart. *Captains of Consciousness: Advertising and the Social Roots of Consumer Culture.* New York: McGraw-Hill, 1976.

Ferguson, Douglas A. "Measurement of Mundane TV Behaviors: Remote Control Device Flipping Frequency." *Journal of Broadcasting & Electronic Media* 38 (1994): 35-47.

Handel, Leo A. *Hollywood Looks at Its Audience: A Report of Film Audience Research.* Urbana: U of Illinois P, 1950.

Herzog, Hertha. "What Do We Really Know About Daytime Serial Listeners?" *Radio Research 1942-1943.* Ed. Paul F. Lazarsfeld and Frank Stanton. New York: Duell, 1944.

Honeycutt, Kirk. "Study: Movies' Role Goes Far Beyond Entertainment." *Hollywood Reporter* 8 Mar. 1995: 6, 72.

Hovland, Carl I., Arthur A. Lumsdaine, and Fred D. Sheffield. *Experiments on Mass Communication.* Princeton: Princeton UP, 1949.

Krugman, Dean M., and Keith F. Johnson. "Differences in the Consumption of Traditional Broadcast and VCR Movie Rentals." *Journal of Broadcasting & Electronic Media* 35 (1991): 213-32.

Krugman, Dean M., Scott A. Shamp, and Keith F. Johnson. "Video Movies at Home: Are They Viewed Like Film or Like Television?" *Journalism Quarterly* 68.1/2 (1991): 120-30.

Lin, Carolyn A. "Exploring the Role of VCR Use in the Emerging Home Entertainment Culture." *Journalism Quarterly* 70 (1993): 833-42.

Lindsay, Vachel. *The Art of the Moving Picture.* New York: Macmillan, 1915.

Pardun, Carol J., and Dean M. Krugman. "How the Architectural Style of the Home Relates to Family Television Viewing." *Journal of Broadcasting & Electronic Media* 38.2 (1994): 145-62.

Priest, Patricia Joyner, and Joseph R. Dominick. "Pulp Pulpits: Self-Disclosure on 'Donahue.'" *Journal of Communication* 44 (1994): 74-97.

Rubin, Alan, and Charles Bantz. "Utility of Videocassette Recorders." *American Behavioral Scientist* 30 (1987): 71-85.

Silverman, Syd. "Entertainment in the Satellite Era." *Variety* 26 Oct. 1983: 13, 99.

Simonet, Thomas. "Industry." *Film Comment* Jan.-Feb. 1978: 72-73.

Sommer, Robert. *Personal Space: The Behavioral Basis of Design.* Englewood Cliffs: Prentice-Hall, 1969.

Xiaoming, Hao. "Television Viewing Among American Adults in the 1990s." *Journal of Broadcasting & Electronic Media* 38 (1994): 353-60.

7

Motion Picture Story Magazine
and the Gendered Construction of the Movie Fan

Kathryn H. Fuller

In December 1910, Vitagraph studio head J. Stuart Blackton announced the founding of *Motion Picture Story Magazine* (*MPSM*), an innovative type of fiction publication dedicated to a new audience, motion picture enthusiasts. Blackton's venture was partly a shot in the dark, partly a calculated risk, for it was not immediately clear who made up the target audience—what was a movie fan? How could fans be attracted to the publication, and how should their interests be identified and served? These were issues with which the editorial staff of *MPSM* struggled. Blackton and *MPSM* editor Eugene V. Brewster created a publicity vehicle that unleashed movie fans' interests and activities in ways they could not have anticipated, and of which they became wary. *MPSM* would change the way some members of the movie audience learned about the movies and made meaning from their moviegoing experiences.

   Examining discussions about the movie fan during the nickelodeon era exposes how unsettled, unfixed, and unformed the category was. Movie fans did not immediately assume the form that has been so familiar since the 1920s; fan magazine readers were not necessarily swooning women and giggly young girls romantically obsessed with actors and the glamour of actresses and Hollywood. The gender and social class of the movie fan became hotly contested issues among film producers, theater owners, magazine publishers, and audience members during the establishment of Hollywood feature-filmmaking. This chapter will examine questions of how the image of readers and their interests appeared to be worked out in *MPSM* in the early years of its publication; those years coincided with the first appearance of the movie fan and a broad conversation about fans in popular culture (Jenkins; Lewis *Gender Politics*; Lewis *Adoring Audience*; Radway; Stacey; Gomery; Fuller).

   In 1911, Blackton was already in the vanguard of American film producers willing to experiment with new modes of publicity and wider forms of audience involvement. The Vitagraph studio in 1910 had commissioned the composition of a Tin Pan Alley song, "The Vitagraph Girl," and had sponsored the publication of accompanying sheet music, arranged personal appearances of the studio's actors at New York city-area theaters, and distributed souvenir photos of studio players. Publishing a magazine was a much more complicated undertaking, so Blackton hired Eugene V. Brewster as editor and partner in the *MPSM* venture, which would be headquartered near the Vitagraph studio in Brooklyn. Brewster was a forty-year-old lawyer, political speaker and an experienced editor of short-fiction magazines ("Brewster").

A short-fiction magazine based on film plots was not a radically new product but one that drew together several trends in early twentieth-century publishing. Since the Civil War, dime novels, story papers, and other cheaply printed, widely distributed publications featuring western, railroad, adventure, and romantic themes, had experienced phenomenal popularity with the expanding audience of working class readers. Mass market publications, however, were undergoing a transformation in the 1910s, adopting more morally upright, genteel subject matter and attracting a more middle-class readership. Dozens of smaller literary magazines and short fiction journals also addressed middle-class and adolescent readers and amateur authors. Novelized versions of Broadway stage plays sold in cheap editions illustrated with photographs of well-known actors were additionally becoming available. Eager to capitalize on these developments, Blackton and Brewster sought to combine an ample supply of action-packed fiction in the translation of movie melodramas to written prose, with an already existing market eager to read such stories. Ironically, the 1900s saw the high-water mark of mass market fiction publishing and the 1920s would bring the decline of dime novels and many of the genre fiction magazines—due to the competition of the movies, historians assert (Denning; Jones; Davidson). Blackton and Brewster not only entered a market in its last glory days, but through their new magazine would promote a rival entertainment form that would hasten cheap fiction's decline.

Blackton and other members of the film industry were increasingly confronted, too, with evidence that some members of the movie audience were not content to remain detached film spectators. These vocal, pro-active viewers sought out additional knowledge and strove to participate in various aspects of film production and in the creation of a movie fan culture. By 1910 and 1911 the studios were being deluged with inquiries from moviegoers who wished to know how to write and sell their own film scripts or "scenarios," and how to master the details of film projection and camera operation. Some audience members wanted to collect souvenir pictures of film actors and go on sightseeing tours of studio film sets. Some hoped to "break into the movies" themselves.

Blackton noted that movie fans wrote to studios wanting to know as much as possible about the plots of current films, desiring to translate visual elements of the entertainment to the written word. They enjoyed the overlap between filmed narratives and written stories, and wanted to reexperience their favorite films in story form. Fans had already begun to seek out plot descriptions in the professional trade journals of movie theater managers ("Stories of the Films"). "The *Moving Picture World* was not known here until I induced a local manager of a news company to handle it and now even the kids buy it to read the film synopses," a Thomasville, Georgia projectionist reported. "One man said, 'When I go to an opera house I have a program telling me of the characters, etc. In a picture show there is nothing but the posters, so every day at lunch time I glance at the titles on the posters, go home and get a copy of the *Moving Picture World*, read the synopsis, and at night I enjoy the photoplay immensely, as I am familiar with the characters and scenes'" ("'Crank Turner'"). This aspect of fan interest seemed to Blackton to be the most profitable to tap and perhaps the least threatening to the balance of power between producers and consumers of motion pictures. It became the focus of his idea for the creation of *MPSM*.

The social status of the prospective *MPSM* audience initially appeared a more important concern than readers' gender. The new magazine followed the compact size and layout of short-fiction magazines like *Century* and *Munsey's*, which appealed to both educated male and educated female readers, and the popular science journals like *Popular Mechanics* and *Scientific American*, which had wide middle-class male readership ("Popular Magazine"). Blackton and Brewster purposely designed the style and content of *Motion Picture Story Magazine* to attract middle-class readers. They optimistically informed the trade journals that "Persons never having been in a moving picture theater will read in the magazine stories that greatly interest them, and the logical consequence will be that they will make it their business to find out where those stories can be seen in picture form and will go and see them." This would both "help raise the standard of the whole motion picture business" and expand the nickelodeon audience ("Increase Your Attendance"). Drawing in more middle-class patrons would especially help urban movie theaters, which had a much less respectable reputation than most rural nickelodeons across the nation. The small town middle class were already enthusiastic motion picture supporters, and further courting the interests of this group and their city cousins, Blackton and Brewster hoped, would be one more way to mollify cultural critics who sniffed in disdain that only illiterate immigrants attended motion picture performances (Fuller).

The inaugural issue of *Motion Picture Story Magazine,* published in February, 1911, resembled a staid fiction journal more than the movie fan magazines of the 1920s. The bulk of the magazine was a dozen seven-page novelizations of one-reel narrative films produced by Patents Trust member studios Vitagraph, Biograph, Edison, Lubin, Kalem, Essanay, Selig and Melies. Each short story was illustrated with several still photos from the film release. "It has been suggested, in addition to the fiction stories to run each month a department devoted to personalities of well known picture players," Blackton and Brewster had gingerly noted in announcing the new magazine to film exhibitors ("Motion Picture Story Magazine"). Uncertain of the reaction of their new readership, the editors tucked a few photographed portraits of film players among the back pages.[1]

Of the more than one hundred film subjects released each month by Patents Trust motion picture producers, the films selected for inclusion in the earliest issues of *MPSM* appear to have been chosen for the "middlebrow" cultural tone of their subject matter. Early issues of the magazine offered plot synopses of recent films on the lives of Moliere and Thomas à Becket, and adaptations of Tennyson, Cooper, and Shakespeare. Historical subjects, especially Civil War films such as *A Dixie Mother* (1913) were published frequently in *MPSM,* as were dramatic melodramas. Also prominently featured, perhaps for their prestige and publicity value, were contemporary muckraking message films that featured crusading reporters, brave doctors fighting disease in the slums, and militant suffragettes (Brownlow; Sloan). Few synopses of slapstick comedies or westerns were included in the early issues, despite their wide popularity with nickelodeon audiences. Brewster and his editorial staff were determined to present a vision of the movies as instructive, uplifting, and wholesome in order for their new magazine to attract and hold a "respectable" male and female readership.

The first issue of *MPSM* was snapped up by movie fans and the magazine was immediately judged a success. Marketed at movie theaters and newsstands nationwide, subsequent issues often sold out within a week of release, and by 1912 circulation had reached 500,000 copies. Since the magazine was doing so well the editors had little reason to alter it. The subsequent rapid evolution of the magazine's content, however, suggests that either the editors were dissatisfied or they were responsive to reader suggestions. Brewster and his editorial staff began to broaden the focus of novelizations to include more fiction based on filmed love stories, westerns, and melodramas. They began to select sce-

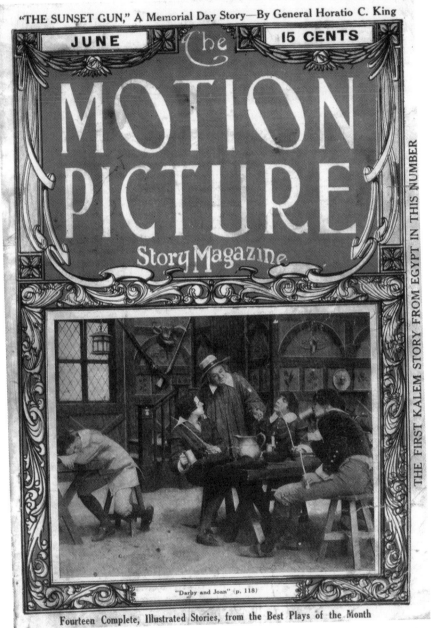

Motion Picture Story Magazine spawned a dozen fanzine publications, running the gamut from artsy photography journals to weekly gossip sheets.

narios based on the quality of the finished film rather than on the subject matter. By the April 1911 issue, a photo portrait gallery of film actors and actresses appeared prominently in the magazine's opening pages. New departments debuted, featuring interviews with players and news of their professional activities. Technical articles about scenario writing, film production and projector optics also appeared in each issue ("Musings"). While there is only sketchy evidence of readers' direct editorial intervention in the shaping of *MPSM*, inclusion of readers' contributions and solicitation of readers' preferences became much more conspicuous and voluminous.

Exactly who the magazine's readers were and what interested them was an issue for the editors as well as for firms that advertised in *MPSM*. Ads in the earliest issues for writers' supplies such as typewriters, ink, and carbon paper, appropriate for the reader-practitioners of a short-fiction magazine, gave way to ads for consumer products like Pompeian Skin Cream, BVD underwear, chocolate bars, Uneeda Biscuits, and Coca-Cola (*MPSM* Feb. 1911, April 1911; "The Actor"). Letters from subscribers such as Mrs. R. A. Stratton of Savannah, Georgia, in August 1911, indicated the success the magazine had found in tapping areas the editors had not necessarily anticipated: "My husband brought me a copy of your magazine a day or so ago (knowing my fondness for the Moving Pictures and everything pertaining thereto), and I was never more pleased with anything in my life—am very "keen" on the pictures and know the faces of the players in them as well as I do those of my friends, can even tell when they change from one company to another" (*MPSM* Aug. 1911 139).

By 1912, *Motion Picture Story Magazine* had become a lively, interactive colloquium for the sharing of movie fans' knowledge and creative interests. Blackton's role in the magazine appeared much reduced after publication was underway, but Brewster seems to have enthusiastically accepted the challenge of making the journal a success. Besides the plot synopses each month, Brewster provided a variety of features concerned with the growing movie culture: regular columns such as "Chats with Photoplayers" and "Green Room Jottings," behind-the-scenes looks at moviemaking, tours of the studios, and editorials criticizing poor films and defending the movie industry against attacks by the press and pulpit. Brewster instituted several innovations that gave readers a larger sense of participation in movie fan culture; he started a never-ceasing round of contests for his readers to vote for their favorite players and the best films, and gave readers space to lobby for their candidates. He crammed the pages full of readers' contributed poems, limericks, and drawings. Thousands of readers deluged Brewster's offices with bits of doggerel about films and favorite actors, mountains of questions about the films and their players, requests for star autographs, and advice on how to enter the movie business. By December 1912, a seemingly astounded Brewster noted, "The popularity of this department far surpassed our anticipations." He announced *MPSM* would give reader contributions on players and films more room, but cautioned "Even now, we cannot hope to publish one-hundredth part of the verses, appreciations and criticisms that we receive" ("Appreciations").

Brewster's most outstanding contribution to the creation of a forum for active fan readership was the Answers to Inquiries column, which premiered in the August 1911 issue. It was presided over by a staff member known only as the Answer Man. Each month's Inquiries department included as many as twenty-five pages of the Answer Man's personal messages to readers. By January 1913 the Answer Man claimed that his office received 2,500 letters a month and he lamented that he could answer only a small percentage of the correspondence in the magazine (*MPSM* Jan. 1913 123). Cartoon drawings show the Answer Man deluged under an avalanche of mail. The Answer Man offered that reader queries could be answered by mail if the correspondent sent an envelope, and a separate bureau was set up at one point to answer many readers' detailed technical questions about how to operate projection equipment or establish nickelodeon theaters.

The differences between the average reader of *MPSM* and these active fans must be noted, for of course they represent a small percentage of all readers, more motivated to respond or to voice their opinions, praise and complaints. They were probably more extreme fans than the passive "lurkers." *MPSM* readers who corresponded with the Answer Man in the early years hailed from both small towns and big cities, were nearly as likely to be male as female, and were interested in a broad diversity of film-related issues. The Inquiries correspondents seemed to represent a geographic cross section of the American movie audience. In September 1911 a contest that awarded monetary prizes for best letters on favorite *MPSM* novelizations illustrated how widespread the magazine's audience was, or at the very least, how widespread *MPSM* editors wished advertisers and the public to perceive the audience to be ("Cash Prize Contest"). Sixty percent of the 85 winning entries came from small-town readers across the country—from Pine Bluff, Arkansas; Huron, South Dakota; Durango, Colorado; Washington, North Carolina; and Oswego, New York. The other 40 percent came from urban readers (a quarter from New York City, where much of the film industry, and the magazine's editorial offices were also located). West Coast readers were somewhat underrepresented. Female winners had a slight edge on the number of male winners (45 to 40). A survey of reader names in the Inquiries column from 1911 through 1916 similarly reveals a fan readership that was 40 percent male and 60 percent female. Whether these portraits of the diversity of *MPSM* readers reflected reality or were orchestrated by the *MPSM* editorial staff, it seems clear that the magazine was not yet solely targeted to the female urban readers that dominated fan magazine discourse in the 1920s.

Consumer goods advertisers, as well, judged a significant proportion of *Motion Picture Story Magazines* readership to be male, as ads for men's personal products appeared prominently next to ads for women's products in the movie fan magazines from 1911 until the late teens. In a typical example, an ad for BVD underwear in sister publication *Motion Picture Classic* in March 1912 was illustrated with a picture of a nickelodeon filled with nattily dressed men who, it seemed, suffered no discomfort in a crowded theater from hot and binding undergarments.

The Inquiries column offered more than just the dry recitation of facts in response to readers' questions. Although to save space readers' letters were not included and responses sometimes read like a one-way telephone conversation, the Answer Man strove to develop an intimate relationship on a mass scale with the magazine's readers, as he researched their most obscure questions about cast members or technical matters and responded to their requests in a confidential, friendly tone. Correspondents held lively debates with him and other readers on such topics as Mary Pickford's acting abilities, the merits or deficiencies of various films, or topical issues such as the war in Europe or national politics. The Answer Man often described his column as an encyclopedia of information about the world of motion pictures, but it also functioned as a meaningful forum for readers' expression of fannish interests. Eighty years later, film historian Edward Wagenknecht recalled with amused pride that his name appears in the January 1912 issue as winner of a letter-writing prize (Wagenknecht). The award of a year's subscription may have been small, but it carried enormous importance to an enthusiastic thirteen-year-old movie fan who reveled in the recognition of his knowledge and talents. His participation gave him a stronger sense of connection with movie fan culture.

There were nevertheless boundaries of permissible discussion in the Inquiries column that led to continuing skirmishes between readers and *MPSM* editors. The Answer Man created editorial rules to deflect certain categories of fans' inquiries. He declined to answer some of his readers' most prying questions about players' marital status and personal habits, which the *MPSM* staff judged to be too invasive of players' privacy. In March 1912 alone, the Answer Man claimed to have rejected 104 inquiries as "inappropriate." That number did include many reader requests for the names of Biograph film actors. Most studios, responding to public demand, had begun promoting the names of their previously anonymous "Vitagraph Girls" in 1909 and 1910, but Biograph remained a particularly stubborn holdout until April 1913, by which time director D. W. Griffith and most of the well-known players had already left. The repeatedly stated restrictions on questions did not deter film enthusiasts from continuing to implore the Answer Man each month to spill the facts about the identities of Biograph's anonymous players, or learn an actor's marital status.[2]

While the Answer Man grudgingly obeyed Biograph's dictums against publicizing the identities of particular actors, rumors of the deaths of prominent players were a different matter. The Answer Man addressed them frequently and repeatedly, resuscitating some film actor or actress in almost every issue of the magazine. Typical is the Answer Man's exasperated, negative response in the August 1912 issue to a fan's letter asking confirmation of a story gotten from a friend's aunt that Maurice Costello had been run over by an auto and killed (170). While many death rumors concerning film players may have been studio publicity "plants," the wild imaginations of movie fans spread the rumors more efficiently and effectively than film producers could ever have orchestrated (Gaines; deCordova).

Movie fans' continued obsession with death rumors of the stars exposed the *MPSM* editors to the dark side of fandom and fame. No wonder then that, following editorial policy and his own preference, the Answer Man himself remained anonymous. As the most tangible link between the growing legion of movie fans and the film industry, he had himself attained a level of celebrity among the film enthusiasts, and he wisely wanted to control their purportedly kind, but dangerously close to overwhelming, attentions. The Answer Man allowed in print only that he was a staff member over seventy years old. This did not keep correspondents from showering him with tins of cookies and cakes, poems and other small trinkets, and pictures of themselves, hoping he could get them on the "inside track" to movie stardom.[3]

Nickelodeon era movie fandom, at least as it was depicted in *MPSM* during its first years of publication, was both sexually undifferentiated and geographically diverse. Almost everyone was invited to be a fan, men and women, young and old, rural and urban, middle-class suburbanites as well as industrial workers. To maintain their profits, motion picture producers and theater owners needed to attract every segment of the American public and deflect cultural critics' concerns. Thus they usually portrayed moviegoers in their publicity materials as adult couples and middle-class families. Beginning in the mid-teens, however, motion picture fan magazines reshaped those images of movie fans into a more narrowly focused reflection of the movie and magazine audience. They began to portray the movie audience in their publications as overwhelmingly dominated by young women. Similar images frequently were being used by consumer product advertisers.

From its first issue, *MPSM* had shown respect for movie fans, addressing its readers knowledgeably, intimately, and confidentially, talking about fans and their interests with a certain admiration for the vast store of knowledge the members of this elite club brought to their study of motion pictures. The editors, writers, and readers nevertheless policed the boundaries of movie fandom, taking potshots at those they considered marginal or unworthy film spectators. Stories, poems, cartoons and tirades railed against audience members who disturbed the fan's concentration, such as the loud and odorous immigrant, the naive country bumpkin (usually male) who had never previously seen a film, or the rude woman who refused to remove her hat in the theater or who gossiped during the show.[4]

While certain female fans were tweaked about disturbing others in the audience while they chattered about the stars' private lives, some male movie fans were even more targeted by *MPSM* for "inappropriate" levels of interest in the movies. It was men, more than women, who were criticized for being too "fanatical." Young boys were depicted in cartoons as the movies' most rambunctiously over-involved fans, shown being mesmerized by dramatic posters and being tossed about during dreams of cowboy and indian chases. Ironically, the magazine's first use of the word "fan" was in a satirical poem in the August 1911 issue titled "The Motion Picture Fan," which included these lines ridiculing the young man's obsessive interest in the mechanics of film technology and exhibition:

> He's very free with strictures, on inappropriate pictures,
> On every mechanism he's *au fait*,
> He can talk about the locus, of the fluctuating focus,
> And let you know the minute it's O.K.
> Should he discourse on shutters, every word he utters,
> You'll find he won't make much of a mistake.
> His original disclosures, on powder and exposures,
> Are anything, believe me, but a fake.
>
> (Hancock)

This image of the male movie fan had parallels in middle-class men's and boys' fascination with electrical inventions like wireless radio, which historian Susan Douglas has characterized as a culture of masculinity. *Scientific American* and *Popular Mechanics*, among other publications marketed to mechanically inclined male hobbyists, devoted many articles to motion picture and radio technology. Motion pictures could be part of a culture of masculinity; nevertheless, here in *MPSM* the knowledgeable male movie fan was spoofed as a pedant who bored everyone around him with technical trivia instead of simply enjoying the show. As the movies evolved into a professionalized, commercialized entertainment form, this image of the movie fan, intimately knowledgeable about the workings of projectors and the writing of film scenarios, was replaced in fan magazines by an image of movie fans as consumers of film, fascinated with the spectacle of the star system. This redefinition helped distance the audience from film production; it also accommodated women and girls more easily than men.

Despite men's continued visibility in the movie audience and demonstrated interest in movie culture, male movie fans increasingly became the fan magazines' targets for criticism or ridicule of fan behavior. *MPSM* more prominently featured letters from male movie fans that made them appear naive and foolish. In the September 1915 issue, fans read that William W. Pratt of Punxsutawney, Pennsylvania, claimed to be shocked to learn that the buildings on the backlot of the new Universal City film studio in California were not real, but merely sets (63). Satiric cartoon panels such as "The Adventures of Flim Flam the Film Fan" ridiculed the male moviegoer whose too-intense attention to a fan magazine led him into Keystone comedy-slapstick types of ludicrous scrapes ("Adventures"; "Dream of a Movie Fan").

That popular culture poked fun at the foibles of men and women in their interaction with new technologies was nothing new. Humor made at the expense of male movie fans was as prevalent in American popular culture as the jokes and comic songs that had earlier skewered foolish male bicyclists and automobile drivers. However, the movie fan magazines now showed a growing unease and confusion over men's roles as movie fans, and seemed to do their best to discourage them. *MPSM* and new rival *Photoplay Magazine* began to reposition themselves, and hence their readership, away from special interest and fan-interactive publishing in another direction, toward the fast-growing, lucrative category of women's magazines that was incidentally attracting far more consumer-product advertising than fan or hobbyist journals.

Several aspects of change were evident as *MPSM* remade itself. In the autumn of 1915 *MPSM* moved away from emphasis on synopses of film scenarios as the featured content. Movies had passed beyond the one-reel film and brief scenario. By 1916 and 1917, the five-reels and longer feature films increasingly would be adapted from popular novels, while novelizations of original film screenplays would stretch to book-length. Brewster dropped the "Story" from his magazine's title in February 1916, simplifying it to *Motion Picture Magazine* (*MPM*). Technical articles on projectors and scenario-writing appeared less frequently. *MPM* became further removed from a hobbyist magazine. After 1916 much of the space devoted to readers' poems, drawings, and comments also disappeared, a move that might have relieved those weary of fan doggerel but removed many of the interactive features that let fans contribute to the publication. Nevertheless *MPM* still offered the enthusiastic reader contests to enter and opportunities to address inquiries to the Answer Man. *MPM* now included more features targeted toward what mass-circulation magazines portrayed as women's interests—advice columns on etiquette, romance, appearance (a "Beauty Hints" department was first published in the September 1916 issue), articles on the stars' clothing on-screen and off, details of players' romances and their private lives, recipes from their kitchens, and breathless descriptions of what cars they drove and what pets they owned.

In September 1915 *MPM*'s new sister publication *Motion Picture Classic*, with the same editorial staff, was launched to meet what appeared to be the inexhaustible demand for news and pictures of film actors. *Classic* led the vanguard of fan magazine editorial changes, as it had a larger page size better suited for glamorous photographic layouts of the stars, a greater number of fashion and women's articles, and "only" fifty to sixty questions answered each month by its Answer Man.[5] In *Classic*, Brewster and his editorial staff first broke previous taboos on discussing film actors' private romantic lives, with articles like "Cupid, Movie & Company, a Popular Firm" (Dench).

The restyled movie fan also made her debut in this period. In November 1916, *Motion Picture Magazine* showcased a letter to the editor from an Ohio reader who told the story of "the truest and most faithful" movie fan, 18-year-old Mary Curtin, daughter of a Columbus, Ohio, car dealer. Mary "has never been known to witness less than 30 movies a week," marveled the writer, "and on the wall of her room has in the vicinity of 450 or 500" movie star portraits (168). Mary attended the movies every day during her school lunch period. She insisted that dates take her to the movies before going on to fraternity dances, and she often lingered so long at the theater that the dance was already over when she and her escort arrived. Yet Mary was not friendless or introverted; a popular young woman and admired for her driving skills, "she has converted many to her habit of almost living at the movies, but none has as yet surpassed her record." This new variety of fan was denigrated by cultural critics for being too absorbed in movies and stars, but she was also criticized for being "too independent" and contemptuous of traditional social rules about woman's ambitions and pleasures. Mary's preference for movie experiences over men's company was both a protest against having to fit into traditional women's roles and a notice that men weren't necessarily wanted in her world of movie fan culture. She jokingly claimed about marriage that "the man I marry must be twice the movie fan I am." When someone warned her she might remain single with those restrictions, "she gave Eva Tanguay's famous cry, 'I don't care!'" (170).

Mary Curtin, movie fan, was a dizzy, off-kilter teenager, but she also represented the New Woman, throwing off traditional roles, daring to do what she wanted. The letter writer mentioned that Mary had traveled all the way to Chicago just to see a film—*The Birth of a Nation* — which had been banned in Ohio. Mary was fiercely independent, and yet very oriented toward leisure and mass culture. She represented the Flapper, a "new and improved" movie fan that would be promoted insistently in the 1920s (Fass).

"Feminine Fads and Fancies," a featured article in the January 1917 issue of *MPM*, illustrates how Brewster and his editorial staff reconceptualized the magazine's purpose and refocused the image of the movie fan. The wide range of interests practiced by fans in 1911 was reduced to young women's overly intense attachments to film actors:

Since the *Motion Picture Magazine* and similar publications have begun to draw the public and the player more closely together, the curiosity of the former, regarding the latter, has been hard to satisfy. The more they know, the more they want to know. The Answer Man, kind old fellow, is bowed beneath the burden of questions, ranging from some one's age to some other actress's salary; from one actor's favorite brand of cigarets [sic] to another's boot size. But since this curiosity is only human, since the players' lives will almost invariably bear the closest scrutiny, and since the players realize that it is the public who provides "the stuff that fills our pay-envelopes," the Magazine has been endeavoring to tell the public—the great, good-natured, benevolent public, who loves deeply and hates fiercely, without, apparently, rhyme or reason—just what it wants to know. (Courtlandt 36)

The repetition of stories like these helped reshape popular opinion about who were movie fans and what were their appropriate interests. As the movies evolved as a professionalized entertainment industry, it had less room for amateur authors or tinkerers. The technologically obsessed male movie fan, intimately knowledgeable about the workings of cameras and projectors, and the writing of scenarios and film criticism, was replaced in fan magazines by an image of movie fans as less involved spectators, consumers, and movie-star worshippers. This redefinition was more able to distance the audience from film production and was more easily focused on women.

By the early 1920s, motion picture fan magazines were doing a booming business (Slide, *Aspects* 102). *MPM* was now one of a dozen publications running the gamut from artsy photography journals to tabloid-like weekly gossip sheets that crowded the racks of the nation's newsstands—*Cinema Art, Film Fun* (published by the humor magazine *Judge*), *Film Play, Motion Picture Classic*, (sometimes simply titled *Classic*), *Motion Picture Journal, Movie Digest, Movie Weekly, Pantomime, Photoplay, Picture Play, Screenland*, and the high-toned *Shadowland* (Slide, *International Film Journals*). Male readers still represented about 10 percent of the question-askers in *MPM*'s and *Photoplay*'s Questions and Answers column. In Cecil B. DeMille's 1920 film *Why Change Your Wife?*, virile husband Thomas Meighan reads fan magazines, much to prissy wife Gloria Swanson's disgust. Men certainly continued to hold up their share of box-office receipts—adult men represented one-third of the American movie audience (women, children and teens the other two-thirds) and surveys indicated that some men did continue to read movie fan magazines throughout the 1920s. Robert and Helen Lynd, for example, found men and boys reading movie fan magazines in the public and high school libraries in Muncie, Indiana (242). Movie fan magazines of the 1920s, nevertheless, would be the major promoters of the image of a female-dominated movie audience and movie fan magazine readership (Studlar). Thus, as the image of the frivolous female fan magazine reader took hold, it became much harder for popular culture to imagine male movie fans or the possibility of their interest in movie magazines or movie fan culture.

Notes

1. Slide notes that the Motion Picture Patents Company was involved in the magazine's founding, contributing $100,000 for initial start-up costs, limiting its coverage to Patents Company films, and requiring a $200 fee from each studio to have a scenario and accompanying photographs published each month. After this initial involvement, however, it is unclear that the Patents Company had a very powerful role in the month-to-month operation of the magazine, and certainly after the Trust disbanded, MPSM continued to thrive for many years (*Early American Cinema* 40-41, 141).

2. For complaints about Biograph's no-name policy, see *MPSM* August 1912 (170), where the Answer Man loses his temper about readers' persistent interest in finding out who Biograph players were; (Slide, *Early American Cinema* 140-43).

3. *MPSM* August 1913 had 613 responses in the Answers to Inquiries column; the August 1915 issue had 344.

4. See "Who's Married to Whom, etc., etc.," in Hansen (247), and Hansen's discussion of the 1902 film "Uncle Josh at the Moving Picture Show" (25-28); see also an "Uncle-Josh"-inspired 1913 cover of the *Saturday Evening Post* reproduced in Bowers (xii).

5. *Motion Picture Classic* was first published as *The Motion Picture Supplement* September 1915; it was often known simply as *Classic*. Although overshadowed by *Photoplay* in the 1920s, *Classic* and *Motion Picture Magazine* remained high quality, popular publications throughout the decade (Slide, *International Film Journals*).

Works Cited

"Actor—Likewise the Actress." *Moving Picture World* 12 Nov. 1910: 1099.

"Adventures of Flim Flam, the Film Fan." Cartoon. *Motion Picture Magazine* Mar. 1916: 159.

"Appreciations and Criticisms of Popular Plays and Players by Our Readers." *Motion Picture Story Magazine* Dec. 1912: 131.

Bowers, Q. David. *Nickelodeon Theaters and Their Music*. Vestal: Vestal, 1989.

"Brewster, Eugene V." *Who Was Who in America* 1943.

Brownlow, Kevin. *Behind the Mask of Innocence: Sex, Violence, Prejudice, Crime: Films of Social Conscience in the Silent Era*. New York: Knopf, 1990.

"Cash Prize Contest." *Motion Picture Story Magazine* Sept. 1911: 141.

Courtlandt, Roberta. "Feminine Fads and Fancies." *Motion Picture Magazine* Jan. 1917: 36-37.

"'Crank Turner' Wants to Know." *Moving Picture World* 2 Dec. 1911: 739.

Davidson, Cathy N. *Reading in America: Literature and Social History*. Baltimore: Johns Hopkins, 1989.

deCordova, Richard. *Picture Personalities: The Emergence of the Star System in America*. Urbana: Illinois, 1990.

Dench, Ernest A. "Cupid, Movie & Company, a Popular Firm." *Motion Picture Classic* Apr. 1916: 33-35.

Denning, Michael. *Mechanic Accents: Dime Novels and Working-Class Culture in America*. London: Verso, 1987.

Douglas, Susan. *Inventing American Broadcasting, 1899-1922*. Baltimore: Johns Hopkins, 1987.

"Dream of a Movie Fan." Cartoon. *Motion Picture Magazine* Nov. 1915: 147.

Fass, Paula. *The Damned and the Beautiful: American Youth in the 1920s*. New York: Oxford, 1977.

Fuller, Kathryn H. *At the Picture Show: Small Town Audiences and the Creation of Movie Fan Culture*. Washington: Smithsonian, 1996.

Gaines, Jane. "From Elephants to Lux Soap: The Programming and 'Flow' of Motion Picture Exploitation." *Velvet Light Trap* 25 (1990): 29-43.

Gomery, Douglas. *Shared Pleasures: A History of Movie Presentation in the United States*. Madison: U of Wisconsin P, 1992.

Hancock, La Touche. "The Motion Picture Fan." *Motion Picture Story Magazine* Aug. 1911: 93.

Hansen, Miriam. *Babel and Babylon: Spectatorship in American Silent Film*. Cambridge: Harvard UP, 1991.

"Increase Your Attendance." *Moving Picture World* 9 Dec. 1911: 829.

Jenkins, Henry. *Textual Poachers: Television Fans and Participatory Culture*. New York: Routledge, 1992.

Jones, Daryl. *The Dime Novel Western*. Bowling Green, OH: Bowling Green State University Popular Press, 1978.

Letters to the Editor. *Motion Picture Magazine* Nov. 1916: 168, 170.

Lewis, Lisa ed. *The Adoring Audience: Fan Culture and Popular Media*. New York: Routledge, 1992.

——. *Gender Politics and MTV: Voicing the Difference*. Philadelphia: Temple, 1990.

Lynd, Robert, and Helen Lynd. *Middletown*. New York: Harcourt Brace, 1929.

"Motion Picture Story Magazine." *Moving Picture World* 4 Feb. 1911: 228.

"Musings of the Photoplay Philosopher." *Motion Picture Story Magazine* Oct. 1912: 140.

"Popular Magazine for Film Fans." *Nickelodeon* 15 Dec. 1910: 339.

Radway, Janice. *Reading the Romance: Women, Patriarchy and Popular Literature*. Chapel Hill: U of North Carolina P, 1984.

Slide, Anthony. *Aspects of Film History Prior to 1920*. Metuchen: Scarecrow, 1978.

——. *Early American Cinema*. Rev. ed. Metuchen: Scarecrow, 1994.

——, ed. *International Film, Radio and Television Journals*. Westport: Greenwood, 1985.

Sloan, Kay. *The Loud Silents: Origins of the Social Problem Film*. Urbana: U of Illinois P, 1988.

Stacey, Jackie. *Star Gazing: Hollywood Cinema and Female Spectatorship*. New York: Routledge, 1994.

"Stories of the Films." *Moving Picture World* 2 Apr. 1910: 502.

Studlar, Gaylyn. "The Perils of Pleasure: Fan Magazine Discourse as Women's Commodified Culture in the 1920s." *Wide Angle* 13.1 (1991): 6-33.

Wagenknecht, Edward. Letter to the author. 29 Oct. 1990.

Part 2

Assessing the Contemporary Cultural Landscape

(Courtesy of the AFI Collection)

Film and television scholarship has undergone a turbulent period during the past two decades with the influx and application of several revisionist perspectives, including various postmodernist, poststructuralist, feminist, psychoanalytic, neo-Marxist, and even neoconservative approaches. Together these diverse critical views have challenged and replaced the more traditional ways of thinking about the popular media and culture. Much of this upheaval, though contentious, has been for the good, as the more static and classical models have given way to methods that are largely grounded on the notions that all aspects of media culture are socially constructed; and movie and TV entertainment is, first and foremost, deeply ideological.

The effects of what is generally grouped together in the aggregate as contemporary critical theory has literally transformed the arts, humanities, and social sciences. Film and television studies as a discipline is no exception. In this way, Part 2 of *In the Eye of the Beholder* addresses an assortment of postmodern and multicultural screen representations, paying closest attention to matters of gender, race, ethnicity, and the disabled. This section underscores many of the most compelling issues being examined in popular film and TV today. For example, Gaylyn Studlar critiques the sexual politics of *Pink Flamingos*, *The Rocky Horror Picture Show*, and *Liquid Sky* in chapter 8. She demonstrates how "femininity" in these features, often enacted by male performers, is linked with perversion in ways that reinforce oppressive attitudes about gender. She also pinpoints how the rise of home video has effectively eliminated these cult films as midnight movie-going experiences.

In chapter 9, J. P. Telotte identifies a fundamental change in the presentation of male and female bodies in the films noirs of the 1940s and 1950s to today's neo-noirs. He argues that the image of the "woman in the door" (frame) which was traditionally coupled with the hard-boiled and dominant male is a myth the culture can no longer sustain. He then links the narrative predictability of the old noirs to cultural stability; and the narrative instability of the neo-noirs to our own present-day cultural impermanence. Laurie Ouellette and Carolyn Anderson profile the cable program, *Talk Soup,* in chapter 10, explaining how it reflects the political economy and aesthetics of postmodern television, whereby TV imagery is recycled, repackaged, and resold in an ongoing loop of symbolic production and consumption. They employ the concept of hegemony to underscore *Talk Soup's* method of ridiculing the more feminized TV talk show culture from a white, male, middle-class point of view, thus reinforcing dominant structures and ideologies.

Jack Nachbar evaluates the movie image of the English on the western frontier in chapter 11. He recognizes a stereotypical consistency over seventy years of film and across genres in which British characters are presented in frontier stories as unhappy or downright evil, corrupted by their restrictive manners and class prejudices. Citing Frederick Jackson Turner's frontier mythos, Nachbar locates the ideological source for Hollywood's tendency of having English characters either forsake European culture and become more American, or pay a heavy price as a consequence. Next, in chapter 12, Martin Norden explores the portrayal of the disabled Vietnam vet in a series of Hollywood films from the late 1980s and early 1990s. He compares *Suspect, Blind Fury, Born on the Fourth of July, Scent of a Woman,* and *Forrest Gump* with the previous cycle of disabled Vietnam vet movies from the late 1970s and early 1980s. Norden considers issues as wide-ranging as rehabilitation, access, sexuality, the redirection of bitterness and rage, and the changing conception of heroism, concluding with recommendations on how to move beyond the age-old stereotypes to more humane depictions.

Rodney Carveth investigates in chapter 13 the role of television news in portraying people living with AIDS. He conducted a detailed content analysis of AIDS-related network news stories between January 1990 and October 1994 as a way of mapping the symbolic terrain. As a result, he distinguishes four successive cycles of news coverage so far, identifies the prevailing stereotypes, and presents suggestions on how to improve future representations along with the public's understanding of HIV and AIDS. William Brown and Arvind Singhal offer an international perspective in chapter 14, examining both positive and negative effects that ensue when the popular media are actively employed for the purpose of guiding constructive social change, rather than maximizing vast profits. They advance seven ethical guidelines for promoting prosocial messages through film and TV programming around the world. As with all seven chapters in Part 2, Brown and Singhal's essay tacitly reminds us that popular film and television are two of the foremost institutional forces in the world for establishing and transmitting human values.

8

Midnight S/excess:
Cult Configurations of "Femininity" and the Perverse

Gaylyn Studlar

Excess defines the midnight movie, a cult phenomenon that seems to catalogue perverse acts with the same enthusiasm as nineteenth-century sexologists such as Richard von Krafft-Ebing, whose *Psychopathia Sexualis* offered detailed clinical descriptions of sado-masochism, fetishism, transvestism, homosexuality, voyeurism, exhibitionism, necrophilia, bestiality, and myriad other sexual "abnormalities" considered to be the essence of perversion. Midnight movies often present a comparable compendium of sexual acts, but their interest in perversion extends beyond clinical curiosity and cataloging. Encompassing everything from the coprophagic antics of Divine in *Pink Flamingos* (1973) to the gender-bending generic pastiche of *The Rocky Horror Picture Show* (1975), these films often use perversion as a means of shocking their audience. However, this exploitation of sexual imagery should not lead us to dismiss automatically cult films such as *The Rocky Horror Picture Show, Pink Flamingos, The Texas Chainsaw Massacre* (1986), *Eraserhead* (1978), or *Liquid Sky* (1983), because the sexual excess of the midnight movie also marks their preoccupation with a culturally ubiquitous problem—that of defining the meaning of sexual difference.

Freud defined perversions as "sexual activities which either (1) extend, in an anatomical sense, beyond the regions of the body that are designed for sexual union or (2) linger over the intermediate relations to the sexual object which should normally be transversed rapidly on the path towards the final sexual aim" ("Three Essays" 7: 150). Consequently, perversion is not only a form of sex that takes a taboo aim or object (such as foot fetishism); it also includes "normal" acts (such as sexual looking as foreplay) that when taken to excess deflect sexuality from the aim of heterosexual genital intercourse. However, as post-Freudians such as Jean Laplanche assert, the meaning of perversion extends beyond the use of bodies in sexual practice or any implied deviation from a universal sexual instinct (23).[1] Perversion reflects on the

117

meaning assigned to the gendered body within a given culture, on the precariousness of "normality," and on the construction of sexuality as a process taking place in the head rather than in the genes or genitalia.

Midnight movies typically crystallize the problem of sexual difference and the s/excess of perversity in a feminine, though not always *female* figure. The three films that form the focus of this article—*Pink Flamingos* (1973), *The Rocky Horror Picture Show* (1975), and *Liquid Sky* (1982)—utilize varying textual strategies to represent sexual difference, but all construct a deeply ambivalent discourse that depends upon "femininity" as a vector point uniting revulsion and fascination, excess and lack, pleasure with the perverse. The precedent for this ambivalent linking of the excess of perversion with female sexuality can be found in many cultural discourses. One unexpected and important source is Freud's work on perversions, "Three Essays on Sexuality."

In the first of these essays, Freud defines perversity as an infantile form of eroticism that becomes abnormal in adulthood when it replaces rather than co-exists with the "normal sexual aim and object," that is, genitally focused heterosexuality (160-61). Children's "aptitude" for polymorphous perversity, remarks Freud, is "innately present in their disposition." Therefore, perversity encounters "little resistance" in children because they have not yet developed the "mental dams against sexual excesses—shame, disgust and morality" that properly control and channel their sexual desires (191).

Freud's remarks are a predictable part of his theory of childhood sexuality, but what is disconcerting is his comparison of children's lack of "mental dams against sexual excesses" with the sexuality of women. "In this respect," he continues, "children behave in the same kind of way as an average uncultivated woman in whom the same polymorphously perverse disposition persists" (191). In the easy comparison between childhood perversity and adult female sexuality, Freud presents us with a conceptual slippage that is not supported by his other studies on perversions.[2] Instead, these comments reveal a stubbornly persistent patriarchal myth, the same sexual ideology that Bram Dijkstra finds in academic painting of the late nineteenth century and Klaus Theweleit locates in the culturally pervasive fantasies of protofascists in twentieth-century Germany. "Uncultivated women," remarks Freud, are easily seduced into finding "every sort of perversion to [their] tastes." Therefore, "the immense number of women who are prostitutes or who must be supposed to have an aptitude for prostitution without becoming engaged in it" proves that "this same disposition to perversions of every kind is a general and fundamental human characteristic" (191). Although attributed to humanity as a whole, the deviance of perversion finds its specific example in women.

Choosing to ignore the deployment of women's sexuality by and for a system privileging male sexual desires, Freud's remarks are consistent with the nineteenth-century belief that women do not have the same sense of sexual and social restraint as men. Freud confirmed this belief in his essay "Some Psychological Consequences of the Anatomical Differences Between the Sexes." He explains that the boy's fear of being castrated by the father teaches him the lesson of sexual prohibition. This "castration complex" proves to be crucial to the development of the superego in men, to their introjection of civilized values. But little girls are already "castrated," so that "the level of what is ethically normal is different [in women] from what it is in men" (193). With little superego constraints on their sexuality, women could be expected to behave like polymorphously perverse children. It was the logical result of their psychosexual development.

In light of this essay, Freud's citation of the "uncultivated woman" in "Three Essays" is significant, for it reveals the assumption that the "disposition" for perversion is actually class specific in women. In *Male Fantasies: Floods, Bodies and History*, Klaus Theweleit finds this same association of perversity with lower-class women underlying the fantasies of the Freikorps, a post–World War I protofascist German military organization that became the core of Hitler's SA. Freikorpsmen divided women into two groups. High-born women could be idealized as pure angels, asexual and nurturing, but lower-class women became the signifier of a dark and degenerate femininity. The body of the proletariat woman was a secret terrain containing "filthy floods" (407). She embodied perverse sexual excess in all its frightful and fascinating possibilities. Theweleit argues that rather than being an anomaly in Western culture, these protofascist fantasies linking perversity with femininity constitute the "equivalent to the tip of the patriarchal iceberg" (171).

The same "patriarchal iceberg" is also evident in midnight movies, but Freud's remarks and Theweleit's examples can serve only as the point of departure for considering the complex representations of femininity and perversion in these films. Some of them, such as *Eraserhead* and *Pink Floyd—The Wall* (1982), represent "normal" heterosexual desire in ways clearly analogous to the Freikorps fantasies. For example, the entire pattern of visual iconography in David Lynch's *Eraserhead* (1983) suggests the "filthy floods" of a menacing femininity, simultaneously a lack (female genitalia as orifice) and fluid (vaginal) too-much-ness. *Eraserhead*'s disturbing dream world is dominated by the hapless protagonist's attempt to nurture a reptilian baby, the abhorrent product of his girlfriend's body.

Eraserhead makes sex a loathsome and repellent thing, but the midnight movie frequently embraces perversion as an outlaw sexuality, a revolutionary excess of desire unhinged from accepted values and celebrated as social deviance. Although its depiction of sex often appears lewd or pornographic, the midnight movie's channeling of sexuality into perversion serves what Eco has termed the "glorious incoherence" of the cult film (4). The de-eroticized visual treatment of varied sexual acts in midnight movies such as *Pink Flamingos, Female Trouble* (1974), and *The Rocky Horror Picture Show* displaces the porno film's predictable climax of/in genital coitus and its presumed spectatorial imperative of arousal. Instead, these films ritualize perversion into a subculture icon of rebellion against bourgeois norms by celebrating the possibilities of sex as ironic play and playacting.

Such an attitude is reminiscent of Herbert Marcuse's view of perversion expressed in *Eros and Civilization*. Marcuse argued that perversions challenge the very foundation of capitalistic society by upholding "sexuality as an end in itself," and by placing sexual practice "outside the domination of society's structuring 'performance principle'"(45-46). Perversions were culturally inadmissible in the capitalist system because they did not fulfill the patriarchal requirement that normal sex must be "socially useful and good." For Marcuse, the commonly held belief that perversions were immoral or unnatural was patriarchal capitalism's predictably repressive reaction to sexual practice focused exclusively on producing pleasure rather than babies.

From a Marcusean perspective, any appearance of perversion in the midnight movie might be regarded as a progressive movement toward subverting the dominant sexual practice sanctioned by the patriarchal bourgeois family, but analysis reveals that most of these films do little to subvert oppressive norms. This can be attributed to the failure to recognize that perversions are easily assimilated into and controlled by dominant culture.[3] However, such a failure can also be read as the result of the films' unwillingness to be perverse enough. Although midnight movies often revel in breaking sexual taboos through homosexuality and inverted sex roles or cross-dressing, these elements suggest a contemporary "sexual revolution" that does not necessarily question the hierarchical status of gender or the patriarchal power imbalance in sexual practice. Mike Brake alerts us to this irony in so-called sexual freedom: "The more sexuality is brought into the open, into a 'liberated zone' freed from puritanism, the more women are open to exploitation by men, unless they too contribute to the sexual debate" (28). Despite the attempt to invoke subculture associations and alternative ideologies, the midnight movie's sexual politics, like those of other youth-oriented media, such as rock videos, are full of the contradictions of patriarchal ideology, contradictions that foreground the difficult negotiation between our lived sexuality and cultural imperatives.

Male Sexuality Unhinged

If she's a girl, then what is my sister?
—Frank Tashlin's *The Girl Can't Help It*

John Waters' films are notorious. Among the first films to achieve cult status as midnight movies, they are archetypal examples of the contradictions of s/excess. Forthrightly described by its director as "the most disgusting film ever made," *Pink Flamingos* exemplifies the midnight movie as aesthetic and sexual shock treatment (Peary 263). The Marquis de Sade once declared that "Art is the perpetual immoral subversion of the established order" (Carter 132). In *Pink Flamingos*, Waters, who readily acknowledges his debt to the Marquis, forges a transparent subculture heterocosm where sexual perversity as social deviance shows up everywhere—especially in his hometown of Baltimore, Maryland.

As with most of Waters' other films, including *Mondo Trasho* (1969), *Female Trouble* (1974), *Polyester* (1981), and *Hairspray* (1988), *Pink Flamingos* employs the talents of Divine, a 300-pound transvestite, to play the film's heroine, Babs Johnson.[4] Babs unites with her family to defend their trailer house and her reputation as the "filthiest person alive." Connie and Raymond Marble challenge her status as the world's filthiest person by sending Babs a gift-wrapped turd on her birthday. Their claim is based chiefly on a cottage industry: they kidnap women hitchhikers to breed babies for lesbian couples. As a sideline, the Marbles push heroin in elementary schools, and Raymond exposes himself in a purse-snatching scam. Confident in her supreme filthiness, Babs accepts their challenge. Before the war for her title is over, she performs fellatio on her son, executes her rivals in a self-styled media event, and munches on dog excrement in the midnight movies' most notorious example of Bazinian spatial unity.

Characterized by Rebecca Bell-Metereau as a "sadistic, domineering female" (123), Babs's character is actually as mercurial as a film noir *femme fatale*. A pastiche of a personality, Babs first appears as a lovingly indulgent daughter to her senile, egg-eating mother. She becomes an enthusiastically incestuous mother, a heartless murderess, and finally, the girl who, as the soundtrack tells us, "can't help it." In his autobiography, Waters disingenuously remarks that Divine is merely an actor who plays women characters; his comment purposefully ignores the ambiguity and complex sexual implications of male transvestism (108). By representing his "heroine" through Divine, Waters extends dominant cinema's manipulation of the female image into outlaw filmmaking; at the same time his film reveals, in a paradoxical way, the deeply problematic construction of femininity in the patriarchy.

In *The Sadeian Woman and the Ideology of Pornography*, Angela Carter asserts that "a woman who pretends to be a man has also cancelled out her reproductive system, like the postmenopausal woman" (62). Carter overstates both the force and predictability of cross-dressing as a signifier, but her remark raises an interesting point: Does Divine prove that something of the reverse is also true? Or is our awareness of the gendered maleness of Divine, like that of any female impersonator, the unalterable difference that inevitably makes his/her sexual jokes and representation of female sexuality "a form of male aggression upon the women he personates" (60)?

Divine's presence relies on the notion that femininity is merely an act in which women and, therefore, anyone can successfully engage. This idea resembles one of the key concepts in modern feminist theory, *the masquerade*, explained by Michele Montrelay as the woman's use of "her own body to disguise herself." Femininity is created with "dotty objects, feathers, hat, strange baroque constructions," the purpose of which is "to say nothing" (93). However, Joan Riviere interprets the masquerade as having another function beyond masking the woman's lack. Women's masquerade of *excess femininity* works to disguise those attributes of masculinity that the patriarchy finds threatening in a female. Feminine accouterments are assumed in excess in order "to hide the possession of masculinity and to avert the reprisals expected if she was found to possess it" (131).

Divine's excess femininity is that of the blonde bombshell whose undulating walk, "cha-cha heels," tight skirt, and clinging sweater define woman as walking sexual minefield. As Babs Johnson, Divine's makeup is so extreme that her hairline must be shaved back to accommodate her sweeping eyebrows, and her huge "breasts," gigantic extensions into free space, are important twin signs of woman's mythical hyperbolized sexuality. Lest her appearance or actions leave any doubt, Babs confirms her polymorphously perverse nature in her declaration that she has "done everything."

Divine's excess femininity hides masculinity, but her possession of the masculine-sexed body alters the meaning of the masquerade. A woman who employs such a masquerade of feminine excess does so to camouflage qualities not believed to be rightfully hers because she lacks the penis, the anatomical signifier of the *phallus,* the patriarchal emblem of power. Divine's masquerade parodies women's performance of femininity, but fails to expose the origins of this performance in patriarchal culture's demand for its construction. Thus, Divine's appropriation of the cultural signs of female subjectivity becomes a symbolic theft and trans-formation that leaves men free to ridicule femininity as a self-styled excess. Her performance does not require men to acknowledge that the feminine behaviors she emulates are actually "the manners they have invented" (Carter 39).

Divine's wo/man, as an act of *bricolage*, parodies the assumption of femininity; it also parodies the "natural" spectacle of women's corpo-real excess, simultaneously too much and yet never enough. She is a parody of a parody, Marilyn Monroe's 1950s bombshell ideal mediated through Jayne Mansfield's mind-boggling too-much-ness. Divine's too-much-ness is convincingly and yet uncomfortably feminine. Bell-Metereau observes, "[W]e must often remind ourselves that 'She' isn't even really a woman . . . we find ourselves thinking of her as feminine" (122-23). So daring is her masquerade that in *Female Trouble*, Divine (as Dawn Davenport) walks to the altar in a transparent lace bridal dress that defies our ability to find the "visually ascertainable" difference that would reaffirm his/her phallic integrity" (Mulvey 13). Regardless of her fake *mons veneris* and gay deceivers, we believe Divine is a woman pri-marily because she is fat. As Noelle Caskey observes, fat is "a direct consequence of her [woman's] sexuality. . . . Fat and femininity cannot be separated physiologically" (176-78). The marker of the "natural" somatic excess of femininity, fat is a sexual liability and social taboo in contemporary America. As Caskey notes, it is also condemned as dis-gusting and a sign of self-indulgence that is class specific (66-67). Squeezed into fake leopard skin, cheap lamé, and stretch polyester, Divine becomes a literalist interpretation of Marx's notion of lumpen proletariat. Her obesity, her self-proclaimed filthiness, and her outra-geously trashy outfits serve as signs of lower-class femininity reminis-cent of the German Freikorps' image of the shameless proletarian woman as their most insistent symbol of perverse femininity: a physi-cally monstrous and grotesque embodiment of woman as political and sexual outlaw (66-67).

If Divine parodies femininity, we can still find a minimally subver-sive function in her attempt to forge her own perverse subjecthood. In *Pink Flamingos*, as the self-proclaimed filthiest person alive, and in *Female Trouble*, as a greedy juvenile delinquent turned into the world's worst mother, she reinvents herself as a Sadeian woman: lewd, orgiastic, aggressively pursuing self-gratification in defiance of feminine cultural norms of self-effacing passivity. In *Pink Flamingos*, Divine orders that Connie and Raymond Marble be tied to a tree. After they are tarred and feathered, she shoots them point blank in the face as reporters from the tabloids watch. Her motto at their execution, "Killing makes me come,"

Divine as Dawn Davenport in *Female Trouble*. In the Sadeian regime, ugliness is venerated as an equally extraordinary excess that challenges a refined bourgeois sensibility. (Courtesy of Museum of Modern Art/Film Stills Archive)

also recalls the Sadeian woman who embraces tyranny instead of martyrdom to challenge "her own socially conditioned role in the world" (Carter 133). Her execution of the Marbles serves as a nihilistic act of aggression that is paradoxically paired with the coprophilic *coup de grace* that confirms Divine's right to be called not only the fictive "filthiest person alive" but also the voice-over narrator cheerfully informs us, "the filthiest actress alive." Femininity and perversity are doubly inscribed in extra-filmic as well as filmic terms.

Although she claims to find sadistic satisfaction in killing, Divine's sexuality is expressed mainly as a narcissistic exhibitionism. Because her exhibitionism breaks free of female passivity and the aim of producing male pleasure, it becomes an autoerotic, perverse act. This recalls the late nineteenth-century belief that narcissism was a distinctly feminine perversion. Painters and novelists of the time obsessively depicted scenes of female self-absorption, while sexologists articulated the idea that the "weaker sex" was susceptible to an autoerotic fixation that would pervert their natural altruism and destroy civilization by unleashing sexual impulses that only men could control (Dijkstra 154-59).

In *Pink Flamingos*, Divine fulfills this description to become a nineteenth-century sexologist's worst nightmare of the effects of female narcissism. She gets "all dressed up to fall in love" and leaves her trailer for an errand in town. Stealing from a meat counter, she walks off with a round steak stuffed between her legs, then defecates in front of a mansion. As she undulates down a crowded city sidewalk to the song "The Girl Can't Help It," the lyrics declare that "the girl can't help it if she was born to please." With her onanistic gestures aimed at no one and everyone, she makes culturally approved feminine exhibitionism perverse because she is so narcissistic that she no longer needs a fetishizing male subject to confirm her objectification.

Divine's spectacle of female carnality elicits incredulity rather than desire from those who observe her on the street. The uglier and fatter Divine gets, the more beautiful she believes herself to be and the more aggressively exhibitionist she becomes. Waters's *Female Trouble* provides the most striking example of this. After being hideously scarred by acid, Dawn Davenport (Divine) takes to the stage in a nightclub act that juxtaposes trampoline tricks with shooting at her audience. By combining ugliness and aggressive female exhibitionism, Waters's films echo the Sadeian spectacle of the grotesque. Usually beauty is venerated as a spectacle of excess, but in the Sadeian regime, ugliness is venerated as an extraordinary excess that challenges rather than confirms a refined bourgeois sensibility (Carter 76). Divine's exhibition of "her" excess of ugliness also reinforces the comic stereotype of the ugly woman who unknowingly elicits ridicule (rather than desire) when she presumes to satisfy the male gaze. The antierotic, parodic treatment of Divine guarantees that the homoerotic possibilities of male looking are averted. The straight male spectator can safely enjoy Divine's "feminine" outrages against social and sexual convention while using the figure of the grotesque wo/man to confirm his own perfection in masculine normality.

In spite of this, Divine still represents a threat to patriarchal norms. While Divine playfully demonstrates that sexual identity has no biological mandate and is not a condition of genitality, she may also echo Freikorpsmen fantasies of a powerful femininity represented as an overwhelming flood, an engulfing tide, the perverse Other that threatens to suck men into the disorder and dissolution of female sexuality (367, 402-06). Any "he" who appears as "she" risks becoming a perverse "feminine body," a soft, flowing, multiple-sited morass of dissolute perverse sexuality that threatens to dismantle the patriarchy's tenuously maintained, phallic-centered subjectivity.[5] Even if initially greeted with derisive laughter, Divine's acting out of such a sexual identity must ultimately be condemned as incoherent—"unhinged"—in a phallocratic order.

The Power of Seduction and Destruction

> Such a perfect specimen of manhood, so dominant!
> —*The Rocky Horror Picture Show*

In *The Rocky Horror Picture Show*, the transvestite alien Frank-N-Furter seduces males and females with equanimity, creates his own ideal sex object, and has everyone emulating his drag queen chic. Yet androgyny has its ironies. Within the generic pastiche of *The Rocky Horror Picture Show*, with its borrowing from horror films, science-fiction, and the musical, Dr. Frank-N-Furter (Tim Curry) represents a gender transformation that assumes perverse possibilities but safely recuperates the revolutionary promise of a homoerotic hedonism through the sexual politics of masculine aggression.

Perhaps the most famous of all cult films, *Rocky Horror* follows the misadventures of Janet Weiss (Susan Sarandon) and her straightlaced fiancé, Brad Majors (Barry Bostwick), as they journey from Denton, "The Home of Happiness," to visit Dr. Everett Scott, their ex-tutor. On a rainy night, they end up at a castle. It is not, as Brad first surmises, "some kind of hunting lodge for rich weirdos," but the home of Dr. Frank-N-Furter and his "foreign" friends—all aliens from the planet of Transexual. Janet and Brad become reluctant witnesses to Frank-N-Furter's "biochemical research" and then rather more willing participants in some sexual research before they escape being beamed back with the castle to the galaxy of Transylvania.

While we may forget that Divine is a man, one cannot forget that Frank-N-Furter, the "sweet transvestite from Transexual Transylvania," is male. A young fan gives his account of why he cross-dresses as Frank: "There's no other role I could play. It's the one that's closest to me. Frank-N-Furter is vicious and likes to be on top. The first time I walked down the stairs to show my mom my transvestite outfit, she was a little upset. . . . It's fun to see people freak out at something that's not that weird" (Bell-Metereau 17).

When he first emerges to greet Janet and Brad, Frank appears in a satin vampire cape. He then sheds this apparel to reveal a black sequined corset and G-string. To escort his guests on a tour of his laboratory, he dons a green laboratory dress. These costumes may signify a transcendence of gender norms, but neither Frank-N-Furter nor his fan who models his "transvestite outfit" for his mom have transcended the cultural contradictions of masculinity. The surface confusion of masculinity and femininity in Frank's costuming and manner does not point to any confusion of the privileges of the category of the masculine vis-à-vis the feminine. Frank-N-Furter is "not that weird" because the perverse Otherness of transvestism and bisexuality are normalized by his comforting sameness—the very apparent masculine qualities that confirm his active, phallic power. When Brad aggressively attempts to remind Frank that his requests to telephone for help have been ignored, Frank ridicules Brad: "How forceful you are, Brad! . . . So dominant. . . . Do you have any tattoos?" Ironically, it is Frank who has tattoos.

In spite of his feminine attire and "swishy" ways, Frank remains a transvestite figure with whom males can safely identify without endangering the power base of their prescribed masculinity. The "master" of his castle, Frank asserts his masculinity in destruction and seduction. When his servants get out of hand, he brings out the whip. When his former lover, Eddie, comes roaring out of an oversize deep freeze, Frank chops him up into a dinner entree. With dissension quelled and his ax put away for the night, Frank proceeds to seduce Brad. He then seduces Janet. By maintaining his status as the seducer and not the seducee, Frank-N-Furter escapes the real danger of gender transformation—that the plurality of perversion might render the male passive, nonphallic, and truly "feminized." However, if, as Lawrence Kubie maintains, human beings are constantly engaged in denying and affirming their gender identities, then Frank-N-Furter may provide a safety valve for unconscious feelings that are normally repressed in straight males (202). Frank-N-Furter himself speaks of the possibility of male identification with, and envy of, culturally inscribed femininity in his song lyrics: "Whatever happened to Fay Wray," he sings, "That delicate satin-draped frame. As it clung to her thigh, How I started to cry. . . . 'Cause I wanted to be dressed just the same!"

Paradoxically, Frank endangers his own power base because he feminizes the archetypal Hollywood image of the mad scientist. As a character remarks, "It was over when he had the plan/To start working on a muscle man." Frank creates a creature, but his mission is for love, not science: He wants a new mate. When his creation, Rocky, prefers Janet to him, Frank cries out: "Oh, Rocky! How could you!" Frank's sexual rejection suggests the melodramatic dilemma of Joan Crawford in *Humoresque* (1946) or Gloria Swanson in *Sunset Boulevard* (1950). In these films, the powerful woman fails in her attempt to forge her young male protégé into a sexually acquiescent partner. But Frank's ladylike disappointment is quickly followed by a vengeful spree in which he zaps Janet, Rocky, and Brad into stony immobility with his sonic transducer. Ultimately, Frank-N-Furter's sexual and scientific escapades are brought to an end by the new commander, Riff-Raff, who declares that Frank's "lifestyle's too extreme!" He shoots Frank with a laser. Imitating King Kong's skyscraper ascent with Fay Wray, a remorseful Rocky carries Frank's lifeless body up the radio tower of the RKO Pictures logo, which has served as the backdrop to Frank's final musical extravaganza celebrating sexual freedom.

Although Frank-N-Furter may provide a way of identifying with a sexually uninhibited and self-expressive character who ultimately evokes a measure of sympathy, the more vulnerable "feminized" side of Frank is not the image with which his fans, male and female, straight and gay, seem to consciously identify. A female fan who dresses up as Frank reaffirms the power politics of the character's sexuality and the appeal of identifying with him through costume. "As Frank, I have a chance to be on top of things, to be a faggot Clint Eastwood. Frank-N-Furter may wear Joan Crawford makeup and high heels, but he's still so masculine there's no way you could mistake him for a woman" (Henkin 23). Frank-N-Furter's fans identify with the Frank who, in juxtaposing the pearl necklace of a demure matron with a sequined lace-up corset, spiked heels, and gartered stockings, evokes Marlene Dietrich's erotic ambiguity in von Sternberg's *The Blue Angel* (1959) while hinting at the tantalizingly taboo possibilities of sado-masochistic bondage. The joke is that Frank would never be caught dead on the bottom, and his fans know it.

Alien Androgyny

> The desire to hide, to be camouflaged.
> To be elsewhere. Other . . . not a person;
> to be done with personhood. . . .

> —Susan Sontag,
> "Fragments of an Esthetic of Melancholy" (116)

Liquid Sky (1982) a sci-fi entry into the midnight movie genre, conceptualizes the problem of sexual difference and desire in a radically different way from either *The Rocky Horror Picture Show* or *Pink Flamingos*. Directed by Russian émigré Slava Tsukerman, *Liquid Sky* clearly understands how sexuality has been invaded by patriarchal power politics. The possibility of a truly revolutionary expression of desire gives way to a dubious sexual "liberation" that produces, as Jeffrey Weeks has remarked, "a false sexuality, which palliates while leaving the real structures of power untouched" (297).

In *Liquid Sky*, this false sexuality fails to even temporarily satisfy its participants, who turn to other forms of gratification. The film focuses on a group of New Wave performers and models who are unaware that an alien space craft (the size of a dinner plate) sits on the Soho rooftop of an apartment occupied by Margaret (Anne Carlisle), a model, and her lesbian lover, Adrian (Paula Shepperd), who sings at a club and pushes drugs on the side. According to a German scientist studying the phenomenon, the alien is attracted to subculture types and this particular site because it feeds on substances created in the human brain during orgasm and heroin use.

In spite of the fact that she appears to have achieved freedom from arbitrary sex roles and gender stereotypes, Margaret, the film's protagonist, is sexually and socially alienated. She and her gay male alter-ego, Jimmy (also played by Carlisle), are fashion models whose sexual ambiguity represents androgyny as the undernourished, emaciated refusal of gender that Dick Hebdige describes in *Subculture: The Meaning of Style* (151). Looking like mirror reflections of each other, Margaret and Jimmy's visual sameness constitutes a personal and cultural paradox centering around the problem of sexual difference. Margaret recognizes one aspect of this paradox in the double standard of gender and aging. When Jimmy says that she is old and ugly, she retorts that Jimmy is "the most beautiful boy in the world." At a photo session, Margaret counters Jimmy's sadistic game-playing with a masochistic act: "I know I'm ugly, you should punish me." He hits her. The photographers encourage their hostilities and dare them to have sex. Jimmy protests, but he is pressured by the group to demand that Margaret "beg for it." She gives him a blow job as Jimmy gazes at himself in a mirror. When he climaxes, he disappears: the alien has killed him.

Since Carlisle plays both Jimmy and Margaret in this disturbing scene, *Liquid Sky* extends both *Pink Flamingos'* transvestism and Tim Curry's bisexuality in *Rocky Horror* into a radical statement on desire and sexual difference. Masculinity and femininity are culturally irreconcilable, even within an ethos of androgyny and bisexuality. Jimmy finds

Margaret sexually repugnant even though she bases her gender identity on a male model. Margaret knows she is following fashion: "I am androgynous not less than David Bowie himself," she comments in self-abasing irony. Thus, *Liquid Sky* does not celebrate the appropriation of punk androgyny into the fashion statement of the 1980s as a liberating blending of male and female traits into an archetype of wholeness but rather as another capitalist cannibalization of the signifiers of a cultural rebellion (punk).

Margaret's attempt to refuse gender stereotyping is also linked to her personal detachment from desire. Margaret rejects sexual puritanism to assume the identity of the profane whore who will permit anyone to do anything to her, but without desire, she is reduced to a commodity, a token of exchange in a game of exploitation. Margaret's college acting teacher and former lover, Owen (Bob Brad) tells her that she has become a "real mean bitch" who looks and acts like a prostitute. Margaret replies that at least hookers are independent. "I'm nobody's victim," she says. However, events belie that notion. To obtain cocaine, Margaret allows a man at a nightclub to pick her up. She is viciously beaten and raped; one of Adrian's junkie clients rapes her just to prove to her that junkies can get it up; Adrian demands that she engage in necrophilia. These events show that although Margaret has increased her field of sexual choices and options for sexual identity, she has not changed the structures of power or oppression.

Within this milieu of sexual brutalization masquerading as liberation, Margaret attempts to detach herself from her past and her middle-class Connecticut roots. Adrian obsessively cites Margaret's past as the reason why she is "an uptight WASP cunt." Memory is cultural excess, the baggage from a past identity. Margaret has failed to distance the past, even as she has failed to successfully reinvent herself within the punk ethos. She remains the victim of patriarchal goals for femininity that shift but continue to place women in a powerless position. She recounts that she was first told to be a suburban housewife, then she was told to be a successful ("free and equal") New York model with a male agent. Her new identity proves as empty as the old, her new "family" as repressive as the original, her female lovers as willing, she says, to step on her as men.

Margaret has replaced one assigned identity with another, currently more fashionable one, but her superficially "genderless" body remains irrefutably exploitable and thus defined as belonging to a specific class: female. Margaret discovers that it is possible to cross the boundaries of sexual difference but not to undo them. The charade of androgyny only obfuscates ideology, as the dominance/submission agenda remains a powerful influence on any relationship under the patriarchy.

Owen tells Margaret that she should "try to be nice," but she says that her defensiveness warns men that "this pussy has teeth." Her figurative remark becomes fact. Before she can escape the burden of her gender, she becomes the ultimate representative of the myth of feminine perversity: the woman who kills with her sexuality. The rooftop alien causes everyone who has sex with her to die. By appearing to turn Margaret into a "killer cunt" the alien merely fulfills the already established myth of female sexuality as a perverse and dangerous mystery.

Inadvertently, Margaret becomes a death hole, but that too can be fashionable. She wryly suggests that she is suitable headline material for *The National Enquirer.* She then uses her hidden weapon as a means of revenge. Like the Sadeian woman, she willingly creates corpses, but she cannot control her new power. Adrian bets that she can fuck Margaret and live: Adrian dies, but Margaret's lack of desire saves her from death.

Although she finds temporary escape in drugs and sex, Margaret finally exhausts all earthly possibilities for escaping her culturally inscribed gender identity. She joins the alien, who becomes her prince, the husband Margaret once dreamed of. She dons a traditional white wedding dress. Begging the departing ship to take her along, she mainlines heroin, known in its best forms as "liquid sky." Caught in a beam of light from the space craft, Margaret dances a tormented dance of erotic self-destruction as she dematerializes. In a transfiguring act of "merging into the nonhuman," she finally finds erotic bliss, the "liquid sky" of orgasm (Sontag 118).

Liquid Sky shows that sex and gender permutations can easily be signifiers of artificial changes, meaningless in themselves, unable to alter woman's social status as victim. Margaret's knowing transgression of the bourgeois norms of her childhood do not make her free. In spite of her subculture "refusal," she has no model for that refusal except a negation that turns into self-destruction. Margaret's final act acknowledges that in a patriarchy, women must always be aliens.

Gender and Generic Pastiche

In attempting to define the cult movie, Umberto Eco has linked its generic and narrative excess to a postmodern impulse, "where the quotation of the topos is recognized as the only way to cope with the burden of our encyclopedic filmic competence (11). As cult films, *Pink Flamingos, Liquid Sky,* and *The Rocky Horror Picture Show* obviously mix generic conventions to create a narrative pastiche, but the image of gender they fashion is also a pastiche, an intertextual and intersexual burden in which cultural signifiers of masculinity and femininity are sometimes scrambled but never disarticulated from their patriarchal connotations. In films like *Rocky Horror* and *Pink Flamingos*, the gender bending of androgyny and transvestism creates a visual disorientation that does not destroy patriarchal law but may serve to disorient it (Hebdige 126).

Although the three films discussed in this article serve as typical examples of the midnight movie's association of femininity with perversion, there are many more cult films such as *The Texas Chainsaw Massacre 2* (1986) and *Day of the Dead* (1986) that mark a similar convergence. Beyond the scope of this discussion, although demanding attention as part of the process explicated here, these films radically refuse to make s/excess pleasurable, and therefore remain marginal—films for hard-core cultists rather than assimilable objects of the Saturday night ritual of midnight movie audiences. Frequently X-rated, these "sick" films, however, may be the most uncompromisingly subversive examples of sexual excess, for their violent fantasies often embrace at least one disturbing truth that the midnight movies discussed here generally avoid: the explicit emergence of perversion from within the patriarchal family unit and its conservative function in maintaining rather than exploding that structure (Stoller 214-17).

With the self-conscious exception of *Liquid Sky*, the sexual rebellion of such "mainstream" cult films as *Pink Flamingos* and *The Rocky Horror Picture Show* shows that gendered power relations are not necessarily subverted by a vision of perversely erotic freedom. On the contrary, femininity and perversity are bound together in a formula that provides the male with a rationale for denigrating "femininity" and female sexuality. What results, finally, in all its contradictions and ambivalences, is a masculinist vision of the mysteries and pleasures of s/excess. Desire unencumbered by difference and division remains a dangerous dream, a "liquid sky," perhaps too much, too overwhelming, too perverse—even for the midnight hour.

Addendum: Sometimes Midnight Is Just Twelve O'clock

In 1990, the year after this article originally appeared, *The Rocky Horror Picture Show* was released on videotape. The promotional copy accompanying the film's release on tape implied that the video was not meant to substitute for the "ultimate movie experience," but that it was best used "to practice all the wild spectator routines and dialogue . . . DREAM IT IN YOUR LIVING ROOM! BE IT IN THE THEATER!" The idea that such a videotape, marketed for home viewing, would create a generation of fans "trained" for midnight movie participation was either completely disingenuous or sadly off the mark.

Soon midnight would become just twelve o'clock at the local mall cineplex, and the midnight movie would largely disappear from America's screens, to be replaced by a late night screening of whatever current release was most popular. The cult movie of s/excess would be displaced to the medium of video to become, like *The Rocky Horror Picture Show*, a part of the domestic entertainment scene, the "living room theater." Americans could go to their local video store to bring home their cult film of choice. They could even emulate the "family" of space travelers of the cult television program, *Mystery Science Theater 3000* who sit alone in their equivalent of a home theater to make fun of outrageous or outrageously bad films.

Even though midnight was no longer set aside for films of s/excess, the attitudes and issues expressed in that dying venue were embraced elsewhere: in television. David Lynch brought the midnight movie ethos to television with his series, *Twin Peaks* (1990). Lynch and John Waters had been mainstreamed into commercial theatrical filmmaking in the 1980s with releases such as *Blue Velvet* (1986) and *Hairspray* (1988). Perhaps more than Waters, Lynch retained the disturbing edge to his work, as evidenced in the controversially violent *Wild at Heart* (1990). Controversial too was *Twin Peaks*. Its basic premise was familiar: a beautiful young woman, Laura Palmer (Sheryl Lee), is found dead, and an FBI man (Kyle MacLachlan) attempts to find her killer. However, what was unfamiliar (to TV) was the program's bizarre tone, dream-like imagery, and surrealistically disturbing (if not blatantly misogynistic) portrait of perverse sexuality in small-town America. These elements helped achieve cult status. In spite of its rather quick demise, the series inspired a theatrical movie in the form of a presequel, *Twin Peaks: Fire Walk With Me* (1992).

Twin Peaks, however, was not television's only adaptation and transfiguration of the midnight movie ethos. Explorations in gender-bending and revelations of "kinky" sexual practice became the raison d'être of the tell-all talk-show trend that came to dominate daytime, "trash" television in the early 1990s. Hosted by Ricki Lake (who had starred in Waters' *Hairspray*), Jenny Jones, Sally Jessy Raphael, Geraldo Rivera, Charles Perez, among others, these programs targeted their appeal as that of the outrageous and unusual presented under the guise of therapeutic revelation and audience education. They offer everything from drag queens and dominatrix transvestites (shades of Dr. Frank-N-Furter) to incestuous "white-trash" couples whose lifestyles unknowingly echo *Pink Flamingos*. Mainstream American life, these programs seem to suggest, contains the essence of the midnight movie, not as a radical, outlaw statement on desire and sexual difference, but as a "freak show" of stigmatized subjectivity and oppressive reality. Like the traditional sideshow talker, the host provides the spiel that arouses curiosity and interest in a display of human difference. The audience may be disturbed, shocked, or mystified, but, unlike the participatory audience associated with the midnight movie, the viewers in the television studio and at home are encouraged to remain emotionally removed. They adjudicate the subject's defiled or deviant behavior that frequently links femininity with perversion. Perversion is discursively defined as pathological and pathetic. This is an important change from the films discussed here, but even so, television in the 1990s clearly demonstrates that there is no longer any need to go to the theater when the clock strikes midnight: s/excess has at last become a marketable spectacle for the light of day.

Notes

My thanks to Bruce Kawin and J. P. Telotte for their comments on earlier drafts of this essay.

1. Laplanche argues that perversion, as the exception to a supposed normative "sexual instinct," ends up by "taking the rule along with it." The result is that "the whole of sexuality, or at least the whole of infantile sexuality, ends up by becoming perversion" (23).

2. Ironically, most of Freud's case studies confirm neurosis or repression as the primary feminine pathology and perversion as predominantly a male syndrome. The only perversion Freud associated consistently with women was masochism. Of course, Freud had no doctor/ patient contact with those lower-class women he cited as so easily seduced into perversion.

3. Marcuse's views can be contrasted with those of Michel Foucault, who contends that modern society actually encourages the "implantation" of perversions and multiple discourses of sexuality; perversions emerge as "the real product of the encroachment of a type of power on bodies and their pleasures" (48); they are managed, categorized, and controlled by modern society so that their subversive potential is neutralized. The subversive value of perversion was questioned by Marcuse himself in his 1966 preface to a new edition of *Eros and Civilization.* See also John David Ober, "On Sexuality and Politics in the Work of Herbert Marcuse."

4. The six film collaborations between Waters and Divine ended with the unexpected death of the latter in March of 1989.

5. Felix Guattari argues for the subversive value of perversion in a controversial essay, "Becoming Woman." He contends that perversion in general and homosexuality in particular have been made into illnesses by psychoanalysis when they should be considered as a revolutionary repudiation of a phallic power. While the latter reduces desire to a binary operation: feminine = passive,

masculine = active, "every 'dissident' organization of the libido" opposes this binary operation and "must therefore be directly linked to a becoming-feminine body; as an escape route from the repressive socius" (86–87). Janine Chasseguet-Smirgel believes that the basis of all perversion is the denial of difference between the sexes and also between the generations. Common to all perversions, she says, is a disavowal of the father's genital capacities (79).

Works Cited

Bell-Metereau, Rebecca. *Hollywood Androgyny*. New York: Columbia UP, 1985.

Brake, Mike. "Sexuality as Praxis—A Consideration of the Contribution of Sexual Theory to the Process of Sexual Being." *Human Sexual Relations*. New York: Pantheon, 1982: 13-31.

Carter, Angela. *The Sadeian Woman and the Ideology of Pornography*. York: Harper Colophon, 1980.

Caskey, Noelle. "Interpreting Anorexia Nervosa." *The Female Body in Western Culture*. Ed. Susan Rubin Suleiman. Cambridge: Harvard UP, 1986. 175-89.

Chasseguet-Smirgel, Janine. *Creativity and Perversion*. New York: Norton, 1984.

Dijkstra, Bram. *Idols of Perversity*. New York: Oxford UP, 1986.

Eco, Umberto. "*Casablanca*: Cult Movies and Intertextual Collage." *Substance* 47 (1985): 3-12.

Foucault, Michel. *The History of Sexuality, I: An Introduction*. Trans. Robert Hurley. New York: Pantheon, 1978.

Freud, Sigmund. "Some Psychological Consequences of the Anatomical Differences Between the Sexes" (1925). *Sexuality and the Psychology of Love*. Ed. Phillip Rieff. New York: Collier, 1963. 183-93.

——. "Three Essays on the Theory of Sexuality." 1905. *Standard Edition of the Complete Psychological Works of Sigmund Freud*. 23 vols. Trans. and ed. James Strachey London: Hogarth P, 1953-1966. Vol. 7. 135-230.

Guattari, Felix. "Becoming Woman." *Semio-texte* 4 (1981): 86–88.

Hebdige, Dick. *Subculture: The Meaning of Style*. London: Metheun, 1979.

Henkin, Bill. *The Rocky Horror Picture Show Book*. New York: Hawthorn, 1979.

Krafft-Ebing, Richard von. *Psychopathia Sexualis*. 1886. Trans. F. J. Rebman New York: Special Books, 1965.

Kubie, Lawrence S. "The Drive to Become Both Sexes." *Symbols and Neurosis: Selected Papers of L. S. Kubie*. Ed. Herbert J. H. Schlesinger. New York: International Universities P, 1978. 195-202.

Laplanche, Jean. *Life and Death in Psychoanalysis.* Trans. Jeffrey Mehlman. Baltimore: Johns Hopkins UP, 1976.

Marcuse, Herbert. *Eros and Civilization.* New York: Vintage, 1962.

Montrelay, Michele. "Recherches sur la feminite." *Critique,* no. 278, qtd. in "Morocco" [A Collective Text]. *Cahiers du Cinema* 225 (1970): 5-13. Reprinted in *Sternberg.* Ed. Peter Baxter. London: British Film Institute, 1980. 81-94.

Mulvey, Laura. "Visual Pleasure and Narrative Cinema." *Screen* 16.3 (1975): 6-18.

Ober, John David. "On Sexuality and Politics in the Work of Herbert Marcuse." *Human Sexual Relations.* Ed. Mike Brake. New York: Pantheon, 1982. 82-107.

Peary, Danny. *Cult Movies.* New York: Dell, 1981.

Riviere, Joan. "Womanliness As a Masquerade." *Psychoanalysis and Female Sexuality.* Ed. Hendrik M. Ruitenbeek. New Haven: College and UP, 1966. 209-20.

Sontag, Susan. "Fragments of an Esthetic of Melancholy." *Art in America* 74 (1986): 116+.

Stoller, Robert. *Perversion: The Erotic Form of Hatred.* New York: Dell, 1975.

Theweleit, Klaus. *Male Fantasies Volume 1: Women, Floods, Bodies, History.* Trans. Stephen Conway. Minneapolis: U of Minnesota P, 1987.

Waters, John. *Shock Value.* New York: Dell, 1981.

Weeks, Jeff. "The Development of Sexuality Theory and Sexual Politics." *Human Sexual Relations.* Ed. Mike Brake. New York: Pantheon, 1982. 293-309.

9

The Woman in the Door:
Framing Presence in Film Noir

J. P. Telotte

> Of all the gin joints in all the towns in all the world, she walks into mine.
>
> —*Casablanca*

The above comment, uttered by the character Richard Blaine in the cult classic *Casablanca* (1942), surely ranks as one of the most famous lines in American film history. And rightly so, not only because it accurately assesses the mix of cynicism and romantic subjection that characterized Humphrey Bogart's popular persona, but also because it neatly points toward a moment of surprise, promise, and possession of which our films in the past have often made great narrative capital. For just after Rick's agonized complaint, we see the "she" in question, Ilsa Lund, Rick's former love, framed in the doorway of his "gin joint," poised to come back into his life and into the story, as it were to "complete" both, gratifying Rick *and* an audience that, by this point in the narrative, wants—and expects—to know more about Ilsa, to gauge her apparent allure and power—which have already been remarked upon by a number of characters. Her appearance thus represents the completion of a narrative promise and the solution to a troubling disturbance in the male protagonist's expected position of power and autonomy.

I note this *locus classicus* not to add to the already substantial discussion of *Casablanca* but rather to suggest a paradigm that might help us weigh some changes that have occurred in American film narrative, particularly with regard to male-female positioning. More specifically, I want to look at some recurrences of this dramatic moment in traditional film noir and in its recent manifestations, in both of which the visual positioning of women seems quite significant—as a defining moment of narrative "trouble." Jacques Tourneur's *Out of the Past* (1947), certainly one of the most often cited examples of classical noir, provides one touchstone here, and the recent effort by Peter Medak, *Romeo Is Bleed-*

137

ing (1993), offers the other. Although the former film has been loosely remade in recent years as *Against All Odds* (1984), *Romeo Is Bleeding* seems a nearer stylistic match with *Out of the Past* and one that can better situate some of the changes that mark recent noir (or neo-noir, as it is beginning to be termed).

Before turning to either film, let me further locate that special narrative moment with which I began in its proper context. The spatially framed character, typically a woman, is commonplace in American film and especially film noir. We might think of the image of Marlene Dietrich casually poised in a window or doorway in works like *Shanghai Express* or *Blonde Venus* (both 1932). Her body, her physical presence, challenges a male spectator within the film—as well as those *of* the film—to try to possess or control her. When Ingrid Bergman's Ilsa Lund appears as a shadowy figure in the door of Rick's Cafe Americain in *Casablanca,* she brings with her some element of that challenge, but also adds a note of vulnerability, of subjectification that was far more common, even expected by this point. Here, Ilsa has come to explain just why she has "walked back into" Rick's life and ultimately to beg for his help. Her appearance in the doorway, this proffering of the self, is significant because it marks the first step in the recuperation of Rick's figure —a recuperation measured by his increasing power over Ilsa, in effect, his *repossession* of her through his possession of her love, and in the process the reconstruction of his very character. Such a reconstruction or regeneration of the male figure through or at the expense of the female is, of course, a common paradigm of classical American films, although one that would meet with many challenges in the emerging film noir of the 1940s.

The dynamic of possession built into this image subtends what David Bordwell terms the "principle of motivation" (70) that drives character interaction in our classical film narratives. That principle moves the central figures via a pattern of causality to achieve "a stable narrative state" (36), that is, one in which the protagonist achieves his goals or restores "an original state of affairs" (16). While it may suggest that complex, at times seemingly conflicting, motivations drive the characters, it also gradually sorts out those motivations, makes them intelligible for us. And it often does so by suggesting the male's implicit need— even his right—to possess or dominate, along with the female's implicit desire to be possessed (or "framed"), as if these poles ultimately constituted some sort of natural order of which our bodies were readily recognizable signs.

This compositional dynamic, buoyed by such unspoken principles of motivation, also intersects with a variety of views about the role of the film spectator and the depiction of women in classical narrative. The key arguments here are obviously those of Laura Mulvey and Gaylyn Studlar on the gaze and the status of the female image.[1] Taken together, their arguments suggest a kind of dynamic tension that crystalizes in and offers another explanation of the visual pattern described here. But my concern, I should note, is not with pursuing the analysis of what we generally term the "psychology" of the cinema, but rather with the shifting narrative function of that framed image of the female body and the moment of surprise attending it, its indication of a disturbance in classical practice that speaks to more recent noir developments.

As critics have often noted, in the film noir the female image seems especially emphasized and in various ways unusually empowered. As Janey Place points out, the film noir marks "one of the few periods of film in which women are active, not static symbols, are intelligent and powerful, if destructively so, and derive power, not weakness, from their sexuality" (35). The very title of a film like *The Woman in the Window* (1944) immediately emphasizes the centrality and importance of this "active" image, one we can note throughout the noir canon, as when Phyllis Dietrichson unexpectedly appears at Walter Neff's door in *Double Indemnity* (1944), when Mildred Pierce walks in on Monty Beragon and her daughter Veda as they make love in *Mildred Pierce* (1945), or when Elsa Bannister suddenly enters the carnival funhouse in *Lady from Shanghai* (1948). In these films and elsewhere the woman suddenly framed in a doorway is indeed an "active" figure, one whose power, it seems, is measured in her ability at that point to shift the very trajectory of each narrative and destabilize it—often by destabilizing or threatening the male figure.

Yet such framing, along with placement deep in the background, typically also suggests something else: limitation, confinement, entrapment. As Place and L. S. Peterson in their classic study of noir styling offer, such "claustrophobic framing devices . . . as doors, windows, stairways, metal bedframes, or simply shadows separate the character from other characters, from his world, or from his own emotions" (31). They help play out a drama well known to students of noir, one in which, as E. Ann Kaplan sums it up, the film "*expresses* alienation, locates its cause squarely in" the woman's "excesses," her "wrong" motivations, her ability to possess or control as men do, and it then "punishes that excess" in order to restore a natural order (3) and narrative stability. It is, in effect, a significant point of narrative tension, one that speaks to the special dynamics of traditional noir narrative.

This pattern seems to describe most accurately the situation found in *Out of the Past*. Told partly in flashback by private detective Jeff

A "framed" pinup—Cora's (Lana Turner) seductive entrance in *The Postman Always Rings Twice*. (Courtesy of the Museum of Modern Art/Film Stills Archive)

Markham/Jeff Bailey, it is a tale of precisely such "excesses," of Kathie Moffett's shooting and theft of $40,000 from her gangster lover, Whit Sterling, and of his attempts to get her back. Hired to retrieve her if not the $40,000, Jeff tracks Kathie as far as Acapulco and there waits for her to show up. From his seat in the back of the bar La Mar Azul, he first spies her in a moment that suggests a kind of epiphany; as he says, "I saw her coming out of the sun—and then I knew why Whit didn't care about that 40 grand."

It is, quite simply, one of the most impressive entrances in any noir film, and a particularly suitable way for inserting this character into the narrative. It seems to clarify the mysterious motivations that have sent Jeff on this case, while presenting Kathie as, at one and the same time, vulnerable and dominating. Bound by the door frame within the film frame, alone and surveyed by the eyes of the bar's male patrons, located at last by the tough detective sent to retrieve her, her silhouetted body seems both exposed and entrapped. And yet her figure dominates the composition, much as her image must dominate Whit's memory and Jeff's impressions. As she stands there, her eyes survey the place as if it were her own, and she seems ultimately comfortable and self-assured, as is illustrated by the easy way she dismisses the guide Jose Rodriguez, rejects Jeff's offered gift of earrings and personal attention, and instructs him in how to *properly* find her—at Pablo's bar. There, two nights later, she repeats her earlier entrance. Framed in the doorway, as Jeff's flash-back notes, "she walked in out of the moonlight, smiling." This time her entrance is pointedly for him, for his "private eye" rather than Whit's, as he seems, with her full assent, to have taken possession of that alluring image.

The dynamic of this scene well suits the larger narrative design of *Out of the Past*. It is, generally speaking, a film about power and subjection, framing and evasion, entry and escape. The narrative details Kathie's power over Whit and his efforts to return her to his control; Whit's plans to get back at both his accountant who is trying to black-mail him and Jeff who had taken his girl; and finally, Kathie's siren-like hold on Jeff and his desire to reassert his autonomy. All of these plot elements dramatize a conflict of motivations, a struggle for power or authority, centered around Kathie's problematic figure. Thus Frank Krutnik uses this film as a central example in his argument that the film noir is essentially about "an erosion of confidence in the legitimising framework of masculine authority" (128). That authority is embodied primarily in "the investigative hero," a figure who typically functions to put things right but who here "is himself contaminated" (125) by the duplicitous and manipulative Kathie, as she wields the power implicit in her framed entry to manipulate Jeff, just as she does, with deadly consequences in each case, both Whit and his henchman Joe Stefanos.

But against that manipulation, *Out of the Past* deploys Jeff's voice-over, flashback narration. One of noir's most common techniques, it here takes the form of an embedded narrative, an extended flashback that takes over part of the larger narrative after Jeff discovers he can no longer hide from Whit, Kathie, and his former life, that *he* remains the subject one. That narration is pointedly an effort, as he says, to get something "off my chest," something "I didn't like any part of." As he related these events out of his past—his seduction by Kathie, his betrayal of Whit, the murder of his former partner Fisher—to his girlfriend Ann, Jeff in effect tries to regain control over his life, to tell it rather than having it told for him in the spurious renderings that are being variously offered by Kathie, Whit, the town gossips, and eventually the police. In this respect, *Out of the Past* clearly illustrates Christine Gledhill's formulation of the dynamic at work in "the typical film noir" as "a struggle between different voices for control over the telling of the story" (16).

More significant for this discussion is the way that struggle plays out visually through a series of entries, through a consistent visual dynamic that emphasizes the conflicting motivations in the struggle of authority and subjection here, in a conflict almost literally between the male and female bodies. It is a pattern that dramatizes Kathie's power, Jeff's recognition of his past situation, and his efforts at regaining his position of authority. We have already noted Kathie's original positioning in the narrative, her deep-focus entry "out of the sun" at La Mar Azul and her matching entry "out of the moonlight" at Pablo's. Following Jeff's flashback account of these events and his meeting with Whit at his Lake Tahoe estate, Kathie once more makes a key entrance from the back of the frame, although this time we remain focused on Jeff, gauging the effect of her presence mainly through his reaction shot—a technique that suggests something of the struggle in which he is involved, a struggle, as it were, of self-possession. Kathie's return later that night, once again coming "out of the moonlight," as she walks in through Jeff's balcony doors, points up her still considerable power and the ongoing contest for autonomy here.

Out of the Past subsequently uses a series of similar compositions to indicate Jeff's deliberate efforts to turn the tables on Kathie. Trying to avoid being set up—as Jeff tells his cabbie friend, "I think I'm in a frame. . . . All I can see is the frame. I'm going in there now to look at the picture"—he literally takes control of the film frame. In a variety of rear-frame entrances that situate him much as Kathie has earlier been situated—in that same dynamic of power and limitation—Jeff breaks into the accountant Leonard Eels's apartment through his balcony door, enters Meta Carson's place through her balcony door, startles Kathie as he emerges from Meta's closet door, and then, back at Whit's Lake Tahoe mansion, suddenly comes into Kathie's room while she is sleeping. In each case, Jeff's ability to easily gain access to the place, even through a locked or blocked door, couples with the "framed," deep-focus presentation of his surprise entry to underscore his own power and the ongoing struggle here to take back what has been lost—his autonomy, his power, even his real identity—from a past and from Kathie who, after killing Whit, lets Jeff know just what she has in mind by asserting that she wants "to walk out of the sun again and find you waiting." Their subsequent deaths, as he sets her up for the police, "framing" her in the only way that he still can, represent his last and only minimally success-ful effort to "take control" over the narrative that is his life.

This deadly spiral that *Out of the Past* describes certainly antici-pates the mutually destructive power struggles that have come to charac-terize contemporary neo-noirs: *Blood Simple* (1984), *King of New York* (1991), *Reservoir Dogs* (1993), *The Bad Lieutenant* (1993), *The Last Seduction* (1994), and *Romeo Is Bleeding*, among others. The last of these affords a particularly revealing comparison, in part because of the way in which it capitalizes on that framed figure and links it to the sort of voice-over, flashback narration we have come to associate so closely with the film noir, and particularly with *Out of the Past*.

While *Romeo Is Bleeding* also employs a voice-over flashback technique, it uses it to frame most of the narrative, in effect, to frame all of the images that ensue and, as is typically the case with such narra-tives, to suggest the narrator's "struggle" for possession of, and control over, all that we see. In this respect, as well as in some of its specific imagery, it recalls such noir classics as *Lady from Shanghai* and *The Third Man* (1949).[2] Yet any sense of mastery over that matter from the past, over all that is here almost elegiacally framed, very quickly disap-pears, when a violent flashback intrudes, out of order, it seems, as the narrator, Jim Daugherty begins telling about "a ghost" he knows, one who "had the strangest story to tell." As in *Out of the Past,* that "ghost" is Jim's previous identity as Sergeant Jack Grimaldi, a cop who was seduced by this work—by the money, power, and women with whom he came in contact—and who, as a result, lost everything—his wife, his mistress, his position, even his identity. When unexplained images from that "ghost's" supposed account suddenly and as if uncontrollably fill the screen, he stops himself and notes: "Hey! Hey, wait a minute! I'm get-ting a little ahead of myself here. Pretend you didn't see that." Right from the start of this narrative, then, it seems that control and authority will prove elusive, the stuff of pretense—on our part and the narra-tor's—and the physical presence of that narrator will carry little weight, even when posed against the "ghostly" bodies of the women he has encountered.

Yet even prior to this "slip" in the narrative, this failure in self-pos-session, *Romeo Is Bleeding* offers a visual warning of sorts about how difficult it might be to "frame" things neatly here, to follow that classical "principle of motivation," to restore "narrative stability." For its opening shot of a desert landscape—which contrasts tellingly with the lush landscapes that introduce *Out of the Past*—leads to a dingy diner, and an interior shot which frames its doorway in the deep background. As that door opens, we cut to a close-up of the bell above it, and then to a long shot that shows the door closing but no one entering. Perhaps it was Jim the narrator, or his ghostly other identity, or simply something he has imagined; in any case, the film has primed us for an entry, for a meaningful human presence in the midst of this desert area, and then, in its own sort of surprise, withheld what we expected to see.

More than just a way of creating a suspenseful atmosphere or of *briefly* blurring the fact that Jim and the subject of his narrative, Jack, are one and the same, this visual pattern becomes central to the film. And as we shall see, the framed entry, although hardly as dramatic as in *Out of the Past*, provides the crucial end points—literally the frame—for *Romeo Is Bleeding*. At this point, though, it primarily points toward the problems of possession and subjection, of embodiment and disembodiment—which possess this narrative as well as its narrator. For framed between these end points, between these desired images of a woman in the door, is a tale of possession on every level. Jack Grimaldi, we learn, "was doing something about" his "big dreams," taking money from the mob in exchange for information. His own corruption, his being "owned" by the mob, apparently follows from his abiding sense that one lives to possess—things, money, others, especially other women. When Jack gets money from the mob, he stashes it in a hole outside his apartment; he terms it "feeding the hole." But as the voice-over points out, when he "fed the hole . . . he made the hole happy," not himself, and he began hearing a kind of "sucking" sound, as if the hole were sucking the very life or substance from him, as if the opening were a kind of black hole. Jack eventually came to feel that his goal was simply to please the hole, and the voice-over describes him finally as a disembodied figure, "a ghost who fell in love with a hole in the ground."

In these circumstances, of course, and in keeping with the noir tradition, love is no less possessive, as Jack's various relationships show. Although he has a loving wife (Natalie) and a girlfriend (Sheri) who caters to his every fantasy,[3] Jack tries to pigeonhole them, to keep them bound to certain limited areas—Natalie in their home, Sheri in her apartment—while he, as his Romeo nickname suggests, pursues other conquests, such as the waitress wife of a fellow he has sent to prison or Mona DeMarkov, the mob killer he is supposed to guard for the government—and shoot for the mob. For Jack, then, love becomes a peculiar intersection of motivations, which makes him see it as "frightening" because "you don't own it; it owns you."

But that is precisely the story that *Romeo Is Bleeding* seems intent on telling at every level: how easily we are possessed by and subject to the very things that we think we possess or control, and how unstable a life—or a narrative—built on such a principle must be. Jack gives orders to his mob contact, but the mob ignores his comments, and in turn the mob boss, Don Falcone, orders him to carry out his instructions or else; so instead of catching killers, he becomes the mob's hired killer. In the short time Mona is in his custody, he tries to seduce her, but she winds up literally on top, controlling him, trying to take his gun, and then laughing at him as FBI agents arrive and take over. Because Natalie likes to keep a photo album—itself a way of *possessing* events, framing them and holding onto them—he gives her a new camera, something with which she might amuse herself and thus leave him alone. However, she is, we later learn, surreptitiously taking pictures of him with his various girlfriends, framing him, documenting his Romeo-like life, and thereby possessing him in the very moments at which he thinks himself most free. And even as Jack tries to make a deal with the District Attorney, giving evidence against Mona in exchange for his freedom, he finds that she has beaten him to it, striking a deal that lets her "walk" while he pays the price of freedom.

This is the narrative pattern that is framed by the framed entry that brings us back to the present and closes the film. For as Jim/Jack finishes his story, as we return to the ironically named Holiday Diner, he stands "waiting for the . . . guest of honor to show," waiting for Natalie to walk through the door in the back of the frame. Her return would, we presume, restore his identity, rematerialize the ghostly Jack Grimaldi, give him back the life and the love that he has lost, and of course end the narrative on a stable note. And his hopes for repossessing the past and Natalie are at least teased out through a series of framing shots here, as the bell above the door sounds, just as in that teasing shot at the beginning of the film. However, it is apparently Mona who enters, a figure suddenly come back from the dead to haunt him, to continue to possess him, even though a reverse-angle shot shows, through a mirror in which we see only an empty door-frame, that she is nothing more than a projection of his psyche. However, that image of the dominant woman, of the figure who, even from beyond the grave continues to possess Jack, gives way to a new long shot of the framing doorway, this time with Natalie indeed standing there, and in this case the same reverse angle seems to confirm her presence by showing her reflection in the mirror. With that confirmation Jim/Jack rushes forward to grab her as she stands framed in the doorway, to repossess her and, as it were, his old life, but that reunion too dissolves into a long shot from his point of view as he looks once more at the doorway, empty as before. The ensuing long tracking shot that ends the film returns us to the empty desert landscape surrounding the diner, the same empty vista with which the film opened, and an image that mocks Jim's hopes at regaining his love, his life, and his identity.

The empty door-frames that frame this film, as well as the desolate desert landscapes onto which that door opens, I have suggested, are most telling. Jean Baudrillard has described the postmodern world as "a place of disappearance," and he notes how today, apparently, it is no longer "the *production* of things which interests us"; rather, "it is the disappearance of things that fascinates us" (Gane 85). That notion of "disappearance" more than literally fits a work like *Romeo Is Bleeding*, for here everything that Jack has—over half a million dollars in cash, his wife, his mistress, his position, his home—disappears, as if it was all sucked down that hole he so faithfully "feeds." The wife he expects to "come walking through that door any day" dissolves into an image of emptiness—an emptiness that speaks to the unavailing and even meaningless nature of all his voice-over assertions, including his final, "bet she still loves me." The empty door-frame marks our inability to locate his motivations ("What is it you want, Jack?" Natalie earlier and repeatedly asked him), to "produce" meaning, to produce the reality we have in classical narratives customarily inhabited—a reality that here is simply slipping away, dissolving into the harsh landscape of impossible desires. Among those now impossible desires is that of a female subjection which might serve the male, help embody him as he longs to be embodied.

Here, in essence, is the shift we might note in the film noir, a change in both *what* we might frame and the surprising effects of that framing activity. For *Out of the Past* and its contemporaries generally sensed that for all of her "excesses," for all of her demonstrated powers, the female might—even should—still be "framed" within a conventional world, that the various powers she represented might be repossessed, that a cultural and narrative stability could in some fashion be reasserted. There remained an ability to sort things out, to "produce" meaning, even from the dark circumstances chronicled in the film noir, even, surprisingly, in the midst of meaning's apparent absence. While Jeff dies at the end of *Out of the Past,* it is a death he has willed, controlled, produced, and one that also generated a freeing fiction for Ann, who—armed with the belief that Jeff did intend to go off with Kathie—should now be motivated to walk back into the life of her old boyfriend Jim and thus begin a new, *normal* life for herself.

In today's darkest noirs we seem fascinated by the absence that invariably prevails, the doorways we cannot fill. Thus in a film like *The Bad Lieutenant* (1992) all the lies and stories the protagonist tells, all the drugs he takes, all the bets he makes, produce only delusions and ultimately death—a death that writes an end to our fascination, as is evidenced by the detached, extreme long shot that places the lieutenant in deep background, framed in his car, as he is shot. *Basic Instinct* (1992) frames several women in its various doorways, one of whom is apparently framing another for a series of murders. We can never be sure, though, which is the murderer or even why the murders were done; all we do know is that one is turning real life into a series of fictions, and the real-life models are being erased by the murderer. With *Romeo Is Bleeding* we return in several ways to the classical pattern of noir, with its voice-over flashback format and its formally arranged figures, its alluring and challenging bodies defiantly placed for our inspection. But the narrative pattern breaks down, cannot hold its course, never reaches stability. The women refuse to be framed and instead simply disappear from the screen, along with all hope for control or possession by the narrator Jack/Jim. And the only real surprise at the film's conclusion is that there is no surprise left to spring; "Of all the gin joints . . . in all the world," no one will walk in here. In its inability to traditionally "position" the woman, and in the process to reembody the ghost-like male while classically resolving the narrative's conflicting motivations, *Romeo Is Bleeding* underscores how our contemporary noirs seem fascinated by what they—and our culture—can no longer contain or frame, by what we can no longer produce.

Notes

1. Mulvey's oft-cited and much-debated argument sees the cinematic experience as centering around a sadistic, subjecting gaze in which an implicitly masculine viewer treats the female as an object of pleasure. In contrast, Studlar interprets it as a submissive, masochistic view in which the female figure acts upon the male viewer.

2. *Romeo Is Bleeding* includes several scenes at the "Wonder Wheel Park," an amusement park with a ferris wheel that instead of the "Fun" and "Games" its signs prominently promise, produces a recurring nightmare for Jack, one in which he is completely in Mona's control as she laughingly rolls dice that will seemingly determine his fate. These images evoke both the amusement park in which *Lady from Shanghai*'s Michael O'Hara finds himself trapped by Elsa Bannister and the giant ferris wheel of *The Third Man* from which Holly Mar-

tins is nearly thrown by his supposed friend Harry Lime. Neither instance, of course, is really a place of fun, but rather the point at which the protagonist's world drops its mask and proceeds to have fun with him.

3. It is worth noting the reflexive element that this film develops in part through its female characters. Natalie, as is noted in the text, is a photographer who is herself constantly trying to "frame" her husband, to capture him on film and to fix him—along with a visual history of his indiscretions—in her photo album. It is, as the missing shots of Mona point up, an impossible task. Sheri, on the other hand, tries to fit within the "frame" of Jack's expectations. Thus we see her, framed in a doorway as she poses for him, striking poses as Marilyn Monroe, "the girl from the Budweiser commercial," and finally, in frustration, offers herself as Madame Curie. However, even that desire to please him at any cost, to be all things to him fails to arouse Jack; the framing, even of the willing female, simply fails here at every turn.

Works Cited

Bordwell, David, Janet Staiger, and Kristin Thompson. *The Classical Hollywood Cinema: Film Style and Mode of Production to 1960.* New York: Columbia UP, 1985.

Gane, Mike, ed. *Baudrillard Live: Selected Interviews.* London: Routledge, 1993.

Gledhill, Christine. "Klute 1: A Contemporary Film Noir and Feminist Criticism." Kaplan 6-21.

Kaplan, E. Ann. Introduction. *Women in Film Noir.* Ed. E. Ann Kaplan. London: BFI, 1980. 1-5.

Krutnik, Frank. *In a Lonely Street: Film Noir, Genre, Masculinity.* London: Routledge, 1991.

Mast, Gerald, Marshall Cohen, and Leo Braudy, eds. *Film Theory and Criticism.* 4th ed. Oxford UP, 1992.

Mulvey, Laura. "Visual Pleasure and Narrative Cinema." Mast, Cohen, Braudy 746-57.

Place, Janey. "Women in Film Noir." Kaplan 35-54.

——, and L. S. Peterson. "Some Visual Motifs of Film Noir." *Film Comment* 10.1 (1974): 30-35.

Studlar, Gaylyn. "Masochism and the Perverse Pleasures of the Cinema." Mast, Cohen, Braudy 773-90.

10

Reading the Talk Show:
The Politics of *Talk Soup*

Laurie Ouellette and Carolyn Anderson

Every weekday on daytime talk shows, ordinary people with diverse backgrounds and interests participate in the production of television discourse, either as guests or as members of a studio audience. Contrary to the one-way flow of most television programming, audience-participation talk shows provide people from marginalized groups an opportunity to share their real-life experiences and viewpoints on a range of social and domestic issues with millions of daytime television viewers across the nation. Numerous critics have suggested that daytime talk television is important because it can function as a space where dominant values are questioned. Sonia Livingstone suggests these programs promote the "lived experience of ordinary people" over the authority of powerful elites (433); Paolo Carpignano et al. describe the talk show as an "oppositional public sphere" (52); and Patricia Joyner Priest, following bell hooks, suggests that marginalized groups who "talk back" on daytime television are engaging in "counter-hegemonic struggle." Perhaps the strongest testimony to such subversive qualities, however, are efforts to make sure daytime talk television is not taken too seriously within the dominant culture.

Stuart Hall, drawing from the work of Antonio Gramsci, offers hegemony as a way to explain how oppositional ideas are safely managed by the ruling groups of advanced capitalist societies ("Culture"). In order to naturalize their economic and social privilege, dominant groups must win the consent of society, a process that always involves some negotiation with marginal groups and oppositional forces. Because hegemony is not predetermined by the given structures of society (for example, capitalism, patriarchy, white supremacy), it must be produced within the realms of signification, ideology, and culture. As the leading ideological apparatus in the United States, television serves dominant interests by reproducing social and political antagonisms, but within "common sense" parameters that do not seriously challenge the status quo. Hence, the diverse and contentious flair of daytime talk television challenges the white, male, and corporate management of society, but the threat is blunted by a variety of internal ideological mechanisms, including the unquestioned authority of the host, the reliance on "experts," the promotion of staged sensationalism, and the framing of widespread social injustice within the logic of therapeutic and personal solutions (Peck; White).

Such modes of containment are, as Todd Gitlin in *Inside Prime Time* and others have argued, a predictable pattern on commercial television, a medium firmly entrenched in ruling interests. But economic and ideological forces are rarely conspiratorial and frequently inconsistent, and hegemony is never completely stable or predictable. As Hall has shown in *The Hard Road to Renewal*, hegemonic power is a sociohistoric phenomenon subject to multiple forms, sites, shifts, challenges, and contradictions. Talk shows are an enormously profitable genre for media corporations but also an extremely worrisome one for the guardians of the social order. As such, they suggest how the contradictory and ever-shifting nature of hegemony is played out within media culture.

From the economic perspective of the cultural industries, the greater inclusion of marginalized groups and antagonistic ideas has been welcomed as an inexpensive means to attract large audiences and accrue profits.[1] The sheer volume of audience-participation daytime talk television now on the air, and the regular appearance of people of color, sexual minorities, women, lower-income people, and other social groups excluded from television discourse on these shows have coalesced to create a steady stream of potential cracks in the dominant order.[2] At the same time, the proliferation of daytime talk television has elicited a troubled response within public discourse, where the shows are charged with the decline of cultural, moral, and journalistic standards.[3] The paternalistic outrage that often surrounds talk shows and their participants in the "serious" news media can be seen as another ideological mechanism, a discursive framework that helps shape the cultural significance or "meaning" of the genre. Still, the "cacophony of voices," in Gloria-Jean Masciarotte's term, ever audible in the world of daytime television continues to contradict and provoke the status quo in ways rarely heard or seen on commercial television.

Talk Soup *as Postmodern Television*

In this essay, we explore *Talk Soup*, a nightly "recap" of short clips from various talk shows, as yet another hegemonic mechanism working to contain the radical impulse of daytime talk television.[4] On this successful E! (Entertainment Television) program, daytime talk television is appropriated for additional profits as well as ideological reorientation. Broadcast images from a range of talk shows are copied, reassembled, repackaged and resold to a cable audience, while real-life guests from diverse social and economic backgrounds are presented out of context, as fodder for mockery by a white, male host. While *Talk Soup* adopts a silly, even haphazard look and feel, the program is more than an innocuous play with imagery. As we will argue, *Talk Soup* is best understood as an ideological phenomenon, a struggle to shape the dominant, "common sense" reading of daytime talk television, while simultaneously capitalizing on the genre's growth and success.

As part of an emerging genre of popular culture now appropriating and reworking symbolic material from television, *Talk Soup* represents a postmodern turn in television's hegemonic role. Postmodernism, to use Gitlin's words, refers to a "certain constellation of styles and tones in cultural works," including pastiche, a relish for copies and repetition, "a knowingness that dissolves commitment into irony," and "acute self-consciousness about the formal, constructed nature of the work" ("Postmodernism" 347). *Talk Soup* adopts a popular postmodern aesthetic by commenting upon the world of daytime talk television with stylized reproductions, the use of ironic quotations from other media, a self-concious awareness of its own production process, and a general tone of parody.[5]

Talk Soup reflects the self-referential, recombinant production process attributed to the "cultural logic of late capitalism," a phrase Frederic Jameson uses to describe, among other phenomena, the unprecedented volume of media messages now populating the cultural landscape and the collapse of traditional distinctions between economic and symbolic production as the cultural industries that trade in images are now among the world's most powerful capitalist enterprises (see also Gitlin, *Inside*). *Talk Soup* exemplifies such a collapse, operating as it does by appropriating television's own symbolic goods as inexpensive raw material for a new round of cultural production. Since the program's debut in 1991, *Talk Soup* staffers have daily taped—off-air and at no cost to E!—up to twenty different talk shows, from which they select "highlights." Reassembled and framed with comic introductions and retorts, the selected clips are resold as original programming (*Talk Soup*) to basic cable subscribers and to advertisers at an extremely high profit margin. Taking the recombinant mode even further, by the summer of 1995, E! was scheduling the same *Talk Soup* episode four times daily, mostly during evening and after midnight hours, and then reassembling the weekly material once more for an hour-long *Talk Soup Weekend* with recycled clips surrounded by new comedy material, programmed up to sixteen times during the course of an average Friday-through-Sunday weekend.

Like the celebrity profiles, behind-the-scenes Hollywood specials, and other entertainment-related programming shown on E!, a network jointly owned by Time Warner and several cable operators, including Tele-Communications Inc. (TCI), Continental Cablevision, Comcast Corp., and Cox Cable, the complimentary talk-show clips were said to serve a promotional function for suppliers, and indeed the early episodes of *Talk Soup* were little more than a string of clips accompanied by promos for upcoming episodes. But in sharp contrast to the celebratory flair of E!'s other programming, *Talk Soup* quickly evolved into a satire of daytime talk shows. Under the scrutiny of hosts who doubled as comedians, the length and frequency of talk-show clips shown were reduced, while sarcastic commentary, jokes, and comical technical manipulations that frame the clips grew more extreme in subsequent seasons.

Why would E! poke fun at daytime talk television while flattering the entertainment industries as a whole? There is much about daytime talk shows that deserves serious critique, especially in an increasingly competitive, ratings-driven environment where sensationalism and spectacle are increasingly the norm. Yet *Talk Soup*'s tendency to highlight the most sensational moments of talk shows, and to ridicule lower-income, female, and nonwhite guests in particular, is a strategy that requires our attention.

Reading the Talk Show

According to E! president Lee Masters, the network's operational philosophy is "to be obscenely profitable, and get into more homes" (qtd. in Kolbert), a goal that was largely fulfilled by the mid-1990s. Between 1993 and 1994 the network tripled its revenue, and by its five-year anniversary in 1995, E! was one of the fastest growing cable networks in the United States with a subscription base of 32.3 million viewers. Much of E!'s growth has been credited to the popularity of *Talk Soup,* the network's highest-rated, most profitable program and the one that as vice president of programming Fran Shea notes, "made viewers aware of E!'s existence" (qtd. in Weinstein). E! executives credit the success of *Talk Soup* to its adoption of an ironic stance, a shift that began when founding host and one-time executive producer Greg Kinnear began offering off-the-cuff sarcastic comments following the introduction and presentation of certain clips ("Welcome, America, a declining cultural and moral black hole, and I've got the show to prove it," went a typical comment from an early season). While not initially planned by

E!, the mockery was strongly encouraged when "vocal and loyal" fans responded favorably by "sending in ideas for gags and jokes" and to "fault the host for missing a perfect one-liner" (qtd. in Weinstein). Despite E!'s generally promotional relationship with the cultural industries, poking fun at daytime talk shows quickly became an exception in the face of financial opportunity and a means to court an upscale cable audience. Thus a complex trajectory of economic interests, audience demographics, and ideological assumptions (as opposed to corporate scheming or premeditated maliciousness) informed and encouraged *Talk Soup*'s parodic spin on talk show culture. "I know this sounds completely odd," Masters once told a reporter, "but we're very confident that we're going to be able to exploit this horrible environment to grow the distribution" (qtd. in Kolbert).

While recognizing the program's multiple points of determination, our primary concern here is how *Talk Soup* functions as a hegemonic mechanism within a postmodern television environment. Although presenting itself as lighthearted and humorous TV pastiche, *Talk Soup* works ideologically by encouraging viewers to distance themselves from people seen and issues raised on talk shows, while simultaneously adopting a white, male, middle-class view on social differences and injustices. What this TV show *about* TV shows offers is a "hegemonic oppositional" reading of talk show culture, an oxymoronic juxtaposition of terms we use to suggest how *Talk Soup* undermines the contradictions of daytime talk television while simultaneously confirming dominant ideologies and power inequities. As reception theorists have shown, the "meaning" of television programs is always a joint production among the cultural industries, audiences, texts, and intertextual references (Morley; Hall "Encoding"; Lewis). Because viewers bring a range of social backgrounds and references (including an awareness of other media texts) to the point of reception, the dominant ideological inflections of television programs may be negotiated and, in some cases, are subject to oppositional interpretations. Contestations over meanings are, as John Fiske and others argue, inextricably related to broader struggles over resources and social power. For members of marginalized groups, reading "against the grain" of television's preferred meanings can function as a counter-hegemonic practice, a refusal of dominant ideologies. In contrast to progressive oppositional readings which challenge dominance, *Talk Soup*'s stance toward daytime talk television articulates its meanings in the opposite direction. *Talk Soup* confirms the authority of the status quo by reading the diversity and counter-hegemonic discourse that renders (at least some of) daytime talk television politically progressive as a joke.

In sharp contrast to the lower-income, mostly female audience associated with daytime television, *Talk Soup* caters to the privileged mainstream, a group of people who, as evidenced by fan mail, "are just amazed at what's happening during this whole daytime subculture while they are away at work or at school" (qtd. in Weinstein).[6] Advertisements and *Talk Soup* promotional discourses court a youthful cable audience for whom abridged talk-show viewing is less informational or habitual than a form of guilty pleasure. *Talk Soup* is "the one show that will respect you no matter how much you tune in," the host assured viewers during one episode. The *Talk Soup* host, who speaks directly to his imagined audience before and after every clip, invokes a media savvy, upwardly mobile, college-educated viewer with his ironic banter. *Talk Soup* staff members addressed on and off camera extend the persona of the host and deepen an implied series of binary oppositions (wry-emotional, attractive-unattractive, intelligent-stupid, male-female, white-black, normal-perverse, middle class–working class) between "us" and "them," a group that includes talk-show guests and, implicitly, less savvy talk-show viewers who do not "get" the *Talk Soup* joke. The entire audience for *Talk Soup*—and even the entire staff, which includes several women (including the producer), an Asian American man and an African American man—need not fit neatly within such binaries to adopt the superior stance toward "others" promoted on the program. Encouraged by an implied equitable relationship with the host, even those viewers who cannot possibly live up to *Talk Soup* standards, and who may read the talk shows quite differently in another context, are invited to join him in an attitude of distance, condescension, mockery, and even contempt toward daytime talk television and its participants.

This ideological stance is masked in official descriptions and promotional materials, where E! defines *Talk Soup* as merely "A look at the best moments from the day's talk shows." When asked his opinion on daytime talk shows, John Henson, who replaced Kinnear as host in 1995, insisted "It's not my role to make an assessment. We just hold the shows up to the light and let the audience decide what they think."[7] In fact, *Talk Soup* routinely chooses some of the most sensational images to be found on daytime talk television for audience consideration, a sample *TV Guide* "Couch Critic" Jeff Jarvis has dubbed a "daily collage of the worst moments in TV's worst genre: the talk show." For the 1992 "Most Memorable Moments" *Talk Soup* special, producers chose, from thousands of possibilities, the following talk show participants to emphasize and, subsequently, ridicule: A woman whose breasts weigh forty pounds (*Sally Jessy Raphael*), a man who ruined his marriage by sleeping with his brother-in-law (*Geraldo*), an insomniac who requires pain to doze so he uses a lit cigarette lighter to burn himself to sleep (*Jerry Springer*), a woman who copes with her husband's death by exposing herself to strange men (*Jerry Springer*) and a "tattoo man" who once hammered a nail through his tongue (*Joan Rivers*).

More subtle but no less condescending is the program's attitude toward "ordinary" talk-show participants who deviate from *Talk Soup*'s presumed white, male, educated, heterosexual, middle-class "norm." Daytime talk television stands alone as a television genre where working-class people and cultures are regularly represented. Ridiculing working-class talk show guests and studio audience members is a favorite form of mockery on *Talk Soup*, one rendered even more noticeable by the fact that middle-class "experts" who also appear on talk shows are missing from clips selected. As Pierre Bourdieu has shown, manners, taste, and "cultural capital" are a product of education and social training but are presented by dominant groups as a natural reflection of superiority and sophistication. Such an attitude permeates *Talk Soup*, where the host routinely makes insulting comments about the physical appearance, dress, and mannerisms of talk-show participants based on unspoken class hierarchies. After showing a clip of a male escort who describes himself as "a god" to women, Kinnear, himself dressed in an expensive suit and tie, commented that he does not "picture God in a gold chain and a Kmart suit." On another episode, John Henson, who is "dressed by Guess" according to program credits, expressed shock upon finding a talk-show guest on *Shirley* wearing a jacket similar to his own.

Clips featuring talk-show hosts who correct their guests for their "offensive language" and even threaten them with expulsion provide additional class-based fodder. "Offensiveness" in such cases refers to vocabulary in violation of "broadcast standards," itself a distinction that assumes only people with educational resources are equipped to describe sexual activity on television. Such moments are magnified on *Talk Soup*, where they are offered as implicit evidence of "bad" manners and "bad" breeding. A related theme revolves around matters of intelligence, with daytime talk-show guests (and, implicitly, viewers) presented as inferior to the *Talk Soup* host, staff, and viewership. One episode ended with a guest comic, billed as a "world renowned psychic," predicting the futures of *Talk Soup* staffers and interns by answering questions such as "Will I graduate *summa* or *magna*?" In contrast, *Talk Soup*'s introduction of a talk-show guest who claimed to "have a very high IQ" was interrupted by an off-screen voice who asked, "If she's so smart, why is she on *Richard Bey*?"

Daytime talk shows are also notable for their representation of women, sexual minorities, and people of color, groups far less visible on other television genres. Couched in self-conscious irony, *Talk Soup*'s discriminatory attitude toward such groups is less explicit than its class-based humor, and can pass by unnoticed even by staff members, as evidenced when a racial slur was changed between its original airing and the weekend wrap-up. (When an African American masseuse was shown giving a sexually provocative massage to a young man on *Jerry Springer,* only to reveal that "she" was actually a man in drag, Henson explained the young man's quick retreat with the retort "Last they saw of him he was running through the heart of the African desert." By the weekend, the quip had been changed to "and thus he ran screaming into the night.") More often, the program reinforces a subtle white, male, heterosexist hierarchy through its selection and framing process. For instance, physical fights among blacks that occur on talk shows are appropriated as a source of amusement. Decontextualized from the structural sources of conflict (and sometimes even from their immediate sources), physically aggressive behavior on the part of people of color is read, through the *Talk Soup* lens, as "primitive" and laughable.

A clip taken from *Ricki Lake* reveals how the politics of class, gender, and race are conflated in such instances. The segment, dubbed "Mind Your Own Beezwax" by *Talk Soup*, presented two working-class African American women whose children share the same father; one blamed the other woman for blocking her ex-husband's parenting. Although only one dimension of the hour-long *Ricki Lake* program, the seconds-long verbal disagreement and subsequent physical fight was chosen for emphasis and, subsequently, re-emphasis. The broader issues discussed on *Ricki Lake* (which could have included single-parenting and child support, two recurring themes on this program, which is particularly popular with young African American women) were not included, or even mentioned on *Talk Soup*. Joking that the women were not "able to patch up their differences," the host proceeded to move on to another clip, only to be interrupted by four young, white *Talk Soup* staffers (three men and one woman) standing in for the imagined *Talk Soup* viewer in the following exchange:

Female staff member. "John, John, aren't we going to see it one more time, in slow motion, please?"

Henson. "Oh, *guys*, look, it's a new year, and my resolution is that we not exploit these childish fights for our entertainment. These are real people whose real lives are being destroyed on TV" [emphasis added].

Male staff member. "Yeah, but that's what makes it fun for us."

Female staff member. "Yeah."

Henson. "Okay, one more time, in slow motion, please."

While the clip replays, Henson narrates by commenting on the clothes worn by the African American bodyguards from *Ricki*'s staff who swiftly break up the fight.

Many of *Talk Soup*'s jokes regarding "attractiveness" are directed toward women of color, a pattern that reinforces oppressive ideologies concerning race, gender, and beauty. While beauty standards are given a special emphasis by *Talk Soup,* the programs from which the clips are culled typically address other issues, including ones that might challenge *Talk Soup*'s own authority. An exception to this pattern was a clip taken from the *Richard Bey Show*, where an African American woman on a panel discussing "beauty bigotry" likened discrimination based on appearance to racism. The beauty debate was, not surprisingly, promptly mocked by the *Talk Soup* host, but often the politics of appearance are less overt. From a *Leeza* program devoted to the subject of "nerds," *Talk Soup* chose to ridicule Regina, a Spanish-speaking woman of color in the studio audience who expressed her pleasure at harassing nerds on a routine basis. On the original *Leeza* episode, the young woman's hostility might have been read as a challenge to the educated, bookish privilege associated with "nerdiness," but on *Talk Soup* such aggressiveness was turned against Regina. Dubbed "I Hate Nerds," the excerpt ended with a white, male panelist warning "It will come back to her some day," at which point the *Talk Soup* host added, "Come back right now," and a series of technical "punishments" began on a close-up of Regina's face that emphasized her eyebrow, nose, and lip rings. Computerized line drawings added more facial piercings, which accelerated in size, culminating with a bone drawn through her nose, all gleefully directed by the host. In this reading, Regina was framed as an unattractive and freakish bully, while the abuse directed at her by *Talk Soup* was presented as both justified and amusing.[8]

Comical labels and crude technical manipulations are the more obvious ways *Talk Soup* frames and directs readings of daytime talk television. More subtle is the program's deployment of a middle-class, white, male gaze while surveying the world of daytime talk television, a viewfinder that encourages the *Talk Soup* audience to read the clips, and the shows, from a similar perspective. A clip focused on rape taken from a *Maury Povich* program demonstrates how viewers are, from the *Talk Soup* vantage point, encouraged to participate in an oppositional hegemonic reading of daytime talk television's progressive moments. In the clip, an African American woman was shown discussing how she prevented a near-rape by grabbing her attacker's penis and twisting his scrotum. Upon return, the host was out of the frame, supposedly doubled up, and then returned with the explanation "It's difficult to listen to, but I feel better now." Here the comic retort at best trivialized the attempted rape; at worst it encouraged gender identification with the woman's attacker.

Within the broader operation of hegemony, *Talk Soup* works to uphold dominant privileges and assumptions routinely challenged on daytime talk shows. While the program is clearly geared toward upscale and, presumably, like-minded viewers, it also has a broader ideological effect as well. As a well-publicized intertextual discourse *about* daytime talk shows, *Talk Soup* contributes to dominant societal understandings of, and expectations for, the genre by routinely putting talk show guests "in their place." But this program can also be contradictory, as evidenced by the inclusion of jokes about the host and the imagined *Talk Soup* audience. After four seasons, the show took on a softer edge with the introduction of Henson, whose self-mocking jokes about bad hair, a nonexistent social life, and a meager salary now run side-by-side with the more biting sarcasm directed at talk show guests.[7] In response to a clip from *Rolanda,* Henson even placed himself, though a chroma key special effect, in a talk-show studio audience, where he imitated an insecure teenage boy who had been shown seeking advice from "Johnny Bravo" on how to become "a pimp daddy." While such cases would appear to extend the mockery to all, they often work to naturalize the pecking order on *Talk Soup.* In the above parody, the teenage boys toward whom many jokes are directed are in turn mocked, but the real target was the subcultural, working-class Johnny Bravo, whose line of advice ("Come out to L.A. and come to one of Bravo's clubs, my son") was replayed several times to cinch the gag. Indeed, many jokes directed toward the *Talk Soup* audience require collegiate-based cultural competencies to appreciate, and as such, work to reaffirm the presumed superiority of the imagined *Talk Soup* viewer. For instance, when the show received a (probably bogus) letter from a viewer claiming he did not "get" one of *Talk Soup*'s mock promotional ads, the host, surrounded by eight laughing white staff men, "deconstructed" the joke ad in a style that mocked continental theory and the French tradition of *explication du texte.*

"To a certain extent we have a bit of that holier-than-talk-show air because, frankly, I personally would like to stand above everything in show business," former host Greg Kinnear once remarked about *Talk Soup*'s ironic stance (qtd. in Weinstein). In fact, *Talk Soup* does not stand above "everything in show business," or even every dimension of the talk-show genre. Rather, *Talk Soup*'s mockery is reserved for the people who participate on daytime shows as guests or studio audience members. Daytime talk-show hosts are rarely the subject of jokes, and when they are, the clips tend to focus favorably on a host controlling or correcting a participant. (One such clip from *Maury Povich* featured a young working class white man, "Torn Between Two Strippers," who evaded his awkward situation by asking "Isn't it about time for the commercial?" Povich's response was swift and direct: "Don't be smart with me. I run the commercial breaks.") Celebrities, experts, and the talk show industry as a whole are also safe from *Talk Soup*'s condescending eye, a pattern reinforced by its flattering treatment of late-night talk shows. While all clips on *Talk Soup* are presented as inherently humorous, the host laughs *at* daytime guests and *with* celebrity guests. Unlike daytime clips, which often must be decontextualized and ideologically re-oriented to ensure comedic effect, late-night clips are presented as straightforward "highlights" of material considered funny on the original program. In contrast to the mockery directed toward daytime talk-show clips, a typical highlight from *Tonight with Jay Leno* titled "Froggie Fun" recapped an occasion when Leno's guest was a frog breeder and the comic situation was "how to determine the sex of a frog."

The Political Economy of Mockery

While powerful, *Talk Soup*'s positioning strategies have certainly not been all-encompassing. Despite its relative success and popularity, *Talk Soup* still reaches a far smaller audience than the combined viewership for daytime talk shows. Moreover, the television industry's response to the program's reading of talk shows has been mixed. In certain quarters, the innovative flair of the program has been praised, as evidenced by several industry awards, including a prestigious 1995 Emmy. The publicity value of *Talk Soup*'s recombinant mode has value to some late night talk show producers who have welcomed representation in the *Talk Soup* mix. But reactions from executives and producers who oversee daytime talk television have grown steadily antagonistic to the increasingly unflattering reading their shows are given on the E! network. In *Talk Soup*'s first few seasons, every daytime talk show in syndication except the *Oprah Winfrey Show* allowed gratis use of its material. Such agreements suggest a degree of complicity, and even support, for the manner in which daytime talk television has been represented nightly on *Talk Soup*. In 1992, for instance, talk show host Maury Povich remarked: "I think it's terrific. It's a great parody. There are serious parts of talk shows and we take ourselves seriously at times, but we have to realize what we are. It's all part of the grand form of entertainment. It's good. It puts us in our place—and we should be put there" (qtd. in Schoemer).

The *Oprah Winfrey Show,* produced by Oprah Winfrey's own Harpo Productions, and a show that has always encouraged a serious reading of its social and political significance, was an early and important exception to the pattern of complicity with *Talk Soup*. Winfrey has argued that her show is about "empowering people, especially women" (qtd. in Livingstone 440). She clearly does not share Povich's view of the "place" of daytime talk shows. Her own personal experience with sexual abuse, drug addiction, racism, and eating disorders, and her commitment to resolving these social problems have fostered more critical discussion than is allowed on most daytime talk shows. When Winfrey refused *Talk Soup* permission to use her material, she prevented her guests from decontextualized mockery, thereby retaining a greater degree of ideological control over readings of her show. Within the broader operation of hegemony, this example demonstrates how important independent media production is to the survival of critical ideas, perspectives, and frameworks.[9]

During the 1994 and 1995 seasons, other successful daytime talk shows, including *Donahue, Sally Jessy Raphael, Geraldo, Ricki Lake, Jenny Jones,* and *Jane Whitney,* pulled their material from *Talk Soup,* leaving E! only lesser-known, and frequently more sensational, programs to ridicule. In contrast to *Oprah,* most of the later pull-outs are owned and syndicated by corporate conglomerates, including Multimedia Entertainment, the Tribune Company, and Warner Brothers, a subsidiary of Time Warner conglomerate which also retains 50 percent ownership over the E! network. These companies have a vested economic interest in preserving their large, loyal, and extremely profitable talk-show viewership. It is not, then, surprising that they pulled their programs from the *Talk Soup* round-up after initial complicity. According to trade reports, accepting the quid pro quo of free clips for free promotion began to wane once the show grew aggressively hostile and more condescending toward talk show guests. At its most condescending, the promotional use-value of *Talk Soup* became increasingly ambiguous and even risky for corporations concerned with maintaining, and not offending, their viewership and advertising base.

Warner Brothers became especially outspoken about the way talk-show guests were ridiculed on *Talk Soup,* despite the corporation's financial stake in the E! network. Such a surprising turn of events raises interesting questions about the contradictory (as opposed to monolithic) operation of powerful media conglomerates. Warner public relations chief Barbara Brogliatti began criticizing *Talk Soup* in *TV Guide* and other public forms before the summer of 1994, complaining that *Talk Soup* "degrades our shows and makes fools of the guests" (qtd. in "Brogliatti"; see also Johnson and Bash). The critique occurred, coincidentally, not long after E! had filed a copyright lawsuit against its parent company for

developing an infotainment program similar in name and scope to E!
Kinnear's response to Brogliatti's accusations was to treat her, a powerful corporate executive, with the same kind of mockery usually reserved
for talk-show guests. The flurry of corporate warnings and apologies
was a rare moment for *Talk Soup,* but a reminder of the continuously
competing, and sometimes contradictory, corporate interests that operate
within the general state of hegemony. For now, the financial imperatives
of the free market have narrowed *Talk Soup*'s scope to the most sensational talk shows still willing to trade self-mockery for free publicity, a
shift that will ironically make it all the easier for *Talk Soup* to read daytime talk shows as a joke.

Conclusion

As Wayne Munson has argued, daytime talk shows represent "one
of the financial economy's most efficient ways to *re*expropriate not only
the everyday resistances and negotiations of popular culture but the
dominant order as well" (10). Despite the numerous regulatory mechanisms operating on the shows (host authority, the reliance on experts, a
"personal" emphasis) the genre allows, and indeed requires, an unprecedented degree of contradiction and social antagonism rarely seen on
commercial television. At yet another level of efficiency, *Talk Soup* sub-
verts those crucial contradictions by encouraging viewers to make
assumptions about the "strange and arcane" world of daytime talk television based on partial and firmly hegemonic understandings. Debates
over serious social, political, and domestic issues permeate most talk
shows, but these aspects are rarely selected for the humorous *Talk Soup*
"recap." With its self-conscious irony and media savviness, *Talk Soup*
makes it extremely difficult (and very "uncool") to adopt a literal reading of daytime talk television, or to take any dimension of the shows too
seriously. Yet, as we have shown, *Talk Soup*'s irreverent mockery works
ideologically by encouraging viewers to distance themselves economi-
cally, socially, and intellectually from the "others" who take part in daytime talk show culture as guests, studio audience members, and audiences. In this sense, the turn toward the most sensational talk shows,
will, within the hegemonic logic of *Talk Soup*, both confirm and justify
the program's self-appointed vantage point.

By drawing on daytime television for its primary production material, *Talk Soup* reflects the political economy and aesthetics of postmodern television, whereby television imagery itself becomes recycled,
repackaged, and resold in an ongoing loop of symbolic production and
consumption. As a TV show about television, *Talk Soup* represents a
potentially radical moment in media culture, a means to question the pol-

itics of representation. A counter-hegemonic parody of daytime talk show culture may, for instance, question the authority of the host, or poke fun at advertisers, or mock the "knowing" attitude of college-educated experts, or reveal the ratings-driven staged aspects of talk show culture. Instead, *Talk Soup* confirms dominant structures and dominant ideologies. With its "oppositional hegemonic" reading of the mostly working-class people, sexual minorities, people of color, and women who are now allowed to contribute to public discourse via the daytime talk show, the program demonstrates how the ambiguities of interpretation signaled by reception theorists can be articulated toward regressive (as opposed to only progressive) readings. Perhaps most important, *Talk Soup* confirms the resiliency of hegemonic struggle in the age of pastiche and simulation. Contrary to postmodern theorists like Baudrillard who equate the sheer pervasiveness of television imagery in contemporary society with the "impossibility" of meaning, *Talk Soup* suggests a proliferation of new sites where ideological struggles over the "meaning" of television (and of class, race, gender, and sexuality) are now being waged.

Notes

1. The daytime talk show was the "most moneymaking type of program on television" in 1992 (Munson 3-4). Real life guests are increasingly used because they routinely match or better the ratings earned by celebrities at far lower costs (see Howard).

2. While in 1981 there were only five audience-participation talk shows on the airwaves (Bickelhaupt), by the mid-1990s such programs totaled at least 20 hours of weekday programming in major cities (Bash). The number of new shows introduced each year has also skyrocketed, leading one industry executive to call the talk show the "most duplicated genre in television."

3. For a typical example of how daytime talk shows are handled in the news media, see journalist Carl Bernstein's critique in the *New Republic*. Critical scholars who attempt to reclaim the oppositional aspects of daytime talk shows are, of course, an exception to the general intellectual response referenced here.

4. The arguments in this essay are based on regular viewings of *Talk Soup*, trade and news reports, and informational and promotional materials received from E! Examples cited from the program are drawn from a videotaped sample of nine 30-minute and four 60-minute weekend programs cablecast between November 1994 and August 1995. Twenty-five different talk shows were excerpted in these thirteen editions. The most frequently excerpted were: *Jerry*

Springer (16 clips), *Rolanda* (13 clips), *Maury Povich* (12 clips), and *Tonight with Jay Leno* (12 clips). An average of seven to nine excerpted clips were featured in each 30-minute show. This figure exceeds the ten to twelve clips one journalist documented in 1993 (McFarlin), suggesting that the 1994 and 1995 seasons expanded the comedy material before and after each clip. Since *Talk Soup* programs are not readily available in archival form we have not included cablecast dates for referenced examples. These dates are available from the authors upon request.

5. For a basic overview of postmodern culture, including postmodern television, see *Postmodernist Culture* by Steven Connor. For an account of how postmodern aesthetics, including parody, have been used by artists, filmmakers, and photographers, see *The Politics of Postmodernism* by Linda Hutcheon. For an excellent introduction to a wide range of critical debates over the politics of postmodernism see *Universal Abandon,* edited by Andrew Ross.

6. Audience demographics obtained from E! list the network's target audience as cable subscribing "adults 18-49." Advertisements placed on *Talk Soup* confirm a youthful viewership. Very few ads feature the domestic cleaning products characteristic of daytime television; many advertisements are aimed at upscale consumers (for example, DeBeers Diamonds ["How else can two months' salary last a lifetime?"], Yoplait Light, Nordic Track). A rare soap ad presents a mininarrative of a young post-graduate who must clean up his act (with Bold) in order to find a corporate job. Promotions for *Talk Soup* merchandise (T-shirts, sweatshirts and mugs) address a similar kind of viewer. Once, while commenting on a daytime talk-show clip, host Greg Kinnear gleefully recognized a *Talk Soup* T-shirt worn by a studio-audience member. Literally separated from the rest of the audience (with special graphics applied to the image), the *Talk Soup* fan was, not unexpectedly, a young, white man (outfitted in the slacker uniform of T-shirt, plaid flannel shirt, and jeans). A mock ad for "*Talk Soup*: The Home Game" depicts a group of white, bored collegiates who turn to a game that promises "All the pain and humiliation of *Talk Soup* in the privacy of your own home."

7. Henson, a twenty-seven-year-old former stand-up comedian, was chosen from 3,000 candidates who auditioned for the job ("The Insider" 8).

8. Because the requirement of a talk-show appearance is often an "experience" that will sell well with audiences, assessments about the authenticity of real life guests are complicated. Contrary to the spontaneous feel of daytime talk shows, the roles people adopt as guests and studio audiences are approved by producers in advance. Most programs solicit guests who meet certain criteria by placing advertisements in local newspapers or by running on-air promotions. Talk show guest booking services emphasize the sensational aspects of everyday life and encourage their clients to do the same as a means to secure participation on the shows (and free trips and hotel accommodations). Studio audi-

ences are also often pre-selected to meet certain criteria, and "coached" before rehearsals and tapings.

9. See Masciarotte for more on how the distinctive discursive strategies employed on *Oprah* operate in gender terms.

Works Cited

Bash, Alan. "America's Talking, and Talking." *USA Today* 30 June 1994: 3D.

Baudrillard, Jean. *Simulations*. New York: Semiotexte, 1983.

Bernstein, Carl. "The Idiot Culture." *New Republic* 8 June 1992: 22-28.

Bickelhaupt, Susan. "Talk Shows Take Over Daytime." *Boston Globe* 21 Nov. 1991: 48.

Bourdieu, Pierre. *Distinction: A Social Critique of the Judgement of Taste*. Cambridge: Harvard UP, 1984.

"Brogliatti and 'Soup' Clips." *Los Angeles Times* 14 May 1994: F7.

Carpignano, Paulo, Robin Anderson, Stanley Aronowitz, and William Difazio. "Chatter in the Age of Electronic Reproduction: Talk Television and the 'Public Mind.'" *Social Text* 25-26 (1990): 33-55.

Connor, Steven. *Postmodernist Culture*. Oxford: Blackwell, 1989.

Fiske, John. *Television Culture*. New York: Routledge, 1987.

Freeman, Mike. "Talk Shows Flourish During May Sweeps." *Broadcasting* 15 June 1992: 11

Gitlin, Todd. *Inside Prime Time*. New York: Pantheon, 1983.

____. "Postmodernism: Roots and Politics." *Cultural Politics in Contemporary America*. Ed. Ian Angus and Sut Jhally. New York: Routledge, 1989. 347-60.

Gramsci, Antonio. *Selections from the Prison Notebooks*. New York: International, 1971.

Hall, Stuart. "Culture, the Media and the 'Ideological Effect.'" *Mass Communication and Society*. Ed. James Curran, Michael Gurevitch, and James Woollacott. London: Edward Arnold, 1977. 313-48.

____. "Encoding/Decoding." *Culture, Media, Language*. Ed. Stuart Hall, Dorothy Hobson, Andrew Lowe, and Paul Willis. London: Hutchinson, 1980. 128-38.

____. *The Hard Road to Renewal*. London: Verso, 1988.

hooks, bell. *Talking Back: Thinking Feminist, Thinking Black*. Boston: South End, 1989.

Howard, Johnette. "Weirdness in Demand on Talk TV-Glut of Daytime Talk Shows Has Producers in Hot Pursuit of the Most Sensational, Outrageous Real Life Stories." *Orlando Sentinal Tribune* 14 Apr. 1992: E1.

Hutcheon, Linda. *The Politics of Postmodernism*. New York: Routledge, 1989.

"The Insider." *Electronic Media* 30 Jan. 1995: 8.

Jameson, Frederic. "Postmodernism, or the Cultural Logic of Late Capitalism." *New Left Review* 146 (1984): 53-92.

——. "Postmodernism and Consumer Society." *The Anti-Aesthetic: Essays on Postmodern Culture.* Ed. Hal Foster. Seattle: Bay, 1983. 111-25.

Jarvis, Jeff. "Talk Soup." *TV Guide* 24 June 1995: 10.

Johnson, Allan. "E! Evolves Into the Voice of Entertainment News." *Chicago Tribune* 17 Oct. 1993: 5C.

Johnson, Peter, and Alan Bash. "Kinnear Says Sorry to Exec for His Sassy Talk." *USA Today* 4 May 1994: 3-D.

Kolbert, Elizabeth. "A Slick Take on Talk Shows Feeds a New Little Channel." *New York Times* 6 June 1994: C11.

Lewis, Justin. "The Meaning of Things: Audiences, Ambiguity, and Power." *Viewing, Reading, Listening: Audiences and Cultural Reception.* Ed. Jon Cruz and Justin Lewis. Boulder: Westview, 1994. 19-32.

Livingstone, Sonia. "Watching Talk: Gender and Engagement in the Viewing of Audience Discussion Programs." *Media, Culture & Society* 16 (1994): 429-47.

Masciarotte, Gloria-Jean. "C'mon Girl: Oprah Winfrey and the Discourse of Feminine Talk." *Genders* 11 (Fall 1991): 81-110.

McFarlin, Jim. "Here's Talking at You, Kids!" *Gannett News Service* 8 July 1993.

Morley, David. *The Nationwide Audience.* London: British Film Institute, 1980.

Munson, Wayne. *All Talk: The Talk Show in Media Culture.* Philadelphia: Temple UP, 1993.

Peck, Janice. "TV Talk Shows as Therapeutic Discourse: The Ideological Labor of the Televised Talking Cure." *Communication Theory* 5.1 (Feb. 1995): 58-81.

Priest, Patricia Joyner. *Public Intimacies: Talk Show Participants and Tell-All TV.* Cresskill, NJ: Hampton, 1995.

Ross, Andrew, ed. *Universal Abandon: The Politics of Postmodernism.* Minneapolis: U of Minnesota P, 1988.

Schoemer, Karen. "The Best, or Maybe the Worst, of the Talk-Show World." *New York Times* 27 June 1993: 2:28.

Weinstein, Steve. " 'Talk Soup' Stirs Up Comedy and Reality." *Los Angeles Times* 12 Nov. 1993: F12.

White, Mimi. *Tele-Advising: Therapeutic Discourse in American Television.* Chapel Hill: U of North Carolina P, 1992.

11

They Went Thataway, Old Chap:
Movie Images of the English
on the American Western Frontier

Jack Nachbar

We expect, as firmly as we can expect anything, that autocracy is by
way of coming to grief and that democracy is waiting to come into its
own, in the realized ideals of that Declaration which puzzled a
belated Englishman like Ruggles, but which is as divinely postulated
as the authority of kings used everywhere to be.

—William Dean Howells reviewing
Ruggles of Red Gap in 1918

In the crucible of the frontier, the immigrants were Americanized,
liberated, and fused into a mixed race, English in neither nationality
nor characteristics.

—Frederick Jackson Turner, 1893

The first English settlers in North America in Walt Disney's 1995
feature-length cartoon, *Pocahontas,* are a thoroughly unpleasant bunch:
vain, patronizing, ignorant, and greedy. Gold is what they're after and if
they have to decimate the 1607 Virginia landscape and slaughter the
local "savages" to get it, well, it is all part of the adventure now, isn't it?
By the end of this very 1990s morality tale, however, most of the
damnable English, through contact with the American land and with
Native Americans, have been redeemed. Hero John Smith has been
taught by the lovely Indian princess, Pocahontas, to "listen to the wind"
of the American environment, usually shown in gigantic open vistas, and
to respect cultures other than the British. The crew of commoners has
discovered democracy. They revolt against their insufferable aristocrat
leader, John Ratcliffe, whom they bind and humiliate. Even Ratcliffe's
snobbish, pampered pet, the English bulldog, Percy, loses his class prejudices, and learns to romp in freedom with Pocahontas's two unrestrained
American pets, Meeko the raccoon and Flit the hummingbird. Only Rat-

cliffe fails to grow a new soul in the American soil, and he is appropriately sent packing, blubbering and unrepentant, back to England where he belongs.

Disney's version of the first English confrontation with the North American wilderness comes as no surprise to most adult members of American audiences because its attitudes and sentiments toward both the English and the American frontier have been familiar ones for over a century. The best-known articulation of these perspectives is, of course, Frederick Jackson Turner's 1893 essay, "The Significance of the Frontier in American History," an essay that virtually defined western American history for the United States for much of the twentieth century and which historian Ray Allen Billington has described as being for periods of time, "virtually unquestioned as the Holy Writ of American historiography" (Billington 3).

Among the ideas presented by Turner in his famous essay was his argument that the frontier was an environment effecting what he called "Americanization." According to Turner, white Europeans were "reborn," on the American frontier. The immigrant began by being European in "thought," but the wild, open land, "takes him from the railroad car and puts him in the birch canoe. It strips off the garments of civilization and arrays him in the hunting shirt and the moccasin." Thus, Europeans trade in aristocratic titles and a mode of status based on class structure for the freedom of open land, and a classless democracy where status is based on skills for survival rather than on a family name.

The result is that to the frontier the American intellect owes its striking characteristics. That coarseness and strength combined with acuteness and inquisitiveness; that practical, inventive turn of mind, quick to find expedients; that masterful grasp of material things, lacking in the artistic but powerful to effect great ends; that restless, nervous energy; that dominant individualism, working for good and for evil, and withal that buoyancy and exuberance which comes from freedom. (Turner 38-61)

Turner's concept of Americanization as reflected in the introduction of English characters to the United States frontier is not only a defining idea in *Pocahontas* but in a number of live-action movies throughout the twentieth century. In all of these films, English men or women confront the primitive coarseness of the frontier and in doing so are reborn, shedding their class consciousness and stuffy manners for individualism, democratic classlessness, and invigorating informality.

Harry Leon Wilson's popular novel *Ruggles of Red Gap* first appeared as a serial in *The Saturday Evening Post*. It became a published novel in 1915 as well as a Broadway play. Wilson's amusing story of a repressed English butler who finds freedom of both soul and employment in the American West was made twice as a silent film, in 1918 and in 1923. The most memorable version of the story, however, is Leo McCarey's wonderfully droll 1935 version with the archetypal Englishman, Charles Laughton, in the title role.

In McCarey's version of the story, Marmaduke Ruggles is a 1908 third generation valet who is in the service of the aristocrat George Van Basingwell (Roland Young), a well-mannered but weakling fop, completely incapable of caring for himself. Ruggles, to his horror, is the stakes in a poker game which Van Basingwell loses to Egbert Floud (Charlie Ruggles), a loud and crude but likable self-made millionaire from the wilds of the town of Red Gap in Washington State.[1] Egbert's social-climbing wife, Effie (Mary Boland), greatly desires a hierarchical class structure for Red Gap modelled on England, and she believes that having a servant like Ruggles will give her a leg up amongst Red Gap's smart set. Egbert, a true Turner American democrat, refuses to treat Ruggles as an inferior, informally calling him, "Bill" or "Colonel" and insisting that the shocked Ruggles sit right down with Egbert and another rough and ready Westerner to get drunk on whiskey.

Once he is ensconced in Red Gap itself, Ruggles undergoes some dramatic Americanization. Egbert allows the town to believe that Ruggles is a real Colonel and invites him to a town dance. There Ruggles meets the feisty widow Mrs. Judson (Zasu Pitts), who is quick to berate Ruggles when he is surprised that the "help" at the party are allowed to mingle freely with the guests. "Nobody minds here, Colonel," she tells him. "It's funny but you're the first one that ever made me feel different from anyone else." Properly chastised for his moment of English snobbery, he whisks the widow off in a waltz. Moments later, in the comic high point of the film, Ruggles further frees himself from the constraints of his English class-consciousness. Effie's socially pretentious brother-in-law demands that Ruggles quit mingling with other guests at the party and return home. When Ruggles refuses, Mr. Charles Belknap-Jackson haughtily kicks Ruggles. In turn, Ruggles, American individualism asserting itself at last, returns the favor and plants his foot squarely in Belknap-Jackson's socially superior keister.

The emotional climax of *Ruggles of Red Gap* comes during a long scene in which Ruggles recites the entire Lincoln Gettysburg Address in a bar full of enraptured ruffians. His basic American credentials thereby established, Ruggles refuses to go back in the employ of Van Basingwell, quits his job with the Flouds, and opens his own restaurant, the Anglo-American Grille. The film ends with the town celebrating the successful Americanization of its new citizen with a hearty round of "For He's a Jolly Good Fellow." Ruggles will in all likelihood retain much of his English sense of decorum, and will never embrace American coarseness. Yet, in his new freedom from a future determined by his .class origins, he has shown a "practical, inventive turn of mind" and a "masterful grasp of material things."

Fancy Pants, the 1950 remake of *Ruggles of Red Gap,* is more of a Bob Hope vehicle in which Hope can perform his bragging coward screen character than it is an illustration of Americanization. Hope's supposedly English butler is in reality an American third-rate actor pretending to be a butler. While McCarey's 1935 film had gently satirized social institutions, the Hope film broadly parodies the British, and white, Native American and Asian Americans equally. No one is spared. Laughs are everything. Hope provides us with only one moment of Americanization, and that occurs during the credits. Hope's credit line, presented to a huge trumpet fanfare, reads, "starring Mr. Robert Hope (formerly Bob)." Hope then appears wearing formal clothes and a top hat. He sticks a pince-nez in his eye, stares offscreen at the audience and snottily intones, "No popcorn during my performance . . . peasants." The rest of the credits then roll. As many people in the 1950s knew, Hope was actually born in London but had earned his fame as a comedian in American radio and movies. The joke, therefore, is that a native Englishman who is now an American is teasing the English by making fun of their mannered arrogance. The Americanized Hope was thus demonstrating the "buoyancy and exuberance that comes with freedom" which Turner defined as a trait of the frontier. It is a joke that Ruggles himself probably would have appreciated.

Twenty years after *Fancy Pants* the cultural climate for stories about the frontier had changed considerably. Hollywood, catering to the values reflected in the social upheavals of the late 1960s and early 1970s, produced westerns questioning traditional Euro-American values, especially on aggressive violence toward indigenous peoples, and presented the wars between Native Americans and whites from a perspective favoring the Native Americans. A hit movie from this cycle of films was *A Man Called Horse* (1970) with Richard Harris[2] as John Morgan, an English lord in the 1820s who is captured by the Sioux and forced by them to be a beast of burden.

For Morgan, the process of Americanization has begun to take place even before the Sioux take him captive. He admires the landscape of the Northwest Territories and tells his guide that he has never earned anything. "Family titles, family property, family position. . . . Everything I ever wanted in life I bought." He knows something is wrong with his

Morgan (Richard Harris) is transformed by the Sun Vow Ceremony in *A Man Called Horse.* (Courtesy of the Museum of Modern Art/Film Stills Archive)

English perspectives. "In England, I look up to God and royalty and down on everybody else," he says of himself contemptuously, and adds that for the past five years he has been "just looking" for something more meaningful.

As might be expected in a movie with a 1970 sensibility, Morgan finds what he is searching for in his captivity with the Sioux. Initially, he finds his own individual initiative. Hoping to engineer an escape he rises above his status as an animal by counting coup on the Shoshone, traditional enemies of the Sioux, thereby gaining the Shoshone horses. Morgan then uses these horses to trade for a bride, Running Deer (Corinna Tsopei), the sister of a noted warrior and his captor, Yellow Hand (Manu Tupou). To be worthy of the marriage, Morgan must undergo a test of courage, the sacred Sun Vow ceremony,[3] in which a man is lifted off the ground supported only by pegs inserted beneath muscles in the chest.

Before the ceremony, Morgan reverts to his English aristocratic attitudes, feelings very much like those expressed in *Pocahontas*, when he tells the Sioux, "To me you were, all of you, mean, vicious, ignorant, superstitious, ugly, benighted savages. To me you were no different from men all over the world." During the famous scene in the ceremonial lodge when he hangs in agony above his captors, however, he receives a vision. A sacred white buffalo tells him, "Speak the truth in humility to all people. Only then can you be a true man and free of your chains." After this advice to, in effect, give up his English air of superiority, Morgan finds what he was looking for in life. He works for the good of his wife and the entire village and near the end of the film, in a dramatic gesture of democratic acceptance, becomes the adopted son of the haggish old woman who initially had beaten him and made him perform the chores of an animal.

In the final scene of *A Man Called Horse*, Morgan, having seen to the ceremonial necessities of his dead adopted mother, leaves the Sioux village at last. He is dressed in the same buckskins in which we first saw him in the film. But gone are the whiskers and the affected "dude" accoutrements of silk scarf and broad-brimmed hat he wore before his capture. Morgan has shed these symbols of his English gentleman status in favor of a more natural look in tune with the American landscape. He has becomes Americanized. It comes as little surprise then that in the 1976 sequel to the film, *Return of a Man Called Horse*, Lord John Morgan grows bored and restless in his vast English estate, and eagerly returns to the Sioux.

Americanization is a process undergone, quite obviously, by English women as well as men. When we first see Catherine Crocker (Sarah

Miles) in *The Man Who Loved Cat Dancing* (1973), she is horribly out of place on the American landscape. She is riding sidesaddle, dressed in formal riding clothes of heavy velvet, wearing a matching top hat and carrying a fancy parasol. As the camera pulls back, we see Catherine alone on a huge expanse of southwest desert and it becomes laughingly clear how Catherine's fancy English riding costume really is inappropriate.

Catherine, we learn, is the daughter of some sort of titled but impoverished Englishman.[4] She is married to a rich American (George Hamilton), who, like Belknap-Jackson, in *Ruggles of Red Gap*, seeks a sudden rise on the social ladder. He has purchased Catherine as his wife as a means to higher status, an obvious sin on the American frontier. Catherine is running away from his coldness and his indifference and, like Morgan in *A Man Called Horse,* is seeking something. And also like Morgan, she finds it after being taken captive.

Catherine is grabbed by Jay Grobart (Burt Reynolds) and his gang of train robbers who are on the run from a big holdup. It is obvious that her aristocratic upbringing has not prepared Catherine for a western life on the run. She can't cook, for example, and she confesses that she does not even know how to make coffee. But slowly she sloughs off the weaknesses of her past and adapts to life on the frontier. This is suggested in the movie mainly through an evolution in Catherine's physical appearance. First the sidesaddle goes, then the fancy-bred horse. Finally the velvet outfit is replaced by basic Western garb that had belonged to a dead member of the gang. During this period, Catherine learns western skills. She takes up cooking and making coffee and even learns to whistle bird calls Indian-style if she senses danger. Her evolution from English lady to western woman is shown in a symbolic baptism when Grobart teases her about trying to wash with dainty propriety at the edge of a cold mountain stream. Catherine flings off her shirt and with gusto throws herself into the pure American water. The ritual concluded, we notice she is falling in love with the American individualist, Grobart.

Catherine's final step in her Americanization comes when she shoots and kills her status-hungry husband in order to save outlaw Grobart who is more at home with the Indians than he is in white society.[5] The film suggests that the two of them may spend their future together in the local Indian village.

Catherine, as well as all of the other English characters described so far, must experience a genuine change of values in order to become truly Americanized. It is not enough to merely exchange a railroad car for a birch canoe. Class consciousness and snobbery, which in these films is invariably seen as essential to the English character, must be exchanged for a genuine appreciation for egalitarian, classless democracy. To fail to develop this perspective leads to a failure in Americanization even though the English character may show certain outward signs of a conversion to American values. Such is the case with English Bob (Richard Harris) in Clint Eastwood's highly praised 1992 western, *Unforgiven.*

English Bob, as a western gunfighter living by his practical skills and his wits, would appear to be clearly in the Frederick Jackson Turner mold. His talents have been perverted, however, by his refusal to bow to democratic principles. Bob makes his living, for example, via racist violence—he shoots "Chinamen" for the railroad. He also bedevils American patriotism by repeating to anyone who will listen to him his theory of why President Garfield has been assassinated. Nobody would shoot the English queen, he boasts, because just to be in the presence of royalty is to be "in awe." "Well, a President," he continues with haughty relish, "I mean, why not shoot the President?" suggesting, of course, that the American president's commoner origins make him not only unawesome, but unworthy of even basic respect.

Big Whiskey, Wyoming, does not cotton to such sentiments in the film. Sheriff Little Bill Daggett (Gene Hackman) arrests English Bob for wearing firearms within the town limits, publicly humiliates him, nastily kicks him into the street, and finally throws him into jail. During most of this violence, an American flag is waving behind Little Bill. In the jailhouse, Little Bill pronounces *The Duke of Death*, a dime novel praising the supposed heroics of English Bob, "The Duck of Death," showing further disrespect for Bob's English identity.

Finally, Little Bill puts Bob on a stage and throws him out of town. Unrepentant of his anti-Americanism to the end, English Bob shouts his final words to Big Whiskey: "A plague on the whole stinkin' lot a ya! Without morals or laws . . . no wonder you all emigrated to America because they wouldn't have you in England. You're a lot of savages, that's what you all are, a bunch of bloody savages! A curse on ya!"

It is difficult to fully know all the nuances of this complex, funny moment in *Unforgiven.* But to anyone watching the film, the emotional response is obvious: we are glad English Bob was brought down off his high horse and we are glad, despite his final protests of his own English superiority, he has been tossed out of town. As he spouts his final curses, an American flag can be seen in the background. Whether it's Ratcliffe in *Pocahontas* or English Bob in *Unforgiven,* it seems that when characters are given the opportunity on the frontier to get with the program of Americanization and they choose not to do it, they simply have to go.[6]

Two observations about the above examples seem rather obvious. The first is the consistency of the image of the English as they experience the American frontier. From silent movies to the films of the present, from comedies to romantic melodramas to cartoons, from lowly menservants to English lords, the pattern remains the same: English characters in all these movies are choked by restrictive manners, and made narrow-minded by class prejudices and faith in a hierarchical social structure. These traits make the characters unhappy or, in some cases, evil. Happiness comes to these characters only when they confront the open spaces and primitive living conditions of the American frontier. This confrontation frees them of their repressive English perspectives and turns them into open-minded, individualistic democrats. Those who do not change on the frontier are seen as unredeemably corrupt and are forced to leave the frontier environment in shame.

The second observation is that these images of the English are stereotypes. The characters are narrowly typed playthings of their creators and their main function seems to be to illustrate the inadequacy of England as opposed to the innate superiority of North America as environments nurturing human perfectability. It is tempting to view these stereotypes as merely a combination of American xenophobia and nationalism. Such a conclusion, however, would probably necessitate ignoring the much more varied images of the English presented in other Hollywood movies.[7] An additional complication is the fact that British actors and actors associated with the British Commonwealth have always been popular in America and some of them, including Sean Connery, David Niven, Errol Flynn, and Anthony Hopkins have played heroic roles in Westerns when their Britishness was not an issue in the film. The reason for the narrow stereotyping of the English characters in the films in this essay apparently lies beyond simple Yankee biases.

A more probable reason why the English are pictured as they are in these films is the power of the vision of Frederick Jackson Turner. Turner's seminal essay has always been questioned by some historians. The recent "new western historians" have been especially strong in their criticism of Turner's ideas, writing him off as all but irrelevant to what actually went on in the West. While admitting Turner's influence on American historians, for example, Patricia Nelson Limerick, perhaps the most vocal Turner critic, finds Turner historically unusable because his concepts ignore Native Americans, privilege Anglo-Americans to the exclusion of most other ethnic groups, and place artificial chronological boundaries in his concept of a frontier. Turner's influence "almost ruined Western history," she concludes (Limerick 72-75). Yet, despite such attacks by academic historians, Turner's perception of the American frontier continues to prevail in the American public imagination. Even Limerick admits that in the discussion among historians about Turner's frontier, "the public is paying no attention to us" (Limerick 79).

Turner's essay continues to be influential because it articulates, in Warren Susman's words, "the official American ideology" (qtd. in Grossman 2). Americans want to believe in their uniqueness as a culture, historian Richard White points out, and Turner, in rich, poetic prose, defined what being an American meant and provided a rich, exciting explanation of how it all came to be in a "clean, dramatic and compelling narrative" (White 11-13). Turner's arguments about Americanization taking place on the sparsely populated, primitive frontier where values of individualism, practicality, and egalitarian democracy could thrive in open, clean space has been a pattern of belief just too attractive for most Americans to forsake. Whether or not it is literally true seems to hardly matter.

English characters on the frontier must forsake their European culture and embrace a new, unique American identity in order to be happy because Turner's frontier mythos demands that they do so. In most Hollywood narratives, English men and women may be and do anything. In frontier stories, however, we require that they become us. If they refuse, tough luck. As with English Bob in *Unforgiven*, we'll enjoy seeing them kicked out, much as we enjoy imagining their leaving at the end of the Revolutionary War, with their hoity-toity tails between their legs.

Notes

1. There are slight differences between the various versions of *Ruggles of Red Gap*. In some versions, for example, Red Gap is located in Arizona, not Washington State, and the name of Ruggles's restaurant is the U.S. Grille.

2. In Dorothy Johnson's short story, "A Man Called Horse," Morgan is not an English lord but a rich Bostonian. In her version, self-respect is the issue rather than Americanization.

3. The Sun Vow ceremony shown in the film was not in actuality a Sioux ritual. The filmmakers had used George Catlin drawings of a Mandan ceremony as a model. The Mandan were traditional enemies of the Sioux. There were Native American demonstrations against the religious inaccuracies in *A Man Called Horse* when it was initially released.

4. The national origin of Catherine Crocker is never given in the film. In Marilyn Durham's 1972 novel of the same title, Catherine is not English. Sarah Miles's accent in the film clearly suggests her British origins, however. In addition, Miles herself would have been identified by 1973 audiences as an actress specializing in British roles. In 1972, she had played the title role in the very British *Lady Caroline Lamb*, named for a mistress of Lord Byron.

5. Grobart had been married to a Native American woman, Cat Dancing, and he robs a train to obtain money to reclaim his two half-Indian children.

6. The six movies discussed in this article are only a sampling of this pattern. Numerous other examples exist. In both the 1936 and 1992 Hollywood versions of *The Last of the Mohicans*, for instance, the British officer, Major Duncan Heyward, is rejected by the central woman character because she has fallen in love with Hawkeye, the American frontiersman. The contrast between the suitors is made especially explicit in the 1992 film. Heyward's proposal to Cora Munro is based largely on his statement that they would be a grand couple in London society. Cora, on the other hand, is most deeply moved by the lure of the American wilderness. "It is more deeply stirring to my blood," she says, "than any imagining could possibly have been." Hawkeye in the film introduces Cora to this land and is played by the British actor Daniel Day-Lewis, who in a symbolic act of Americanization, has completely lost his English accent. Not surprisingly, at film's end, Heyward, after several acts of haughty incompetence, is dead, and Hawkeye and Cora head into the forest, undoubtedly to begin a frontier American family.

7. In 1933, for example, two years before McCarey's *Ruggles of Red Gap*, the film *Cavalcade*, with an all British cast, featuring two families of Londoners over two generations, presented a wide variety of English characters. The film was a huge box-office success in the United States and won the Academy Award as Best Picture of the Year.

Works Cited

Billington, Ray Allen. *The Frontier Thesis: Valid Interpretation of American History?* New York: Holt, 1966.

Durham, Marilyn. *The Man Who Loved Cat Dancing.* New York: Harcourt, 1972.

Grossman, James R., ed. *The Frontier in American Culture.* Berkeley: U of California P, 1994.

Johnson, Dorothy. "A Man Called Horse." *The Second Reel West.* Ed. Bill Pronzini and Martin H. Greenberg. Garden City: Doubleday, 1985. 98-110.

Limerick, Patricia Nelson. "The Adventures of the Frontier in the Twentieth Century." *The Frontier in American Culture.* Ed. James R. Grossman. Berkeley: U of California P, 1994. 66-102.

Turner, Frederick Jackson. "The Significance of the Frontier in American History." *Frontier and Section: Selected Essays of Frederick Jackson Turner.* Ed. Ray Allen Billington. Englewood Cliffs: Prentice-Hall, 1961.

White, Richard. "Frederick Jackson Turner and Buffalo Bill." *The Frontier in American Culture.* Ed. James R. Grossman. Berkeley: U of California P, 1994. 6-65.

Wilson, Harry Leon. *Ruggles of Red Gap.* Garden City: Doubleday, 1915.

12

Hollywood's Disabled Vietnam Vet Revisited

Martin F. Norden

As I observed in my 1985 essay "The Disabled Vietnam Veteran in Hollywood Films," American movie stereotypes of Vietnam veterans as junkies and sadistic killers finally began giving way during the late 1970s and early 1980s to more sensitive depictions, led by a particular subgroup: those veterans disabled by the war. The reasons are complex, but generally speaking, disabled vets as constructed in such films as *Coming Home* (1978), *The Deer Hunter* (1978), *Cutter's Way* (1981), and *Modern Problems* (1981) avoided the gross characterizations Hollywood ascribed to their able-bodied brethren.[1] Appearing just a few years after the war's conclusion, these films represented a major step forward in disability depictions as they grappled with such issues as rehabilitation, access, sexuality, the redirection of bitterness and rage, and changing notions of heroism.

During the late 1980s and early 1990s, Hollywood created another cycle of movies that represented disabled Vietnam vets. This round included *Suspect* (1987), *Blind Fury* (1989), *Born on the Fourth of July* (1989), *Scent of a Woman* (1992), and *Forrest Gump* (1994), and it is worth asking if these films, some with exceptionally high profiles, have followed the lead of the earlier ones. I concluded my original article with the thought that "as we continue to gain chronological distance on the conflict that tore apart U.S. society like no other since the Civil War, we will hopefully see other films that will build on the reasonably realistic portrayals of disabled Vietnam veterans that Hollywood has offered thus far" (23). Has this happened? What in particular have been the concerns of these more recent films as they pertain to disabled veterans and how do they connect with the others? In a sense, this current essay picks up where my earlier one left off by assessing such items as the factors that effectively signaled the end of the first cycle, the second set of films themselves, and the circumstances that led to their creation. My hope is that this investigation will lead to a better understanding of the evolving relationship of mainstream society and its disabled Vietnam-vet population as constructed in the movies.

179

In a number of respects, 1978 seemed to be shaping up as the year of Hollywood's disabled Vietnam veteran. Not only did the two key films of the first cycle, *Coming Home* and *The Deer Hunter*, appear then but several other related projects were in the works: *Born on the Fourth of July* and *Inside Moves* (1980). A brief reassessment of this period should prove a helpful prelude to our study of the films of the late 1980s and early 1990s. As we shall see, the respective fates of the two films noted above suggest that a general moviemaker antipathy toward disabled vets was already underway even as *Coming Home* and *The Deer Hunter* were scoring their successes.

The first of these film projects was related directly to the much-discussed *Coming Home*,[2] and it is worth briefly tracing the overlap of these productions. After wrangling with Nancy Dowd over her commissioned but unusable script, *Coming Home* producers Jane Fonda and Bruce Gilbert found themselves in over their heads as neophyte movie executives and turned to the producer-director-writer team behind the successful 1969 movie *Midnight Cowboy*—Jerome Hellman, John Schlesinger, and Waldo Salt—to help bring their movie to fruition. Though Schlesinger would soon leave the project (a Briton, he felt the material would be better handled by an American), Hellman and Salt became integrally involved in the project. They cast aside much of Dowd's work except for its central concept, with Salt eventually spending more than a year and $50,000 of his own money interviewing hundreds of disabled Vietnam vets in his quest to make *Coming Home* as authentic as possible.

Though busy writing a screenplay draft, Salt found the time to work closely with one of his interview subjects: an erstwhile gung-ho soldier paralyzed from the mid-chest down named Ron Kovic. Something of a father figure for the antiwar veteran (he was then in his early sixties while Kovic was around thirty), Salt helped him through a project that would soon become Kovic's autobiographical book, *Born on the Fourth of July*. "Ron was floundering and looking for a way out of his own problems," noted Hellman. "He frequently stayed at Salt's suite at the Chateau Marmont [in Los Angeles] and got emotional as well as literary support from him" (qtd. in Collier 253). Salt and Hellman had even lined up Kovic as a technical adviser for their film, but the vet had other plans; after finishing *Born on the Fourth of July* he sold its movie rights to Al Pacino, an actor coming off star turns in *Serpico* (1973), *The Godfather Part II* (1974), and *Dog Day Afternoon* (1975) and whose on-screen persona, by turns brooding and explosive, seemed well suited to the literary self-portrait Kovic had developed. Kovic thought the movie would be further enhanced by the work of Oliver Stone, a screenwriter and fellow Vietnam veteran who had recovered from several severe war injuries.

Luke Martin (Jon Voight) and Sally Hyde (Jane Fonda) in one of Holywood's seminal disabled Vietnam veteran films, *Coming Home*. (Courtesy of the Museum of Modern Art/Film Stills Archive)

Unfortunately for all concerned, the film's financial backers developed a case of cold feet. With William Friedkin slated to direct, Stone to write, and Pacino to star, the moviemakers were a mere four days away from the start of principal photography in 1978 when the funding for the film fell through, dashing their hopes. Though it seemed that Stone might be able to get the project moving again after a burst of attention in 1979 for his *Midnight Express* screenwriting Oscar, he hit a low point with an ill-fated exercise in psychological horror called *The Hand* (1981) two years later. "I'd been hot, and all of a sudden I was cold," Stone said. "*The Hand* kind of buried me" (Stone, "My Brilliant Career" 60). Kovic was obviously chagrined by the turn of events but had some cause for optimism. "At the time, Oliver promised me, 'If I ever get the opportunity, if I'm ever able to break through as a director, I'll come back for you, Ronnie,' " he remembered (qtd. in Seidenberg 56).

Another film that went into development in 1978 had quite a different outcome. Producer Robert Evans had just purchased the movie rights to a novel published that year by Tod Walton called *Inside Moves,* about a Vietnam vet named Roary who notes his disabled status point-blank on the book's first page: "I got hurt in Vietnam. This land mine blew a hole in my upper back and destroyed some vertabrae and part of my spinal cord and part of my brain." The person scheduled to direct, Richard Donner, felt uneasy about the book's Vietnam dimension, however—"I didn't want to do another Nam story, really," he said ("Dialogue" 58)—and while he went off to Great Britain to direct the epic fantasy *Superman* (1978) Evans had screenwriters Valerie Curtin and Barry Levinson eliminate all reference to Vietnam in their adapted script. When the movie, also called *Inside Moves,* finally appeared in 1980, the lead character (played by John Savage, who coincidentally had played the role of *The Deer Hunter*'s severely disabled veteran) had been converted into a depressed young civilian who becomes permanently disabled after a suicide attempt off a tall building.

Hollywood ambivalence toward disabled Vietnam vets only increased with the production of the problem-fraught *Cutter's Way* and *Modern Problems* and their release in 1981. Though *Coming Home* and *The Deer Hunter* had scored well at the box office and on Oscar night several years before, these other films, mishandled in various ways, left only a minimal footprint at the box office. Realizing that films with disabled Vietnam veterans were no longer hot box-office commodities, at least for the time being, Hollywood backed off from the topic for several years.[3]

After a rather lengthy dry spell, the second round of disabled Vietnam vet films began on a highly tentative note in 1987 with *Suspect,* directed on location in Washington, D.C., by Peter Yates from a screen-play by Eric Roth. Irish actor Liam Neeson played Carl Wayne Anderson, a homeless Vietnam vet who lost his hearing and speech during the war and who is accused of killing a D.C. office worker. A major force behind the movie was Cher, who starred as Kathleen Riley, the public defender assigned to the deafened vet's case. "A script has to mean something to me," she said. "I loved the idea that the story was about a homeless man, and I thought it said something about the condition of homelessness. And I felt like Kathleen and the homeless man, they're the same kind of char-acter, people who are caught in the human condition doing the best they can" (qtd. in Weber 56). Despite Cher's pronouncements and the fact that he is the movie's title character, however, Carl distinctly plays a support-ing role to his lawyer and a smooth-talking jury member (Dennis Quaid) who illicitly work together to solve the crime of which the vet has been accused. Yates and Roth perceived the film primarily as a vehicle for Cher. As Roth noted, the movie pivots on her performance: "Others in *Suspect* are better actors, maybe, but it's her persona that shines through" (qtd. in Weber 56). Though Neeson's performance benefited greatly from his work with audiological specialists at Gallaudet University and Viet-nam veterans who had suffered hearing loss (Norden, *Cinema* 299), most critics ignored his characterization or mentioned it only in passing. Sheila Benson of the *Los Angeles Times* was one of the more generous with this brief description: "Working entirely without dialogue, Neeson's tragic, homeless vet becomes a fully fleshed-out and powerful character" (9). The relationship of his impairment to Vietnam, and all the ramifications arising therefrom, went largely unacknowledged.

Blind Fury (1989), a movie produced two years later, elevated its disabled Vietnam vet to main-character status but the result was hardly an improvement. Starring Rutger Hauer as Nick Parker, a soldier blinded in battle twenty years prior to the film's main narrative, *Blind Fury* pre-sents its vet as a seer-like figure given to uttering such quasi-profundities as "Unreasonable men make life so difficult." Aided by the able-bodied son of a Vietnam comrade, the mystical and violent Nick uses a preter-natural ability for wielding a sword to wreak vengeance on assorted criminals who have violated his moral code. To illustrate Nick's adept-ness with his weapon, the movie actually shows him slicing off a crimi-nal's eyebrows at one point. Loaded with verbal cheap shots ("I'm gonna put that blind man in a wheelchair" snarls one crook, while another tauntingly labels Nick "a walking advertisement for hiring the handi-capped"), *Blind Fury* seldom rises above the level of a comic book and proved so problematic that its distributor, Tri-Star Pictures, decided to release the film directly to video and pay-cable.

If Hollywood filmmakers were not exactly plumbing the depths of the disabled Vietnam vet experience during this time, the topic made a roaring comeback in late 1989 in the form of the long-delayed *Born on the Fourth of July*.[4] After hitting it big with *Platoon* (1986) and *Wall Street* (1987), Oliver Stone gained the clout necessary to revive the Ron Kovic project that had been languishing for more than a decade. "After *Platoon* I knew that Oliver could have done any film that he wanted to do," recalled Kovic. "I got a phone call and he said, 'Ronnie, come to New York. We're gonna go out to Massapequa. We're gonna try to make this film again'" (Kovic, *Today Show*).

After securing stable financing with co-producer A. Kitman Ho through a distribution deal with Universal, Stone began working on a new screenplay with Kovic (the two eventually shared screenplay credit on the final film) and set about casting the newly reborn *Born on the Fourth of July*. For the central character, Stone hired a young actor who seemed an unlikely selection at first: Tom Cruise, prince of Hollywood glamor-boy roles. "I chose Tom because he was the closest to Ron Kovic in spirit," he said. "I sensed that they came from the same working-class Catholic background and had a similarly troubled family history. They certainly had the same drive, the same hunger to achieve, to be the best, to prove something. Like Ron too, Tom is wound real tight. And what's wrong with that?" Kovic, too, was impressed. "I was amazed the first day I met Tom Cruise," he said. "I was surprised how great an understanding he had of what I had gone through: my suffering, my hurt, the difficulties that I had to overcome to be in this world after Vietnam" (Kovic, *Today Show*). Stone had Cruise work with a wheelchair on and off for a year in preparation for the part and found him quite willing to do almost anything to capture the essence of Kovic's character. "I put a lot of pressure on Tom," he said. "Maybe too much. I wanted him to read more, visit more hospitals. I wanted him to spend time in that chair, to really feel it. He went to boot camp twice, and I didn't want his foxhole dug by his cousin. At one point I talked him into injecting himself with a solution that would have totally paralyzed him for two days. Then the insurance company—the killer of all experience—said no because there was a slight chance that Tom would have ended up permanently paralyzed. But the point is, he was willing to do it" (qtd. in Corliss 79).

Shot mostly around Dallas and in the Philippines, *Born on the Fourth of July* poignantly details the stages of Ron's life over a twenty-five-year period: his youth in Massapequa, Long Island; his service in Vietnam that included an accidental killing of a fellow American and ended when a bullet severed his spine; a soul-shattering trip to Mexico; his rejection of United States policy in Vietnam and forcible ejection from the Republican National Convention in 1972; and his triumphant speech at the 1976 Democratic convention. Ron's transformation from hawkish superpatriot to impassioned war protestor, the movie's key narrative element, was a process that in real life took years. "Ron, when he came back from the war, was still very prowar," said Stone. "I mean, we didn't make it easy: that just because he got shot [and then used] a wheelchair that he changed overnight. It wasn't that easy. It took four, five years for him to deconstruct his mind, and to change the mind, to go from one bias to the other bias" (Stone, *Today Show*). The filmmakers did offer a bit of foreshadowing, however, through a tip of the hat to a famous antiwar author and filmmaker; during the scene in which a doctor tells Ron he'll never walk again, the camera glides over to a copy of Dalton Trumbo's *Johnny Got His Gun* on a tray near the vet's bed.

Though it does not shrink from such issues as the sexuality of paraplegics and prejudice against wheelchair users (Ron travels to a Mexican brothel that caters to injured veterans, for instance, while a security guard at the Republican convention dumps him out of his vehicle, an act that fails to diminish its user's resolve), the movie like its spiritual twin *Coming Home* gradually de-emphasizes the lead character's impaired mobility in favor of other dimensions of his life, particularly his antiwar activities. Ron comes across as a complete human being, not one defined solely in terms of a disability, and it's a quality strongly enhanced by the work of Stone's cinematographer, Robert Richardson. Though the highly mobile, often dizzying camerawork does include a few brief objectifying shots of Ron (mainly from his mother's and girlfriend's perspectives), they are far outweighed by the numerous low camera angles from the vet's point of view, low-angle shots that bestow a sense of heroism on him, and frequent tight close-ups of his face. These shots strongly encourage members of the audience to identify with Ron and help them understand the range of his experiences and emotions.

The film's symbolic dimensions further inspire the audience to look beyond Ron's use of a wheelchair. He and the United States were coincidentally "born" on the same day, and the sense of Ron-as-America from the 1950s to the 1970s is central to both the autobiography and the movie. As Cruise pointed out, *Born on the Fourth of July* is more than a personal, coming-to-terms kind of story: "The film isn't about a man in a wheelchair. [It's about] the country, what it went through, was, became. You know, an invalid. . . . It was a crippling time for this country, and you had to get beyond this man and a chair" (Cruise, *Today Show*).

For Kovic, the film represented the chance to make people aware of the terrible legacy of Vietnam and the importance of never getting involved in something like that again. "When Oliver called me up and told me that we were going to do this film again, it was like being given a second life," he said. "I could never quite reconcile being in this wheelchair after Vietnam. I could never quite understand how my sacrifice could have any kind of meaning at all. Working on the script with Oliver was the first time that I began to understand that my sacrifice, my paralysis, the difficulties, the frustrations, the impossibilities of each and every day would now be for something very valuable, something that would help protect the young people of this country from having to go through what I went through" (qtd. in Seidenberg 28).

With its power, sensitivity, and willingness to confront controversial (or ignored) issues, *Born on the Fourth of July* represents a milestone in the depiction of disabled veterans, but subsequent films did little beyond exploiting some long-standing disability stereotypes. Such was the case of *Scent of a Woman*, a 1992 movie written by Bo Goldman and produced and directed by Martin Brest. Al Pacino, who had lost out on the opportunity to play a disabled Vietnam vet in the aborted *Born on the Fourth of July* project in 1978, got a second chance by playing Lt. Colonel Frank Slade, an Army career officer accidently blinded in a stunt with a grenade after being passed over for promotion. He proclaims himself "just your average blind man," and from Hollywood's perspective, he is just that; highly embittered and verbally abusive, Frank lives in an isolated, alcoholic, venomous "splendor" in a shed behind his niece's home in New Hampshire. He soon encounters an able-bodied caretaker with problems of his own: Charlie Simms (Chris O'Donnell), a well-scrubbed prep-school student who faces possible expulsion and the loss of a Harvard scholarship if he doesn't inform on some classmates. The unlikely two become mutually helpful buddies, but not until after Frank tricks the youth into accompanying him to New York where he plans to rent an expensive hotel room, enjoy an extravagant meal, make love to a "top of the line" prostitute, and then kill himself. *Scent of a Woman* is replete with attributes that disability activists have long fought against, particularly its equation of disability with bitterness and utter despair. (After Charlie stops Frank from committing suicide near the end of the film and tells him to get on with his life, Frank responds: "What life? I got no life! I'm in the dark here. D'ya understand? I'm in the dark!") In the tradition of so many other movies with blind characters— *Blind Fury* very much among them—it also includes the near-obligatory and entirely tasteless scene of a blind person driving a vehicle. Despite Pacino's Oscar-winning performance as Frank, *Scent of a Woman* left disabled audience members extremely divided over its merits.[5]

The substantial dollops of bitterness and rage that characterize *Scent of a Woman*'s veteran also served as major defining factors for an

Army officer severely wounded in a Vietnamese ambush in *Forrest Gump* (1994), a highly episodic movie based on the like-titled novel by Winston Groom. Scripted by *Suspect*'s Eric Roth and directed by Robert Zemeckis, *Gump* spans about thirty years and focuses mainly on the titular figure (Tom Hanks), a young man with an IQ of 75 who grows up in Alabama during the 1950s. An idiot-hero in the tradition of Voltaire's Candide, Forrest eventually ends up a soldier in Vietnam after a series of highly improbable incidents and later earns the Congressional Medal of Honor for inadvertently saving half his unit during an attack. One of those rescued is his commanding officer, Lieutenant Dan Taylor (Gary Sinise), whose loss of both legs during the ambush had been foreshadowed in a rather mean-spirited way. (While admonishing his charges to change their socks frequently, he had observed that "the Mekong will eat a grunt's feet right off his legs.") Dan becomes a most embittered soul after his disablement, but Forrest redeems him after both have returned to civilian life; Forrest keeps a promise made to a dead war buddy to run a shrimping boat on the Gulf Coast and, in the interest of helping Dan, signs him on as his first mate.

Though so many of the film's commentators tended to dwell on the special-effects trickery that allowed the able-bodied Sinise to look like a double amputee, others observed that the emotional Dan serves as an effective foil to the bland central character well beyond the duo's service in Vietnam. "His life and Forrest's continue to intersect as the film unfolds," noted Bernard Weinraub of the *New York Times,* "and in contrast to the stoic Forrest, the big-hearted, slightly crazy Army officer goes through a series of intense emotions—rage, despair, bitterness, resignation" (1). Director Zemeckis said he "saw characters [in *Forrest Gump*] as metaphors for different aspects of the American character" (qtd. in Adler 59), and he clearly wanted to use Dan to represent its darker side. Wishing to keep Forrest an innocent at all costs, Zemeckis and his *Gump* colleagues ascribed the majority of the Vietnam "baggage" to the former lieutenant. As a *Boston Globe* critic noted, the character of Dan "begins with the usual resentment and anger, but becomes more than just another of the alienated survivors we've been seeing ever since Marlon Brando's disabled World War II vet in *The Men*. Because Sinise's character carries the tragic vision and rueful awareness of the Vietnamese aftermath, Hanks's Forrest Gump can remain innocent and not affront us with his innocence" (*Forrest Gump* 73).

What does this new round of disabled Vietnam veteran films tell us? It is a mixed bag of portrayals to be sure, with the best and the worst of the lot—*Born on the Fourth of July* and *Blind Fury*—coincidentally appearing the same year. These films continue a tradition established by the earlier cycle by exhibiting a set of attitudes markedly different from the ones present in the disabled-vet films of World War II. In movies such as *Pride of the Marines* (1945), *The Best Years of Our Lives* (1946), *Till the End of Time* (1946), *The Men* (1950), and *Bright Victory* (1951), the vets are endowed with a mantle of heroism and members of mainstream society are generally portrayed as sympathetic to them and share in their victory when the vets inevitably triumph over the physical and psychological problems. These qualities—very much related to that special post–World War II *Zeitgeist*—are conspicuously underrepresented (if present at all) in both sets of Vietnam vet films. We are treated instead to a parade of extreme social misfits who attempt to maneuver through a society by turns indifferent and hostile.

Other concerns go beyond war-related issues to the revival of a long-standing cliché about disabled people in general: that they are forever boiling over with bitterness and rage. As these movies amply demonstrate, moviemakers continue to define their disabled characters in terms of such qualities. Indeed, all of the films discussed in this essay depict their vets with varying degrees of resentfulness and anger or show them having difficulty containing their violent tendencies. One might argue that such powerful emotions make for greater dramatic tension, but it's also clear that this assumption reflects a deeply entrenched able-bodied bias. As social scientist Nancy Weinberg has observed, "The general public tends to believe that people with physical disabilities have suffered a terrible tragedy and are forever bitter about their misfortune" (141). It's a view often at odds with the way disabled people themselves feel about their disabilities and adapt to them.

Conspicuously linked with this stereotype is the idea of having an able-bodied peer or mentor "save" the disabled character. *Boston Globe* reporter Betsy Lehman summed up this point well by noting that "leaders of the disability rights movement say that this theme—an enraged and bitter disabled person who must be redeemed by an able-bodied companion—is depicted again and again in movies, books, plays and television shows. It's a depiction, they say, that has real-life implications, isolating the disabled even more from the able-bodied, and subtlely [sic] blaming the disabled for the frustrations they experience" (29). Without question, the movies discussed in this essay hinge on this antiquated notion.

As bleak as all of this may seem, there is at least one positive aspect of these films worth noting: most have followed the lead of the earlier disabled Vietnam vet films by going beyond the basic stereotypes to show the vets channeling their energies and emotions into activities other than "overcoming" their disabilities. Ron Kovic leads a protest against government policies at the 1972 Republican National Convention, for example, while Frank Slade goes to bat for his young friend Charlie at a prep-school disciplinary hearing, and in both instances the characters' disabled status has become incidental to the narrative. In my humble view, this is precisely the direction that movie depictions of disability should take, and perhaps the Americans with Disabilities Act—passed in 1990 and implemented in stages throughout the early 1990s—will serve as an impetus for continuing such depictions. It is too early to assess the impact of the ADA on moviemaker attitudes as of this writing, but as the act's positive effects continue to be felt across the country, Hollywood will—it is hoped—continue to develop disability depictions that move beyond the age-old stereotypes to emphasize the characters' humanity and convictions.

Notes

1. Quart and Auster have provided a lead by suggesting that the severely injured vets may have been "perceived by others as bearing the stigma of guilt for the whole society" (31).

2. See Norden, "Disabled," for an overview of the movie's narrative.

3. For articles on the content and troubled history, respectively, of *Cutter's Way*, see Norden, "Portrait," and Norden, *"Cutter's Way."*

4. Additional insights into this provocative film may be found in Lipkin (183-86).

5. For a sense of the varying reactions of disability activists to this film, see Lehman (29, 31).

Works Cited

Adler, Jerry. "'Tis a Gift to Be Simple." *Newsweek* 1 Aug. 1994: 58-59.

Benson, Sheila. Rev. of *Suspect* . *Los Angeles Times* 22 Oct. 1987, sec. 6: 9.

Collier, Peter. *The Fondas: A Hollywood Dynasty.* New York: Putnam, 1991.

Corliss, Richard. "Tom Terrific." *Time* 25 Dec. 1989: 74-79.

Cruise, Tom. *Today Show* interview. NBC-TV 19 Dec. 1989.

"Dialogue on Film: Richard Donner." *American Film* May 1981: 57-63.

Rev. of *Forrest Gump. Boston Globe* 6 July 1994: 69, 73.

Kovic, Ron. *Today Show* interview. NBC-TV 21 Dec. 1989.

Lehman, Betsy A. "The Hurtful Stereotypes About the Disabled." *Boston Globe*
     5 Apr. 1993: 29, 31.

Lipkin, Steve. "The Object Realm of the Vietnam War Film." *Beyond the Stars 3: The Material World in American Popular Film.* Ed. Paul Loukides and Linda K. Fuller. Bowling Green, OH: Bowling Green State University Press, 1993. 175-86.

Norden, Martin F. *The Cinema of Isolation: A History of Physical Disability in the Movies.* New Brunswick: Rutgers UP, 1994.

——. "*Cutter's Way* and the Problem of Distributional Censorship." *CommOddities: A Journal of Communication & Culture* 1 (Apr. 1994): 53-58.

——. "The Disabled Vietnam Veteran in Hollywood Films." *Journal of Popular Film and Television* 13 (Spring 1985): 16-23.

——. "Portrait of a Disabled Vietnam Veteran: Alex Cutter of *Cutter's Way.*" *From Hanoi to Hollywood: The Vietnam War in American Film.* Ed. Linda Dittmar and Gene Michaud. New Brunswick: Rutgers UP, 1990. 217-25.

Quart, Leonard, and Albert Auster. "The Wounded Vet in Postwar Film." *Social Policy* 13 (Fall 1982): 24-31.

Seidenberg, Robert. "To Hell and Back." *American Film* Jan. 1990: 28-31, 56.

Stone, Oliver. "My Brilliant Career." *Time* 26 Jan. 1987: 60.

——. *Today Show* interview. NBC-TV 22 Dec. 1989.

Weber, Bruce. "Cher's Next Act." *New York Times Magazine* 18 Oct. 1987: 42-46+.

Weinberg, Nancy. "Another Perspective: Attitudes of Persons with Disabilities." *Attitudes Toward Persons with Disabilities.* Ed. Harold E. Yuker. New York: Springer, 1988. 141-53.

Weinraub, Bernard. "A Takeoff Fueled by Passion." *New York Times* 27 July 1994, sec. C: 1, 7.

13

The Role of Television News
in Portraying People Living with AIDS

Rod Carveth

In February 1995, Greg Louganis, winner of the 1984 and 1988 Olympic gold medals in diving, announced in an interview with ABC's *20/20* (February 24, 1995) that he knew he was infected with Human Immunodeficiency Virus (HIV) before the 1988 Summer Olympics in Seoul, South Korea. Since then, Louganis's infection has developed into Acquired Immune Deficiency Syndrome (AIDS). Louganis said he was very concerned when he hit his head on the board during a dive and shed blood in the pool. Louganis did not inform the doctor, who stitched up the two-inch cut without wearing protective gloves, that he was HIV-positive.

Network and tabloid news coverage of Louganis's announcement shared a common visual theme in presenting the story—video of the dive in which Louganis hit his head. What is also significant was what was not covered. What is missing from the story is his abusive stepfather, his dyslexia, the ugly taunts Louganis endured because of his Samoan heritage, his suffering from clinical depression, and three suicide attempts (Sandomir; Wilbon). Instead TV news coverage focused on the dramatic image of Louganis hitting his head on the diving board and his failure to protect his doctor from being infected with an almost certainly fatal disease.

Since the early 1960s when household television ownership passed the 90 percent mark in this country, Roper Poll results have revealed that Americans receive most of their news from television. Roper respondents generally indicate that they find TV news more believable than newspapers. What is troubling about these findings is that the typical TV network nightly newscast contains only about 22 minutes of actual news (minus time for commercials and other nonprogram material). Studies also show that viewers have great difficulty remembering what they see and hear on TV news (Robinson and Levy). For example, researchers found that the more viewers relied on TV for news of the Persian Gulf

Conflict, the less they knew about the basic facts of the conflict (Lewis, Jhally, and Morgan).

News coverage of Human Immunodeficiency Virus (HIV) and Acquired Immune Deficiency Syndrome (AIDS) has often been criticized (e.g., Shilts), but its importance in defining this disease and shaping society's response cannot be challenged. News organizations help determine how and when AIDS reaches the public agenda (Dearing and Rogers; Hertog and Fan; Hertog, Finnegan & Kahn). News organizations are also the principal sources of information about AIDS for most people worldwide.

Thus, the media possess an enormous responsibility. If they inform their audiences accurately about HIV and how it is and is not transmitted, the media can enable individuals to reduce their risk of infection. Conversely, if the media provide ambiguous or inaccurate information, they may contribute to placing people at increased risk of AIDS.

Evolution of Coverage of AIDS

AIDS may be the first national "media disease." Previous epidemics—especially cholera and polio—have attracted journalists' attention, but this coverage has tended to be more localized and limited in scope (Berridge). AIDS has not only triggered an unprecedented volume of news media reports but is the first epidemic of the television age.

One reason for the volume of this coverage is that AIDS is presently incurable, and treatments for slowing the progression of the disease are limited. A second reason for such coverage is that the methods of combatting the disease involve confronting (and overcoming resistance to confronting) potentially uncomfortable aspects of our social identity involving gender, sexuality, and race/ethnicity. Finally, AIDS is a disease that involves both sex and death, two primary ingredients of sensationalist news copy.

Though journalists have responded to the epidemic by reporting AIDS with much greater frequency than other diseases, they have also tended to report about AIDS within their own boundaries and prejudices. For example, *Newsweek* first reported on the disease because the reporter's brother had AIDS, not because of the significance of the disease or its "victims" (Kinsella). Thus, AIDS first came into the news as a problem of "others"—gay men, foreigners (Haitians), intravenous drug abusers—rather than as an urgent threat to all.

A number of analyses of news coverage of AIDS have been conducted; however, many of these have been limited in scope. Only a few studies have examined the content of news reports in a systematic and comprehensive fashion. Of these, the studies by Rogers et al., Konick, and Colby and Cook are the most useful because together they describe and clarify the phases of development of news coverage of AIDS.

Taken together, these studies reveal that network news reporting of AIDS tended to occur in cycles. For example, the hallmarks of reporting in the early 1980s were ignorance, denial and moral panic (Colby and Cook). In the early 1980s, network television news virtually ignored the disease. For the first two years of the AIDS epidemic—1980-1981 when the disease was still referred to as GRID, or Gay Related Immune Deficiency Syndrome—no network news coverage existed on the malady. Only six network news stories appeared in all of 1982.

Coverage did rise dramatically in June 1983 due to two factors. First, there were the revelations that in addition to gay males, heterosexual individuals—hemophiliacs, intravenous drug abusers, and children—were contracting the disease. Second, reports from the Centers for Disease Control documented the exponential climb in AIDS cases. Most of the network news stories focused on the "AIDS hysteria" that this mysterious malady brought about. As Colby and Cook argue, however, network news coverage was not sensationalistic. Rather, TV network news tried to reassure the public that scientific progress was being made in controlling the epidemic. However, the progress being focused on in the news stories was not the search for a treatment for those already afflicted with AIDS (that is, gays) but for a vaccine for "everyone" (that is, heterosexuals).

After the temporary rise in network news coverage in 1983, coverage slowed until 1985, thus completing the first cycle of network news reporting on AIDS. The second cycle began with the reported illness and subsequent death of film (*Giant, Pillow Talk, Seconds*) and television (*McMillan and Wife*) star Rock Hudson. His 1985 death signaled an alarm because, even though Hudson had long been rumored to be gay, he portrayed the macho, heterosexual matinee idol, so esteemed by the societal mainstream. Overwhelming media attention focused on AIDS in the aftermath of Hudson's death. Each network began examining the disease in detail on nightly newscasts and special reports (one of the first was a 1985 NBC special entitled *Life, Death, AIDS*), with the principal message being how the average audience member (seen as a white, non-drug-abusing heterosexual) might contract and/or prevent AIDS through self-precautions.

Though the coverage spawned by Hudson's death helped legitimize AIDS as a news story, this second cycle of AIDS coverage differed from the first in three ways. First, there were far more stories about AIDS that aired on the three major networks. The coverage was almost frenetic, in which virtually any event or scientific development was seen as news.

While reporters' knowledge of the subject was improving, readers and viewers were presented a roller coaster of alternating optimism and despair, as claims of breakthroughs mixed with apocalyptic projections of HIV infections and death rates.

Second, the coverage tended to be more event-driven rather than topic-driven (Colby and Cook 236-39). After the first few AIDS stories, rather than airing new aspects of continuing stories about AIDS, reporters more often relied on "pseudo-events"—news conferences, protests, etc.—to tell their stories. As a result, authorities such as governmental officials and noted doctors became crucial sources for information and opinions on AIDS.

Third, the thematic content of stories presented varied widely. Konick (1994) identified eight major network news story themes: AIDS as policy issue (22 percent), AIDS as plague (20 percent), uncaring society (20 percent), AIDS as scientists' fight (8 percent), AIDS as a disease of non-mainstream "fringe" groups (8 percent), caring society (8 percent), times are getting better (3 percent) and AIDS as business opportunity (2 percent). Konick found that the thematic content of news stories varied according to the eras that they aired. For example, the number of stories about AIDS as a policy issue and AIDS as scientists' fight increased during 1987, while stories about the uncaring society declined.

The third phase, beginning around 1989, has seen a slight decline in the volume of reporting that nevertheless leaves AIDS higher on the public agenda than other health issues. There is now a tendency to report AIDS as another running story in the policy arena. News organizations plan their reporting around prearranged events such as the international AIDS conferences and World AIDS Day.

Within each of these broad phases of AIDS coverage, there have been variations. Television news organizations have given AIDS saturation coverage only intermittently, usually when the disease looked less like a disease of "others" and more like a threat to the general public. Thus, reporting has tended to be cyclical, with peaks of coverage interspersed with longer periods of routine, more reactive reporting. For example, news peaked worldwide in 1985, when actor Rock Hudson sought treatment for AIDS and the disease first became a real issue to most Americans. News coverage peaked again in late 1991, when National Basketball Association star Magic Johnson announced he was HIV-infected.

AIDS is certainly not unique in its cyclical coverage. The pattern appears to be a feature of the media's response to many policy stories and is known as the issue attention cycle (Berridge). For example, coverage of global warming has tended to rise and fall; each rise comes when the media find a new angle. With AIDS, as with other subjects, the cycle is driven by news values and the agenda of the media, rather than by actual trends. For example, published research into HIV has increased consistently, first sharply, and now much more slowly, ever since 1981. News coverage has been much more erratic, however; the volume of reporting has not matched trends in the numbers of people affected by the pandemic.

The Present Study

The present investigation seeks to update the work of aforementioned authors. In order to explore the type of coverage presented by network news, an examination of network news stories appearing on ABC, CBS and NBC from January 1990 to October 1994 was conducted.

Data was obtained by accessing online the Network News Archive at Vanderbilt University. The first stage of analysis was to explore the frequency and pattern of coverage during the nearly five years. The number of stories per month for the period is illustrated in Figure 1.

As Figure 1 demonstrates, network news coverage about AIDS is characterized by both predictable and unpredictable peaks and valleys. For example, the number of AIDS stories predictably increases each June or July to coincide with news coming out of the annual international AIDS conference. Unpredictable, breaking events also spur coverage. For example, the number of AIDS stories peaked in June and again in November of 1991. The reason for the June increase was due to the

Figure 1

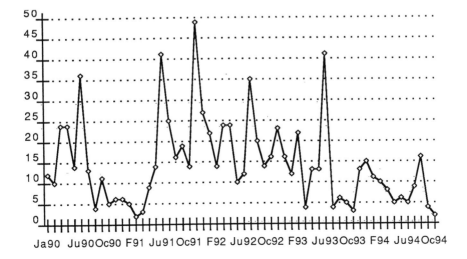

Ja90 Ju90Oc90 F91 Ju91Oc91 F92 Ju92Oc92 F93 Ju93Oc93 F94 Ju94Oc94

charge by Kimberly Bergalis that her HIV-positive dentist, Dr. David Acer, had infected her with the virus. News coverage peaked again in November 1991, when National Basketball Association star Magic Johnson announced he was HIV-positive. Johnson made a huge media impact not only in the United States but across the world. Coverage increased again in March-April 1992 due to the revelation, and subsequent confirmation, that tennis star Arthur Ashe had AIDS.

Overall, this analysis revealed that the erratic, cyclical news coverage that characterized network news reporting of AIDS in the 1980s has continued in the 1990s. In fact, from November 1991 to October 1992, there were 261 network news stories. The subject of 50 of these stories was Magic Johnson, and an equal number was devoted to either Kimberly Bergalis or Arthur Ashe.

A more detailed analysis was conducted for stories airing from January 1993 to October 1994 (the last date for which story descriptions were available online). The reason for picking this period was that it was a period of time in which no major media personality revealed s/he was HIV-positive, nor were there any significant breakthroughs in the fight against AIDS.

Each story listed was coded for the date of the broadcast, the network that the story aired on, the type of story, the length of the story, the reporter for the story, and the city where the story originated. Identified were 227 stories. Of these, 151 aired from January 1993 to December 1993, and 76 aired from January 1994 to October 1994.

Few differences were observed for the number of stories aired on the networks; NBC aired slightly more stories during that time period than did ABC or CBS, though the difference was not statistically significant (see Table 1).

Table 1
AIDS Stories Broadcast by Network, 1993-94

	Frequency	Percent
ABC	71	31.3
CBS	73	32.2
NBC	83	36.6
Total	227	100.0

Length of Stories
The length of stories ranged from 10 seconds to six minutes and 10 seconds. The average story length was 1 minute, 51 seconds. Nearly half the stories (45.3 percent) were between 1.5 minutes and 2.5 minutes in length. Over one quarter of the stories 28.6 percent) were 30 seconds or less, and slightly under one quarter (21.7 percent) of the stories were over 2.5 minutes (see Table 2).

There were no statistically significant differences in the length of stories among the three networks. ABC's 71 stories averaged 2 minutes, 4 seconds, CBS's 73 stories averaged 1 minute, 49 seconds and NBC's 83 stories averaged 1 minute, 41 seconds.

Overall, the networks together averaged slightly over 10 stories and 18 minutes per month, or about 6 minutes per network per month.

Story Topics
As seen from Table 3, themes of stories broadcast on AIDS roughly paralleled those of Konick. Of the stories, 50 (22 percent) were about new developments in combatting AIDS, particularly new drugs to fight the disease. Planned events, such as the International AIDS conferences and World AIDS Day were covered in 21 stories. Policy issures were dealt with in 50 stories, though 11 of them were about the formation and appointments to the AIDS Commission. Almost a third of the policy stories, 16, dealt with immigration issues, while 15 dealt with issues of AIDS funding.

Table 2
Length of Network News Stories about AIDS

Story Length (in seconds)	Frequency	Percent
0-30	65	28.6
31-60	3	1.2
61-90	7	2.9
91-120	66	29.1
121-150	37	16.2
151-180	13	5.4
>180	34	15.0

Table 3
Types of Stories Presented on Network News
January 1993 - October 1994

Story Type	Frequency	%
Medical Developments	50	22.0
Special AIDS Events	21	9.2
International AIDS Conferences	18	7.9
World AIDS Day	3	1.3
Policy Stories	50	22.0
AIDS Funding	15	6.6
AIDS Commission	11	4.8
AIDS Programs	2	.9
Immigration	16	7.0
Condoms	6	2.6
Surveys on AIDS Behavior	15	6.6
International	18	7.9
Personalities	22	9.6
Magic Johnson	7	3.1
Arthur Ashe	6	2.6
Miss America	1	.4
Randy Shilts	5	2.2
John Curry	1	.4
Nureyev	2	.9
Contracting AIDS	19	8.4
David Acer	3	1.3
AIDS & Health Workers	2	.9
Doctors & AIDS	2	.9
AIDS Transmission	12	5.3
AIDS Protests	8	3.5
AIDS & Legal Issues	12	5.3
Other	12	4.4
Sports	2	.9
Floods & AIDS	2	.9
Entertainment	3	1.3
AIDS & Religion	2	.9
Benetton Ads	1	.4
AIDS Victims Network	1	.4
Theron Brown	1	.4
Total	227	100.0

Issues surrounding the transmission of AIDS were dealt with in 19 stories,including three stories about Dr. David Acer; 18 stories reviewed AIDS in other countries, though 16 of those stories dealt with blood bank scandals in Germany and France.

Of the 227 stories, only two, about the AIDS Victims Network (an AIDS support service) and about Theron Brown, an HIV-positive person running a youth program, really dealt with people living with AIDS

Reporters

Of the stories surveyed, 82 were reported by the news anchors in the studio (either as "tell" pieces or voice-overs). The remaining 145 stories were reported by 68 different correspondents. Aside from network medical correspondents—ABC's George Strait with 21 reports, NBC's Robert Bazell and Robert Hager with 20 reports, and CBS's Bob Arnot with 17 reports—no other correspondent had more than three stories. While it appears on the one hand that the networks have assigned a variety of correspondents to covering the AIDS crisis, it could be argued that the networks have sacrificed depth of reporting for breadth of reporting.

Location

Eighty-three stories originated from the three various network studios; 34 stories originated from Washington, and 26 came from New York. Therefore, almost two-thirds of the AIDS stories originated from the two network "news capitals." Of the remaining cities, 15 reports came from Berlin (where the 1993 International AIDS conference was held), 9 from San Francisco and eight from Los Angeles. Overall, 80% of all the stories came from five locations: the nation's capital, three of the cities in the United States with the highest number of AIDS cases, and the site of an international AIDS conference. As such, AIDS could be seen as an "urban disease," not one directly affecting viewers in the suburbs and rural areas of the country.

Discussion

Results of this study suggest that network news coverage of AIDS has not changed as it enters the second decade of the disease. Coverage has been dominated by two types of stories: science's unsuccessful quest for a cure, and the impact of AIDS on celebrities, people who are psychologically close to the audience. This may reflect a judgment by network news editors that HIV and AIDS is no longer a novel disease, but a chronic, *routine* one.

Such coverage thus follows two broad themes that parallel what Elizabeth Fee described as the two primary societal reactions to the syphilis outbreak in the early twentieth century: the scientific response and the moral response. While network news coverage of AIDS has focused a great deal of attention in the quest for a cure—the scientific response—reporting those types of stories face certain obstacles. The process of scientific research is complex, slow, and hard for TV news to portray as dramatic. In order to visually portray this process, network news organizations are limited to interviews with scientists (who are not prone to providing easy-to-digest "sound bites"), footage of lab work and graphics.

Stories involving the "moral response" are inherently more dramatic. Such stories present social struggles of "good" versus "bad." For instance, a number of stories about Magic Johnson's announcement that he was HIV-positive noted his admitted promiscuous sexual behavior. The underlying message here is that anyone so sexually careless "deserves" to get the disease. Similarly, the Kimberly Bergalis–Dr. David Acer story focused on the "outrageous" act of a dentist who not only did not inform Bergalis that he was HIV-positive but also was careless enough to transmit the virus to her. The resultant news coverage helped prompt stricter guidelines governing the activities of HIV-positive medical personnel, though the case of Dr. David Acer was the only known case of a member of the medical profession transmitting the virus to a patient. Incidently, a 1994 *60 Minutes* report suggested that Kimberly Bergalis (as well as four other of Acer's patients) acquired HIV from a sexual partner, not Dr. Acer.

It is not surprising to see how network news covered Greg Louganis's announcement that he had AIDS. Among the famous athletes who have said they have HIV or AIDS, Louganis is the first who has talked openly of his homosexuality, having publicly acknowledged this at the 1994 Gay Games in New York City. As a result, there was some question among many people in the TV audience (as well as within TV news organizations) as to Louganis's moral character. The primary angle presented about Louganis's announcement was a question of his character: in not warning his doctor. This issue was visually emphasized by the repeated image of Louganis hitting his head and bleeding in the water. Despite the fact that the chlorine in the pool would have immediately killed HIV, and that both Louganis's personal physician and his coach discouraged him from telling the U.S. Olympic Committee (USOC) about his condition, the dominant theme was that Louganis, a social "other," committed an act of questionable ethics, one with dangerous implications to innocent people (or "us").

Network news coverage of HIV and AIDS has shaded toward a conservative moral tilt. Television news tends to be supportive of the "mainstream" of America. Opinion polls have revealed that the majority of Americans supported the pro-family agenda of Reagan/Bush (and now Gingrich) administrations (Singer, Rogers and Glassman). Hence, by continually portraying an America that is profamily—and, by default—antigay—the networks have established and reinforced the dominant sociopolitical ideology of U.S. society. Thus, the hegemonic process of network television trivializes and symbolically marginalizes societal "deviants" such as gays and injection drug users (IDUs) (Gitlin, 1979; Tuchman, 1978).

The focus of network news on the moral response to the disease may also be in response to competition in an information marketplace. Tabloid news shows such as *A Current Affair* (1986-1991), *Hard Copy* (Feb. 1987–July 1987), and *Inside Edition* (1988-1990) tend to be sensationalistic in their coverage. For these tabloid producers, AIDS is a disease that involves both sex and death, two primary ingredients of sensationalist copy. Therefore, in order to compete for viewers, network news shows have to become more dramatic, both in individual story content and in the types of stories that are covered. For example, during January-October 1994, over twice as much time was devoted to the coverage of the Nancy Kerrigan–Tonya Harding controversy than was devoted to stories about HIV and AIDS. The Kerrigan-Harding story was a classic story of "good" (Kerrigan) versus "evil" (Harding); the impact of the story, however, was largely limited to these two women, while the impact of AIDS affects millions. This suggests that the line between "news" and "entertainment" is becoming increasingly blurred.

Storylines for TV-movies are often ripped from the headlines. The relationship between TV entertainment and TV news, however, goes beyond the made-for-TV movies on the lives of famous celebrities (Rock Hudson, Liberace) or "cause-celebre-ities" (Ryan White). Stories based on the news weave their way into the plotlines of various TV dramas. Consider, for example, two AIDS transmission stories that played prominently on the nightly network news. The first involved Gaetan Dugas, an HIV-positive flight attendant identified as "Patient Zero" in Randy Shilts's book, *And the Band Played On*, and later on *60 Minutes*. Dugas knowingly passed on the virus to unsuspecting sexual partners, evem though he knew he had AIDS. Many of the early patients afflicted with HIV were contact-traced to Dugas. This story formed the storyline of two different TV dramas, *Midnight Caller* (1988-1991) and *Equal Justice* (1990–1991) (Buxton, Carveth [in press]). A second prominent network television news story that made it into a series story-line was the Kimberly Bergalis–Dr. David Acer story. The news story became the principal storyline for an episode of *Picket Fences* (1992-

1996) (Carveth, in press). Thus, the frame adopted by network news in telling the AIDS story in this country has been virtually copied by TV entertainment.

The Impact of News Portrayals

The impact of news coverage on people's perceptions of people living with AIDS is difficult to assess. While such portrayals may support the status quo, they can also perform a disservice to those groups who are impacted by AIDS. Because AIDS is yet incurable, and because the majority of people living with HIV come from groups considered to be socially deviant, there is a tendency for many in the public to "blame the victim" (Herek and Capitanio).

Several studies (e.g., Pryor, Reeder, Vinacco, and Kott) have shown that negative feelings about homosexuality are strongly related to negative reactions to an HIV-positive person, whether the infected person was depicted as contracting the disease through heterosexual intercourse or by other means. Additionally, negative feelings about homosexuality were related to rating AIDS as "immoral, disgusting and dirty." Subjects with negative attitudes toward homosexuality tended to agree with the statements that "AIDS is God's punishment of homosexuals," or that gay persons with AIDS "deserved" to have contracted the disease.

These tendencies to blame the victim may stem, in part, from the images of people living with HIV presented by the news media. Previous research on both adolescents and college students (e.g., McDermott et al. 1987) shows that television and magazines are the most relied-upon sources of information about HIV and AIDS for these age groups. Carveth (1991) found that the more TV news college student respondents watched, the more likely they were to say that the following types of individuals "deserved" to have AIDS: gay men, female partners of intravenous drug abusers (IVDAs), male partners of IVDAs, IVDAs and customers of prostitutes. These relationships held up even when controlling for gender, class standing, knowledge of AIDS, and knowing someone with the disease. In addition, Coleman (1993) found that increased network TV news consumption was associated with greater feelings of the personal risk of acquiring AIDS. Fear of AIDS has been shown to have a strong relationship with the tendency to blame people with AIDS for getting the disease (O'Hare, Williams, and Ezoviski, 1996).

Another study demonstrated a relationship between network news coverage of AIDS and the volume of calls to AIDS hotlines. The National AIDS Hotline usually averages 7,000 to 8,000 calls per day. The day after basketball star Magic Johnson announced he was HIV-positive, calls to the National AIDS Hotline numbered over 119,000 and averaged close to 60,000 for a week thereafter (Mann, Tarantola, and Netter).

The volume of these calls indicates an overall impact, but says little about individual understanding of the story. A survey conducted by the Glasgow Media Group determined that AIDS has various meanings for different audience groups. The study found that the term "bodily fluids" led to a great deal of confusion among members of the audience. Some thought bodily fluids referred to semen and blood, while others thought it meant urine or saliva. Part of the reason for this confusion may rest with the reluctance on the part of editors to be more precise. Overall, these studies indicate that network news has contributed to informing the public about HIV and AIDS; however, such coverage may have also contributed to misunderstanding and misperceptions about the disease on the part of the viewers.

It is naive to propose that a monolithic media system acts upon an equally homogeneous society. It is also erroneous to conclude that specific coverage is causally linked with specific policy changes, or that the process works in one direction only. Journalists' sources, such as politicians and other officials, can manipulate reporters to cover an issue from a particular angle, thus helping to set the political agenda (Colby and Cook). Scientists, too, can manipulate reporters who still tend to view their word as gospel. This may lead to so-called expert opinion being reported as fact or to minor developments being portrayed as major breakthroughs.

Dearing and Rogers (1992) suggest that peaks in news coverage have stimulated shifts in policy in the United States. These policy shifts have occurred, however, only where news coverage has been at a saturation level and reassurance has been outweighed by concern. Thus, these coverage peaks, not the number of AIDS cases or a critical mass of scientific concern, have placed AIDS on the public agenda. Some peaks may have had a clear effect: the publicity surrounding the revelation by Magic Johnson of his HIV status triggered a surge in demand for HIV tests in the United States and a consequent promise of more funds for testing. The impact of other peaks, meanwhile, has been much less obvious. For example, despite the Rock Hudson furor, the U.S. government did not recognize AIDS as a national emergency in 1985. Recently, coverage critical of the U.S. immigration and travel authorization policies on people living with HIV has failed to shift the administration position.

Conclusion
Up until now, network television news coverage of HIV and AIDS has been less than ideal. The major shortcoming in television news cov-

erage is that while the networks do a adequate job in reporting (albeit high-profile) people becoming infected with HIV and dying of complications related to AIDS, coverage of the challenges facing people living with HIV/AIDS is virtually nonexistent. In other words, HIV infection is treated in much the same way as a death sentence: reporters cover the verdict, and then the execution. For example, people generally rallied around Greg Louganis, and stories about AIDS prevention were in the news. Once the initial flurry of news coverage dies out, however, everything goes back to business as usual. The next time Greg Louganis receives a significant amount of media attention will be when he dies.

Consequently, viewers see little about living on "Death Row" (that is, living with the disease). While such portrayals occasionally appear, nothing in the coverage approaches the day-to-day story of HIV-positive Pedro Zamora, the late star of MTV's *Real World*. As more and more people become infected, the audience is going to want to know more about living with HIV rather than waiting to die. The audience hopes that the next famous person to have the disease will be able to rally some sustaining support in the fight against AIDS.

There are signs that things may begin to change, albeit slowly. For example, a television commercial for Nike features a runner named Ric Munoz. The spot describes Munoz as someone who runs "80 miles every week" and "10 marathons every year," and then, incidentally, as someone who is HIV-positive. Nike advertising director Joe McCarthy said that the company was not making a statement about HIV or AIDS. "We wanted to tell an inspirational 'Just do it' story, and this seemed like a story that could appeal on a very emotional level. And it's grounded in sports, making it a story appropriate for Nike to tell," he explained. McCarthy also noted, "Eighty, 85 percent of the comments are positive, applauding Nike for having the courage to make this statement" (Elliott D19). What is important about this spot is the recognition by at least one sector of the advertising industry that people living with HIV are a vital segment of our society. Perhaps now network executives will be more comfortable in establishing the next era of AIDS news coverage as the "living with HIV" era.

Works Cited

Basil, Michael, and William Brown. "Interpersonal Communication in News Diffusion: A Study of 'Magic' Johnson's Announcement." *Journalism Quarterly* 71 (Summer 1994): 305-20.

Berridge, Victoria. "Aids, the Media and Health Policy." *Health Education Journal* 50 (1991): 179-95.

Buxton, Rodney. "'After It Happened . . .': The Battle to Present AIDS in Television Drama." *The Velvet Light Trap* 27 (1991): 37-47.

Carveth, Rod. *Television Viewing and Blaming the Victim: An Exploration of the Link Between TV and Attitudes Toward PWAs.* Paper presented at the annual convention of the Western States Communication Association, 1991.

——. "Amy Fisher and the Ethics of 'Headline' Docudramas." *Journal of Popular Film and Television* 21.3 (1993). 121-27.

——. "From 'Their' Disease to 'Our' Disease: Portrayals of AIDS on Prime Time Television." *Mass-Mediated AIDS*. Ed. Linda Fuller. Amherst: HRD Press (in press).

Colasanto, Diane, Eleanor Singer, and Theresa Rogers. "Context Effects on Responses to Questions about AIDS." *Public Opinion Quarterly* 56 (1992): 515-18.

Colby, David, and Timothy Cook. "Epidemics and Agendas: The Politics of Nightly News Coverage of AIDS." *Journal of Health Politics, Policy and Law* 16 (Summer 1991): 215-48.

Coleman, Cynthia-Lou. "The Influence of Mass Media and Interpersonal Communication on Societal and Personal Risk Judgments." *Communication Research* 20 (Aug. 1993): 611-28.

Dearing, James, and Everett Rogers. "AIDS and the Media Agenda." *A Communication Perspective on AIDS*. Ed. Timothy Edgar, Mary Anne Fitzpatrick, and Vicki Freimuth. Hillsdale, NJ: Erlbaum, 1992. 173-94.

Elliott, Stuart. "Advertising: From Nike, a Real World Ad with an H.I.V.-Positive Runner." *New York Times* 2 Mar. 1995: D19.

Fee, Elizabeth. *AIDS: The Burdens of History*. Berkeley: U of California P, 1988.

Gitlin, Todd. "Prime Time Ideology: The Hegamonic Process in Television Entertainment." *Social Problems* 26 (Feb. 1979): 251-66.

Herek, Gregory, and John Capitanio. "AIDS Stigma and Contact with Persons with AIDS: Effects of Direct and Vicarious Contact." *Journal of Applied Social Psychology* 27 (1997): 1-36.

Hertog, James, and David Fan. "The Impact of Press Coverage on Social Beliefs." *Communication Research* 22.5 (Oct. 1995): 545-74.

Hertog, James, John Finnegan, and Emily Kahn. "Media Coverage of AIDS, Cancer and Sexually Transmitted Diseases: A Test of the Public Arenas Model." *Journalism Quarterly* 71 (Summer 1994): 291-304.

Kinsella, James. *Covering the Plague.* New Brunswick, NJ: Rutgers UP, 1990.

Konick, Steven. "A Visual Thematic Analysis of Network News Coverage of AIDS." Paper presented at the Annual Convention of the Association for Education in Journalism and Mass Communication (1994).

Mann, Jonathan, Daniel Tarantola, and Thomas Netter. *AIDS in the World.* Cambridge: Harvard UP, 1992.

McDermott, R., M. Hawkins, J. Moore, and S. Cittadino. "AIDS Information Sources among Selected University Students." *Journal of American College Health* 35 (1987): 222-26.

O'Hare, Thomas, Cynthia Williams, and Alan Ezoviski. "Fear of AIDS and Homophobia." *Social Work* 41 (1996): 51-58.

Price, Vincent, and Mei-Ling Hsu. "Public Opinion about AIDS Policies." *Public Opinion Quarterly* 56 (1992): 29-52.

Pryor, John, Glenn Reeder, Richard Vinacco, and Teri Kott. "The Instrumental and Symbolic Functions of Attitudes toward Persons with AIDS." *Journal of Applied Social Psychology* 19 (1989): 377-404.

Robinson, John, and Mark Levy. *The Main Source.* Beverly Hills: Sage, 1985.

Rogers, Everett, James Dearing, and Soonbum Chung. "AIDS in the 1980's: The Agenda-Setting Process for a Public Issue." *Journalism Monographs* 126 (1991).

Rogers, Theresa, Eleanor Singer, and Jennifer Imperio. "The Polls: Poll Trends." *Public Opinion Quarterly* 57 (1993): 92-114.

Sandomir, Richard. "Louganis, Olympic Champion, Says He Has AIDS." *New York Times* 23 Feb. 1995: B11.

Shilts, Randy. *And the Band Played On.* New York: St. Martin's, 1987.

Singer, Eleanor, Theresa Rogers, and Marc Glassman. "Public Opinion about AIDS Before and After the 1988 U.S. Government Public Information Campaign." *Public Opinion Quarterly* 55 (1991): 161-79.

Stipp, Horst, and Dennis Kerr. "Determinants of Public Opinion about AIDS." *Public Opinion Quarterly* 53 (1989): 98-106.

Tuchman, Gaye. *Making News.* New York: Free Press, 1978.

Wilbon, Michael. "No One Is Immune." *Washington Post* 23 Feb. 95: D1.

Witt, L. Alan. "Authoritarianism, Knowledge of AIDS and Affect Toward Persons with AIDS: Implications for Health Education." *Journal of Applied Social Psychology* 19 (1989): 599-607.

14

Ethical Guidelines for Promoting Prosocial Messages through the Popular Media

William J. Brown and Arvind Singhal

The use of popular media to address important social problems and influence audience members' beliefs and behaviors raises important ethical issues.[1] Consider the following examples of popular films and television programs designed to promote social change:

At movie theaters across southern Africa, thousands of Africans respond to the rave reviews of the Zimbabwe film *More Time,* nominated for eight MNET film awards and winner of the best film award at the Southern African Film Festival in 1993. Targeted toward teenagers, the film weaves the captivating yet realistic story of Katomeni, a 15-year-old Mbare school-girl ready to fall in love while encountering the dangerous world of alcohol, sex, and HIV/AIDS. As she seeks to avoid the dangers of growing into a young woman, Kotameni creates a discourse with the audience by revealing the social pressures, complex emotions, and family ties that come to bear on her journey to adulthood. The film's prosocial message encourages teenagers to be morally responsible and to communicate closely with parents as they face the moral pressures of young adulthood. (Smith 1-18)

Traffic flows in Delhi noticeably decrease as *Hum Log* (*We People*) comes on the air on Doordarshan, India's National Television Network. The first long-running soap opera on Indian television, *Hum Log* achieves audience ratings of 90 percent in Hindi-speaking areas. The program becomes so popular that when the audience learns of an engagement between one of the daughters of the *Hum Log* family and a dishonest man seeking to take advantage of her, thousands of viewers contact Doordarshan and demand that the engagement on the program be broken. Monahar Joshi, the scriptwriter, complies with the audience request and has the daughter break the engagement and marry a loving and honest man. The soap opera wedding inspires parties all over India and thousands of congratulatory letters, faxes, and gifts are sent to the soap opera characters who play the newlyweds. (Singhal and Rogers 331-50)

207

At movie theaters in Bangladesh, thousands of people line up to see an entertainment film, *Sonamoni* (*Golden Pearl*). The film tells the story of Gafur and his wife Rohima, who lose access to the source of safe drinking water in their village. Their baby soon suffers dysentery and dehydration, a consequence of drinking polluted water from the village pond. While the child's life is threatened, Gafur and Rohima learn about oral rehydration therapy (ORT) and save the child's life. Through this popular film, millions of Bangladeshi families have learned about ORT. (Riber 1-2)

Across Eastern Europe and the former Soviet Union, millions of television viewers tune their television sets after dinner to the popular animated television series *Superbook*. In Kiev, over 100,000 viewer letters are received each week in response to this series of stories from the Old Testament. Michael Little, President of CBN, Inc., the producer of *Superbook*, reported that even in Albania, a former militant atheist nation by law some eight years ago, the series, broadcast on the government's national television network, rated as one of the most watched television programs in the country's history.[2]

These four examples illustrate the marriage between popular entertainment media and prosocial messages intended to promote social change. By 1995 over fifty developing countries were actively engaged in media projects that disseminate educational messages through entertainment programs. These programs, variously called prodevelopment, prosocial, enter-education, edutainment, and infotainment, promote persuasive educational messages through the use of entertainment media. The use of entertainment media to promote prosocial messages is more generally referred to as the entertainment-education strategy in mass communication (Brown and Singhal, "Ethical Issues" 268-80). A prosocial message is defined as any communication that depicts cognitive, affective, and behavioral activities considered to be socially desirable or preferable by most members of a society (Rushton 248-58). National governments throughout the world, especially in developing countries, are highly interested in increasing the prosocial message content of popular media (Brown, *Use of Entertainment* 253-66).

The growth of entertainment media products throughout the world is unprecedented. The rapid diffusion of new communication technology such as communication satellites, VCRs, cable television, and so forth provide multiple entertainment options for media users. The pervasiveness of the American film industry has affected the world's cultural landscape (Turner R6). Although most of the popular media is commercially driven, the use of films and television programs to promote social change is steadily increasing (Brown, "Sociocultural" 157-71). Ethical concerns centering around the antisocial effects of graphic sex and excessive violence in entertainment media products are pressuring governments and private organizations to call for a more constructive and responsible use of the media (Brown and Singhal, "Influencing" 334). In countries that are decimated by the AIDS epidemic, uncontrolled substance abuse, ethnic hatred and strife, and civil disorder, the need to use the popular media to help solve social problems is especially acute.

In this chapter, we describe how popular films and television programs are used to promote social change and the ethical issues of using popular media for social influence. We also present ethical guidelines that writers, producers, media professionals, and government officials should consider.

The Global Influence of Entertainment Media

The past fifty years of communication theory and research reveal that entertainment media have a profound and measurable influence on the attitudes, beliefs, and behaviors of media users (Bineham 230-46; Chaffee 246-49). The impact of popular films and television programs on individual and societal beliefs and behaviors will continue to increase as satellite technology, broadcast and cable television, and VCRs diffuse rapidly in developing countries.

Television audiences have greatly expanded during the past few decades. About thirty years ago, only 5 percent of the world's television sets were found in developing countries; by 1993, the numbers had increased to 50 percent. In two of the world's most populous countries, China and India, television now reaches a combined one billion people. The distribution of video recorders is also increasing rapidly in developing countries. Wang Wei of the Beijing Broadcasting Institute reported in 1993 that in many urban areas of China the diffusion of VCRs had reached 50 percent.[3]

Paralleling the rapid diffusion of television sets and VCRs has been the growth of the worldwide entertainment industry. A large percentage of the United States GNP comes through its entertainment industry, which in 1992 recorded a $4 billion trade surplus (Turner R6). U.S. revenues from films and ancillary entertainment activities are growing at a faster rate for foreign product sales than for domestic consumption (Gregor R16). The sociocultural impact of films and other entertainment products will increase in the future as VCRs rapidly diffuse in developing countries and as video-on-demand technology becomes available in Japan, the U.S., and Europe.

The influence of entertainment television will also continue to increase as broadcasting systems in developing countries allow more entertainment programming. In virtually every country where television has been introduced and allowed to privatize, entertainment television programs and movies eventually dominate the broadcasting time because of their great popularity and success in attracting commercial funding. The present trend indicates that the entertainment orientation of the international film and television industry will increase, even in developing countries that are committed to using the media for educational purposes.

The use of the entertainment media to promote prosocial change is also a growing trend (Singhal 1-25). Advertisers have a successful history of using marketing communication strategies to influence attitudes and behavior through the mediums of film and television. More recently, a social marketing approach has been employed to promote prosocial beliefs and behaviors through media (Solomon 87-104). During the past two decades or so, classical product marketing strategies have been used to market good citizenship, fire safety, exercise, seat belt use, smoking cessation, responsible drinking, condom use, sexual responsibility, political beliefs, environmental awareness, women's equality, and dozens of other important social beliefs and behaviors.

Communication theory and research has also been employed to create entertainment programs that promote prosocial beliefs and behaviors (Brown, Singhal, and Rogers 43-47). Mexico was one of the first nations to systematically apply theories of social science to produce prosocial media messages. Communication theory provided the theoretical framework for eleven dramatic television series that addressed important social problems in Mexico. These television programs, called *telenovelas* (literally "television novels"), were produced by Televisa, Mexico's private national television network. From 1975 to 1981, Mexican *telenovelas* promoted adult literacy, good health practices, family harmony, sex education, nationalism, women's status, better treatment of children, good citizenship, and family planning (Rogers, Singhal, and Brown 149-65).

After Mexico's positive experience with *telenovelas,* other nations experimented with dramatic television serials to promote prosocial goals such as the adoption of modern agricultural practices (in Nigeria), women's status and family harmony (in India), self-reliance and respect for the elderly (in China), family planning (in Turkey), the prevention of substance abuse (in Brazil), and adult literacy (in Pakistan).

In recent years U.S. television networks have broadcast programs to raise social concerns about AIDS, drunk driving, drug abuse, crime prevention, and child abuse. Hollywood films have also promoted social concern for physically impaired individuals and for those battling terminal diseases such as AIDS. Kathyrn Montgomery's study of Hollywood shows that a number of private organizations have established Hollywood offices to actively lobby film and television producers to address social issues (*Target Primetime*).

Sarah Pillsbury and John Riber are among the film producers who have used motion pictures to address specific social needs. Pillsbury, who believes every film has an ideology or world view, won an Oscar for a short dramatic film about a child with Down Syndrome (Rogers, Vaughan, Shefner-Rogers 19). She has produced several films to address important social issues like teenage violence and women's abuse. Riber, a U.S. film producer living in Zimbabwe, has produced over a dozen films in Africa and Asia to improve the treatment of women, increase adult literacy, promote family harmony, encourage safe health practices, and educate teenagers about sexual responsibility (Smith 1-18). One of Riber's films, *Bor Holo, Dor Kholo* (*It's Dawn, Open Your Door*), was broadcast twice on national television in Bangladesh and encouraged over ten million Bagladeshis to join literacy programs within two years of its release.

Educational institutions have also contributed to the use of popular film and television to promote prosocial messages. Harvard University's School of Public Health helped to develop the "designated driver" television campaign to prevent drinking and driving. The designated driver concept diffused rapidly, appearing in 70 different prime-time television series in the U.S. by early 1990.

In 1986, a unique entertainment-education project developed by Johns Hopkins University's Population Communication Services (JHU/PCS) resulted in the launching of "Cuando Estemos Juntos" ("When We Are Together"), a Latin American rock music video. The song, which promoted teenage sexual abstinence, became number one on the pop music charts within six weeks of its release in Mexico and became a top-rated song in eleven other Latin American countries (Brown and Singhal, "Entertainment-Education" 81-101).

In 1991, a popular award-winning film called *Turtle Races* was produced to tell the story of a young long-distance runner who works with handicapped children though the Special Olympics program. The film, intended to promote a better understanding and treatment of the physically impaired, was entirely produced by film students at Regent University in Virginia. A year later, film students at Regent produced *Crowning Glory (1992),* another award-winning film about the struggles of a family helping their daughter fight the physical and emotional battles of cancer. These are just a few examples of how educators are using the film and television media to address important social issues.

Ethical Dilemmas

The use of the entertainment-education communication strategy to promote prosocial change presents several ethical dilemmas with which communication scholars, mass media officials, and national policy-makers must wrestle (Brown and Singhal, *Ethical Issues* 268-80; Brown and Singhal, "Ethical Considerations" 92-99). Given that five billion people (over 80 percent of the entire global population) presently consume some form of modern and/or traditional communication media, the ethical dilemma becomes complicated.

While use of the entertainment-education communication strategy is expanding in developing countries and elsewhere, literature on the ethics of utilizing the entertainment-education strategy is scarce. Existing work on the ethics of media message content focuses mainly on specialized genres (for example, television news, soap operas) and antisocial media effects, and does not discuss broad ethical questions on the use of media for social influence (Cooper 450-55).

The process of social influence through media messages, whether intended or unintended, needs to be guided by ethical principles. Ethical communication upholds and protects an individual's freedom, equality, dignity, and physical and psychological well-being (Brown and Singhal, "Ethical Issues" 268-80). If the communication media fail to uphold and protect these basic human values, or if they limit people's access to resources for their basic needs, then the ethical basis for responsible media use is insufficient. Producers of prosocial messages need an ethical framework for social influence.

The entertainment-education communication strategy presents at least seven important ethical dilemmas (Figure 1): (1) the prosocial development dilemma—how to respond to those who argue it is unethical to use media as a persuasive tool to guide social development; (2) the prosocial content dilemma—how to distinguish prosocial from antisocial media content; (3) the source-centered dilemma—who should determine the prosocial content for others; (4) the audience segmentation dilemma —who among the audiences should receive the prosocial content; (5) the oblique persuasion dilemma—how to justify the "sugar-coating" of educational messages with entertainment; (6) the sociocultural equality dilemma—how to ensure that the prosocial media uphold sociocultural equality among viewers; and (7) the unintended effects dilemma—how to respond to the unintended consequences of prosocial media. Most of these ethical dilemmas are represented in the following question: Who is to determine for whom what is prosocial and what is not?

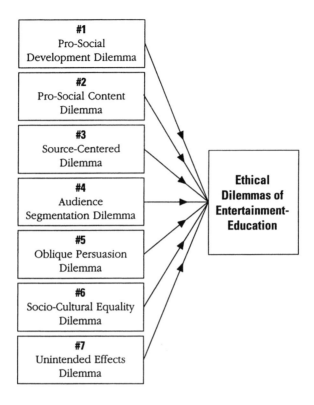

Fig. 1. The ethical dilemmas associated with entertainment-education programming.

The Prosocial Development Dilemma

The foremost ethical dilemma associated with the use of the entertainment-education strategy centers around the fundamental question: Is it right to use media as a persuasive tool to guide social change? Media critics argue that it is virtually impossible to produce "value-free" or "socially innocuous" entertainment programs (Bryant; Thoman). The idea that persuasive communication is unethical and therefore should be avoided ignores decades of media effects research showing entertainment media are imbued with persuasive messages. For example, we know that audience involvement with television programs can persuade audience members to think and do certain things; but how much it persuades is debatable. We also know persuasive messages can have positive and negative influences. Regardless of the degree of social influence, if even one percent of a population is persuaded to change a belief or a behavior on account of watching a television program or seeing a film, that is still an important change. Persuasive communication is an integral part of everyday life in a free society; therefore it can not and should not be restricted on the grounds that some bad people may try to manipulate audiences through the media (Bettinghaus and Cody 21-30).

Arguing that it is unethical to use popular television and film to promote prosocial beliefs and behaviors seems unreasonable and inconsistent with democratic freedom. However, unequivocal promotion of an entertainment-education communication strategy for prosocial development can also represent an untenable ethical position. When disagreements exist about the "rightness" or "wrongness" of a social message, it becomes obvious that what is considered to be "prosocial" by one set of people (whether that group represents the majority of a population or the highest court of the land) should not be uncritically promoted by the media. Whether or not it is ethical to produce entertainment-education programs depends on a number of factors, including the nature of the belief or behavior being promoted, who decides the prosocial status of a certain belief or behavior, and what effects the promotion of a certain belief or behavior are likely to have on an audience.

Thus the ethics of using entertainment-education as a persuasive tool for bringing about prosocial development is inextricably intertwined with several other ethical dilemmas, which are discussed below.

The Prosocial Content Dilemma

The prosocial content dilemma centers around the problems of distinguishing between prosocial and antisocial content. What may be construed as "prosocial" by certain audience members might be perceived as "antisocial" by another audience group. The issue of abortion can help illustrate this dilemma. Pro-abortion groups, who support a woman's choice in controlling her life and the life of an unborn child, will consider a television sitcom episode (for example, a famous episode of *Maude*) promoting abortion rights as "prosocial," whereas anti-abortion groups, who support the rights of the unborn child over the wishes of the mother, will consider that same episode to be "antisocial." Labeling an issue as "prosocial" or "antisocial" obviously involves a value judgment on part of the source of the message, which can present problems from the receivers' perspective.

The Source-Centered Dilemma

The source-centered dilemma centers around the question: Who decides what prosocial messages should be promoted? In most developing countries, including those broadcasting entertainment-education programs, the source of decision-making is typically the national government which decides what is prosocial, which messages should be promoted through the media, who should be targeted, etc. History tells us of several national governments who have abused the media to promote antisocial beliefs and behaviors (and also about other national governments who have used the media ethically and responsibly for prosocial purposes).

Unfortunately, the assurance that the media will be used for prosocial purposes, that is, to benefit society, is not any greater in nations where the responsibility for prosocial messages is left to television producers and commercial advertisers rather than to national governments. Such a responsibility shift creates problems for television producers and advertisers who usually avoid addressing controversial social and educational issues. For instance, until recently, U.S. television networks opposed the broadcast of condom advertisements, even though network soap operas depict numerous sexual acts on television every day (Lowry and Towles). The reconciliation of prosocial media messages in free market economies like the United States (where television systems are commercially driven) is part of the ethical dilemma.

The Audience Segmentation Dilemma

The fourth ethical issue concerning the use of entertainment-education programs is associated with targeting educational messages to particular audience segments. Audience segmentation represents an important communication strategy intended to help producers to fine-tune messages to fit the needs of a relatively homogenous audience segment in order to maximize its effects. For instance, media messages on family planning in developing countries are often targeted to fertile-aged couples, who obviously represent an important audience segment for the educational value that is promoted.

However, such "fine-tuning" of media messages risks alienating other important audience groups (for instance, adolescents and teenagers, sexually active singles) who could also benefit from messages on sexual responsibility. Another ethical dilemma associated with audience targeting centers around the methodological considerations of evaluating the effects of prosocial media messages. For instance, the desire to have a treatment and control region as part of a natural field experiment motivated the program producers and researchers of *Twende na Wakati* (*Let's Go With the Times*), a family planning/AIDS radio soap opera in Tanzania, to block out radio broadcasts of the soap opera (for two years) in the Central Dodoma region of Tanzania. Individuals in this control area may have unwanted pregnancies and may contract HIV during this two-year broadcast period, events that otherwise could have been prevented (Rogers, Vaughan, and Shefner-Rogers 1-21). These and other ethical problems of "targeting" media messages that may occur in field experiments need to be recognized and debated.

The Oblique Persuasion Dilemma

The entertainment-education strategy takes a somewhat oblique route to audience persuasion in that education is "sugar-coated" with entertainment in order to break down the learning defenses to the educational message content. So audiences might think that they are being entertained, while subtly they are being educated about a prosocial issue or topic. Using entertainment to captivate the audiences' attention while the underlying motive is one of education, represents an important ethical dilemma.

The Sociocultural Equality Dilemma

A sixth ethical dilemma in using the entertainment-education communication strategy concerns the problem of ensuring socio-cultural equality, that is, providing an equal treatment on television of various social and cultural groups. Sociocultural equality means regarding each social and cultural group with the same value or importance (Gudykunst and Kim 264-66). In nations with a high degree of homogeneity, there is a high degree of consensus regarding a society's normative beliefs and behaviors. In Japan, where cultural homogeneity is 99 percent, people are expected to have fewer problems agreeing on what is prosocial than people in the United States, where the homogeneity index is perhaps 50 percent or less (Kurian 48).

Ensuring sociocultural equality through prosocial television is especially important but problematic in such socioculturally diverse countries as India. While the *Hum Log* television series, within the limits of a patriarchal social system in India, confronted viewers' traditional beliefs about women's status in Indian society, the viewers' ethnicity, linguistic background, and gender were found to be important determinants of beliefs about gender equality (Brown, "Prosocial Effects," "Sociocultural Influences," "Use of Entertainment"; Singhal and Rogers, "Television Soap," "Ethical Issues"). The subservience of women is still considered to be socially and culturally acceptable in many Indian households, a result of the highly patriarchal and patrilineal social structures. However, such is not the case all over India. So television's treatment of all viewers as socioculturally "equal" in India represents an ethical dilemma.

The sociocultural equality dilemma lies at the heart of the unresolved debate on cultural imperialism, whereby mass media programs, with their accompanying cultural baggage, are exported from one country to another. When U.S.-produced cultural products are consumed in countries that have radically different socio-cultural environments, frustration and anger can result on part of the viewing audience. For instance, in a particular episode of *I Love Lucy* that was broadcast in China, Lucy overspent her allotted funds on new furniture, upsetting her husband Ricky. What made the program culturally inappropriate was that the amount of money Lucy spent on furniture in half an hour was more than two years of average wages in China (Brown and Singhal, "Ethical Considerations"). The realization of socioeconomic disparity is not always welcomed by national governments of countries where people daily struggle for adequate food, safe drinking water, and shelter.

The inappropriateness of imported mass media programs may not necessarily be unethical; however, the creation of desires for material possessions that can never be obtained by large audience segments is certainly an ethical concern that should be carefully considered.

The Unintended Effects Dilemma

A seventh ethical dilemma brought about by the use of the entertainment-education communication strategy is the problem of unintended effects. Social development is a complex phenomenon whose consequences are not always predictable. Undesirable and unintended consequences can result from the diffusion of prosocial messages. Reluctance to broadcast condom advertisements and address sexual responsibility on U.S. television demonstrates how a fear of unintended consequences can discourage prosocial messages. Many fear that content intending to promote sexual responsibility might encourage sexual promiscuity instead (Dannemeyer).

It is not easy to forecast audience responses to seemingly prosocial messages. For example, when one of the authors showed the Tatiana and Johnny music videotape to a media effects class at the University of California at Los Angeles, pointing out how successful the rock music campaign was in persuading teenagers to say "no" to sex, a student replied: "I thought it said 'yes' to sex." As mass media audiences continue to expand in developing countries and as the number of prosocial programs increase, an understanding of the ethical dilemmas associated with the entertainment-education strategy becomes crucially important.

Ethical Guidelines for the use of Prosocial Media

In response to the seven important ethical dilemmas discussed here, we offer seven ethical guidelines for consideration by sponsors, producers, distributors, and broadcasters of entertainment-education media designed to promote prosocial beliefs and behaviors. We encourage those who use entertainment media to promote social change to—

1. Consider opposing perspectives of a social issue that is addressed by an entertainment-education message and when representing opposing perspectives do so fairly and accurately. (For example, many high schools that teach teenagers sexual responsibility and discuss condom use also discuss abstinence and the significant risks of condom use for HIV/AIDS prevention).

2. Create entertainment-education programs in close consultation with community leaders of the target audience.(Producers of the entertainment-education radio soap opera *Twende na Wakati* consulted closely with community leaders during the pre-production phase of the program.)

3. Help audiences to understand potential beneficial and detrimental persuasive influences of popular media. (Producers need to depict how media influences viewers through entertainment-education media.)

4. Carefully consider the advantages and disadvantages of targeting audience segments with entertainment-education messages while excluding other segments. (Government development officers who sponsored *Twende na Wakati* and researchers who studied the radio programs debated the pros and cons of having control groups in the study who did not receive the HIV/AIDS prevention messages.)

5. Encourage audience members to recognize the beliefs and behaviors promoted by entertainment media. (Producers of the Indian soap opera *Hum Log* ended episodes with an epilogue by a famous Indian film star who explained to audiences the important prosocial message of each program.)

6. Carefully consider the sociocultural impact of entertainment-education messages on potential audiences. (Several national governments such as Thailand have sponsored national conferences to discuss the sociocultural consequences of imported and domestically produced entertainment media.)

7. Anticipate potential unintended effects of entertainment-education messages on potential audiences and seek to reduce potentially detrimental influences. (After experiencing a mad rush for literacy booklets after an episode of a popular Mexican *telenovela,* creating a huge traffic jam in Mexico City, more planning was given to the printing and distribution of educational materials for future prosocial media programs.)

Tatianna and Johnny, a popular teenage couple in Mexico, embrace in their hit music video as they sing about the importance of sexual responsibility. (Courtesy of Johns Hopkins Center for Communication Programs)

Although it is nearly impossible to satisfy all audience members and sociopolitical groups with the prosocial content of entertainment-education media efforts, many ethical conflicts regarding media content can be avoided by employing the ethical guidelines provided here. While some topics are easier to address ethically with prosocial messages than are others (for example, entertainment-education programs that promote literacy like the Mexican *telenovela Ven Conmigo* and the Bengali film *Bor Holo, Dor Kholo* have a very high prosocial legitimacy and low risk of negative unintended effects), there are too many critical social needs to avoid addressing other more difficult topics.

Conclusion

In summary, whether or not it is ethical to produce and distribute prosocial entertainment media products depends on a number of factors, including the potential benefits of the beliefs or behaviors being promoted, the degree of consultation with targeted audiences regarding the prosocial messages being promoted, and the potential intended and unintended effects of the prosocial messages on the targeted audience. Thus the ethical issues concerned with producing popular media to guide social development must be discussed within the context of shared community values and beliefs. The ethical use of popular media must be based upon the imperative of protecting people's freedom, equality, dignity, and physical and psychological well-being. To promote prosocial change through the media requires that producers make a moral commitment to protect the public from media content that encourage destructive beliefs and behaviors (Weiser).

The popular media already have a powerful persuasive influence. To purposefully discourage the production of entertainment-education programs because of the ethical dilemmas associated with their effects makes little sense. The important question is not whether prosocial messages should be disseminated through popular media but whether to allow market forces or community values and consensus to shape those messages. Community leaders must actively help guide the entertainment industry in promoting prosocial beliefs and behaviors that benefit society. Despite the risks of unintended consequences, popular films and television programs with prosocial messages can improve the quality of our lives and help alleviate societal problems.

If we are to encourage the use of entertainment media to promote prosocial messages, then the responsibility for producing entertainment media products cannot remain solely on the shoulders of commercial sponsors and media conglomerates who may be insensitive to community values (Medved 320-45). Nor can we depend on government officials who can arbitrarily decide what is prosocial and what is not. Ultimately, the public and each community must fulfill an important role in the production and distribution of the cultural media products that they and their children will consume.

Note

The authors thank their colleagues at Regent University and Ohio University for their contributions to the debate on the ethical issues of popular media culture; and especially thank film critic and author Michael Medved for raising that debate to the national agenda with his insightful book, *Hollywood vs. America: Popular Culture and the War on Traditional Values.*

The present article draws upon two previous works by the authors: "Ethical Dilemmas of Prosocial Television," published in 1990 by *Communication Quarterly*; and "Ethical Considerations of Promoting Prosocial Messages through Popular Media," published in 1993 by the *Journal of Popular Film and Television.*

Works Cited

Bettinghaus, Erwin P., and Michael J. Cody. *Persuasive Communication.* 5th ed. New York: Holt, 1994.

Bineham, Jeffery L. "A Historical Account of the Hypodermic Modelin Mass Communication." *Communication Monographs* 55 (1988): 230-46.

Brown, William J. "Prosocial Effects of Entertainment Television in India." *Asian Journal of Communication* 1 (1990): 113-35.

——. "Sociocultural Influences of Prodevelopment Soap Operas." *Journal of Popular Film and Television* 19 (1992): 157-71.

——. "The Use of Entertainment Television Programs for Promoting Prosocial Messages." *Howard Journal of Communication* 3 (1992): 253-66.

Brown, William J., and Arvind Singhal. "Entertainment-Education Media: An Opportunity for Enhancing Japan's Leadership Role in Third World Development." *Keio Communication Review* 15 (1993): 81-101.

——. "Ethical Considerations of Promoting Prosocial Messages through the Popular Media." *Journal of Popular Film & Television* 21 (1993): 92-99.

——. "Ethical Issues of Prosocial Television." *Communication Quarterly* 38 (1990): 268-80.

——. "Influencing the Character of Entertainment Television: Ethical Dilemmas of Prosocial Programming." *America's Character: Recovering Civic Virtue.* Ed. Don E. Eberly. Lanham, MD: Madison, 1995. 333-46.

Brown, William J., Arvind Singhal, and Everett M. Rogers. "Prodevelopment Soap Operas: A Novel Approach to Development Communication." *Media Development* 36 (1989): 43-47.

Bryant, Jennings. "Message Features and Entertainment Effects." *Message Effects in Communication Science.* Ed. James J. Bradac. Newbury Park: Sage, 1989. 231-62.

Chaffee, Steven H. "Differentiating the Hypodermic Model in Mass Communication." *Communication Monographs* 55 (1988): 246-49.

Cooper, Thomas W. "Ethics, Journalism and Television: Bibliographic Constellations, Black Holes." *Journalism Quarterly* 65 (1988): 450-55, 496.

Dannemeyer, William E. "AIDS and Public Policy." *Salt and Light.* Ed. David J. Gyertson. Dallas: Word, 1993. 237-58.

Gregor, Anne. "Entertaining Numbers: A Statistical Look at the Global Entertainment Industry." *Wall Street Journal* 26 Mar. 1993, eastern ed.: R16.

Gudykunst, William, and Young Yun Kim. *Communicating with Strangers.* 2nd ed. New York: McGraw Hill, 1992.

Kurian, George T. *The New Book of World Rankings.* New York: Facts on File, 1984.

Little, Michael. "The Amazing Story of *Superbook.*" Public address at Regent University, May 1993.

Lowry, Dennis T., and David E. Towles. "Soap Opera Portrayals of Sex, Contraception, and Sexually Transmitted Diseases." *Journal of Communication* 39 (1989): 77-83.

Medved, Michael. *Hollywood vs. America: Popular Culture and the War on Traditional Values.* New York: Harper Collins, 1992.

Montgomery, Kathyrn C. *Target Primetime: Advocacy Groups and the Struggle over Entertainment Television.* New York: Oxford UP, 1989.

Riber, John. *Synopsis of the Film Sonamoni (Golden Pearl).* Columbia, MD: Development through Self-Reliance, 1992.

Rogers, E. M., Arvind Singhal, and William J. Brown. "Entertainment Telenovelas for Development: Lessons Learned." *Serial Fiction in TV: The Latin American Telenovelas.* Ed. Anamaria Fadul. Sao Paulo: School of Communication and Arts, U of Sao Paulo, 1993.

Rogers, Everett M., Peter Vaughan, and Corinne L. Shefner-Rogers. "Evaluating the Effects of an Entertainment-Education Radio Soap Opera in Tanzania: A Field Experiment with Multi-Method Measurement." Paper presented at the International Communication Association, Albuquerque, NM, May 1995.

Rogers, Everett M., Subashis Aikat, Soonbum Chang, Patricia Poppe, and Pradeep Sopory. *Entertainment-Education for Social Change.* Proceedings of the Conference on Entertainment- Education for Social Change. Los Angeles: Annenberg School for Communication, U of Southern California, Mar.-Apr. 1989.

Rushton, J. Philipe. "Television and Prosocial Behavior." *Television & Behavior: Ten Years of Scientific Progress and Implications for the Eighties.* Vol. 2. Ed. D. Pearl, L. Bouthilet, and J. Lazar. Bethesda, MD: National Institute of Mental Health, 1982. 248-58.

Singhal, Arvind. *Social Change through Entertainment.* Athens, OH, unpublished manuscript.

Singhal, Arvind, and Everett M. Rogers. "Prosocial Television forDevelopment in India." *Public Communication Campaigns.* 2nd ed. Ed. Ronald E. Rice and Charles K. Atkin. Newbury Park: Sage, 1989. 331-50.

——. "Television Soap Operas for Development in India." *Gazette* 41 (1988): 109-26.

Smith, Steven C. *Media Development Trust Presents "More Time."* Columbia, MD: Development through Self-Reliance, 1993.

Solomon, Douglas S. "A Social Marketing Perspective on Communication Campaigns." *Public Communication Campaigns.* 2nd ed. Ed. Ronald E. Rice and Charles K. Atkin. Newbury Park, CA: Sage, 1989: 87-104.

Thoman, Elizabeth. "Media Education: Agenda for the 90s." *Media Ethics Update* 2 (1989): 8-9.

Turner, Richard. "Hollyworld." *Wall Street Journal* 26 Mar. 1993, eastern ed.: R6.

Vidmar, Neil, and Milton Rokeach. "Archie Bunker's Bigotry: A Study in Selective Perception and Exposure." *Journal of Communication* 24.1 (1974): 36-47.

Wei Wang. Personal Interview. 20 Mar. 1993.

Weiser, Dennis. "Two Concepts of Communication as Criteria for Collective Responsibility." *Journal of Business Ethics* 7 (1988): 735-44.

Part 3

Additional Sources in Popular Film and Television

(Courtesy of the Museum of Modern Art/Film Stills Archive)

The complex interaction between people, popular culture, and media technology is a global phenomenon as we approach the new millennium. Just over one hundred and fifty years ago, information moved only as far and as fast as men and women could carry it. Today, in contrast, we see the new digital language of instantaneous communication everywhere. Many social theorists have written about how Americans and members of other Western societies have radically transformed themselves and their cultures since World War II. They describe these various changes and the resulting new era by a number of fashionable terms, such as post-industrial age, media age, or postmodernist age. Whatever one chooses to call this era, America has profoundly changed since 1946, redefining the way people conduct their home life, work, and leisure time; how they partici-

225

pate as citizens and consumers, and for the purposes of this section of the book, conduct research and process information.

Commentators have spent the last fifty years speculating about an "atomic age," when the single, most important technological development resulting from the effort surrounding the Second World War is arguably the digital computer, more so than the bomb. The computer, in tandem with the new television and video technologies and along with older forms of electronic, motion picture, and print media, has eclipsed our nuclear obsession with a more fundamental and persuasive agenda, especially as we move farther away from the urgencies of the Cold War.

In this spirit, therefore, we are including both conventional and online resources for the further study of popular film and television, including two selective bibliographic surveys as well as a listing of useful internet sites. Peter Rollins supplies both "sources" and "strategies" for additional film research in chapter 15. His overview is thorough, easy to use, and spiced throughout with useful editorial suggestions. Robert J. Thompson furnishes a similar review of the literature for television in chapter 16. His insightful compendium includes both scholarly and general interest titles, reflecting the inclusive spirit of popular culture studies as a whole.

In addition, the following twenty websites provide easy access to masses of information when researching popular film and television topics. This inventory is certainly not complete since the Internet is expanding exponentially each month. These homepages and databases should be helpful, however, and most of these sources also have corresponding links to related websites of interest:

Academy of Motion Picture Arts and Sciences
http://www.ampas.org/ampas

American Communication Association (scholarly links)
http://www.uark.edu/dept/comminfo/www/film.html

American Film Institute
http://www.afionline.org

Cinemedia
http://www.afionline.org/CineMedia/cmframe.htlm

Cross-Cultural Film Guide
http://newton.library.american.edu/collects/
media/afderhe/aufderhe.htm

Director's Guild of America
  http://www.leonardo.net/dga/dganews

Film & History
  http://h-net2.msu.edu/~filmhis/

History of Communication Media Technologies
  http://www.mediahistory.com

Internet Movie Database
  http://us.imdb.com/

The Hollywood Reporter
  http://www.hollywoodreporter.com/

Library of Congress Early Motion Picture Site
  http://lcweb2.loc.gov/papr/mpixhome.html

List of cinema/mass media journals
  http://alpha2.csd.uwm.edu/Dept/English/jclist.html

Microsoft Cinemania Online
  http://Cinemania.msn.com/Cinemania/Home.asp

The Motion Picture Guide
  http://www.iguide.com/movies/mopic/pictures/

Museum of Broadcast Communication
  http://www.neog.com/mbc/

ScreenSite: Film and Television Resources
  http://www.sa.ua.edu/TCF/contents.htm

Take Two (internet guide to film and television)
  http://www.webcom.com/~taketwo/

UCLA Film and Television Archive
  http://www.cinema.ucla.edu/default.html

Women in Cinema
  http://poe.acc.virginia.edu/~pm9k/libsci/womFilm.html

Yahoo (search engine) for movies, films, television
  http://www.yahoo.com/Entertainment/

15

Selective Bibliography for Researching Popular Film: Sources and Strategies

Peter C. Rollins

The title of the collection you are reading, *In the Eye of the Beholder,* suggests that the method selected for a film research project often will influence the kinds of answers yielded. This guide to sources will outline some of the methods of film study.

Credits and Facts

Conscientious reviewers need accurate credits for actors and the characters they play; writers will profit most from the "Quick Reference" books and CDs listed (100a). In the age of home viewing, our television speakers are often small; the pronunciation and spelling of a character's name can often be in doubt. (For example, is the villain in *Billy Budd* (1961) John Claggart or John Claggard? Does Peter Ustinov —screenwriter, star, and director for the film—play Captain Vear or Captain Vere? The spelling of the Captain's name has special meaning because he is a symbolic figure, as a seeker after veritas, the truth, but if the novella by Herman Melville is not handy, getting the spelling right can be a problem.) In addition, the quick reference items will have details about producers, directors, screenwriters, etc. These details will lead thoughtful writers to imaginative connections to other films by the same creative talents. The "Auteur Studies" section lists critical studies which explore the impact of individual artists (400d).

Beginning researchers are often unclear about the actual function of specialized artists and artisans listed in movie credits. A section on "Specific Jobs and Roles in Filmmaking" will translate the argot of even the most esoteric job title (600). (For example, what is the difference between a cameraperson's responsibilities and those of the director of photography?) A section on "Screenwriting" leads to studies of the people who put the film concepts into dialogue and (proposed) action (1002).

A Film in Its Own Time

The "Contemporary Reviews" (200) section provides responses to films when they were first assayed by critics. Books from the "Film in Context" (400c) and "Decade Studies" (400e) will be especially helpful in drawing lines from the cinematic texts to their cultural contexts. Consideration of these reactions informs and sharpens the insights of culturally aware viewers. Like all important works of art, motion pictures reflect the attitudes and world views of their eras—even when they attempt to transcend them.

Film and the Pressure of Institutions

Because films are such expensive products, there are many institutional and market pressures at work—shaping the design of plots, determining the kinds of characters who will appear, and forcing writers, directors, and actors to adjust their artistry to conform to (the perceived) tastes and tolerances of audiences.

Overviews of film history will provide some information of this issue, but the pressures of the movie colony will be best addressed in sources listed under "Institutional Approaches" (500). Over time, studios took on their own distinctive styles and specialized in the kinds of films that interested their lead directors, producers, and executives. In addition, the box office was very important to an expensive medium as was the bond between studios and theaters (until 1948, when studios had to divorce themselves from distribution). Voluntary and imposed censorship contributed to the types of characters, dress, and action reaching the screens of America; indeed, the "Censorship" (900) section tells much about changing values in the twentieth century as America sometimes recoiled at the reflection it found in its cinematic mirror.

Films and the Social Conscience

It is not true that motion pictures can escape the major issues of their time nor is it true that Hollywood films directly confront social issues. Politics, ideology, prejudice intrude into even the most well-meaning projects so that John Steinbeck's activist novel *The Grapes of Wrath* (1939) (as produced by Darryl Zanuck and directed by John Ford in 1940) closes with a happy ending! Topics below such as "The Social Problem Film (800), "Minority Images" (1000) and "Vietnam" (1001) will expose readers to the variety of approaches to political and moral issues. The section on "Documentaries" (700) reveals that even so-called factual films are highly interpretive works of art—and that news is an interpretive genre.

A 3-D movie audience from the 1950s: special eyes for *these* beholders. (Courtesy of the Museum of Modern Art/Film Stills Archive)

The Genre Approach

The "Genre Studies" approach examines how motion pictures conform to existing formulas—the western genre or the action-adventure genre or the buddy-film genre, etc—and how they deviate from the standard patterns (400f). Because film is a commercial medium, filmmakers walk a tightrope: if they imitate an existing formula too closely, they may not grab audience attention; on the other hand, if they are too inventive, a popular audience may become confused and not know how to respond—resulting in a bad bottom line. For scholars of popular film, both tendencies are revealing—the effort to conform as well as the daring to experiment. Many of the essays in this collection are sensitive to the impact of formula; the "Genre Studies" section is particularly detailed to reflect that interest.

Long-term Follow-up

There are a number of exciting journals that will lead those with long-term interests to the most recent research of popular film. A "Journals and Periodicals" section lists the best ones; many of the authors in this collection will be found in their pages (2000).

Reference Works (100)

Quick Reference (100a)

Katz, Ephraim. *The Film Encyclopedia.* 2nd ed. New York: Harper Reference, 1994.

A revised, older work, but very handy. Alphabetical listings by film title, director, technical term, industry union, or institution. Often sold at a reduced price.

The Motion Picture Guide CD-ROM. New York: CINE Books, 1995.

A CD containing full credits, full awards, and—in some cases—very detailed plot summaries plus critical remarks. Very useful for teachers who wish to give students basic credit information since the CD allows a "print" function for the computer. Quality of writing is good to fair, but the convenience of this resource is hard to match.

Cinemania 96. (CD-ROM) Microsoft Corporation, 1995.

A rich film resource that includes 20,000 capsule reviews by Leonard Maltin; 2,000 essays by Roger Ebert; 2,800 reviews by Pauline Kael. Also has terms from Baseline's *Encyclopedia of Film;* James Monaco's *How to Read a Film;* and Ephraim Katz's *Film Encyclopedia.* Additional biographies, stills, and some famous clips. Updated yearly by online subscription.

In-Depth Reference (100b)

Film Literature Index. Eds. Vincent Aceto and Fred Silva. Albany: Filmdex, 1973-
  Begins coverage in 1971 and surveys 240 periodicals using both title and subject categories.

Furtaw, Julia. *The Video Sourcebook.* 2 vols. 16th ed. Detroit: Gale Research, 1994.
  The best resource for tracking down videos for purchase. Has multiple outlets listed and precise address data for distributors of 130,000 programs. Indexed by subject and credits. For example, 35 entries for "John Ford."

Magill's Survey of Cinema. 13 vols. Englewood Cliffs: Salem Press, 1980- .
Covers silent and sound eras with credits and signed essays by film students and scholars. Very useful. Also available in networked database through Dialog and Knowledge-Index. (Gateway to the latter is provided through CompuServe.)

Contemporary Reviews (200)

The New York Times Film Reviews (1913-1974). 19 vols. with biennial supplements. Boston: Garland, 1975- .
  Reviews of films as they were released by an important source of elite opinion. Indexed. Not always reliable, but evokes how reviewers first responded to a film.

Variety Film Reviews, 1907-1980. 16 vols. New York: Garland, 1983- .
  The industry evaluation of Hollywood films; often takes unexpected perspectives on technical aspects. Frequently written in industry slang—which can be fun.

Magill's Cinema Annual. Englewood Cliffs: Salem. 1092- .
  Major films of the year covered with a perspective not available to daily reviewers.

Basic American Film History (300)

Mast, Gerald. *A Short History of the Movies.* 5th ed. Rev. by Bruce Kawin. New York: Macmillan, 1986.
  A long, short history.

Bordwell, David, Kristin Thompson, and Janet Staiger. *The Classical Hollywood Cinema: Film Style and Mode of Production to 1960.* New York: Columbia UP, 1985.

A model history for its balance of industrial history, production history, and aesthetics.

Belton, John. *American Cinema/American Culture*. New York: McGraw, 1994.
The companion volume to the PBS series. Extensive links between film and broader cultural shifts.

Everson, William K. *American Silent Film*. New York: Oxford UP, 1978.
Survey before sound by a true enthusiast.

May, Larry. *Screening out the Past: The Birth of Mass Culture and the Motion Picture Industry*. Chicago: U of Chicago P, 1983.
Evolution of films and theaters in a cultural context.

Interpretive (400)

Contemporary Hollywood (400a)

Medved, Michael. *Hollywood vs. America: Popular Culture and the War on Traditional Values*. New York: Harper Collins, 1992.
A controversial interpretation that describes Hollywood as a "poison factory."

Ryan, Michael, and Douglas Kellner. *Camera Politica: The Politics and the Ideology of Contemporary Hollywood*. Bloomington: U of Indiana P, 1988.
An assessment of the political meaning of American films from 1960 to the mid-1980s.

Feature Film Overviews (400b)

Bordwell, David, and Noel Carroll, eds. *Post-theory: Reconstructing Film Studies*. Madison: U of Wisconsin P, 1996.

Braudy, Leo. *The World in a Frame: What We See in Films*. Garden City: Doubleday, 1976.
Especially sensitive to westerns, musicals, and the evolution of genre within historical contexts.

Edgerton, Gary, ed. *Film and the Arts in Symbiosis: A Resource Guide*. Westport: Greenwood, 1967.
Explores the relationship between motion pictures and radio, television, video, the new media technologies, literature, theater, painting, the graphic arts, photography, classical music, and popular music.

Jowett, Garth. *Film: The Democratic Art.* Boston: Little, Brown, 1976.

How movies—and legislation with regard to them—exhibit changing values, 1890s-1950s. A must for Americanists interested in film in a cultural context. Documents the earliest controversies about the connections between film and audience behavior.

O'Brien, Tom. *The Screening of America: Movies and Values from Rocky to Rain Man.* New York: Praeger, 1992.

Sklar, Robert. *Movie-Made America: A Cultural History of American Movies.* New York: Random House, 1994.

A pioneer book revised in 1994. Panorama of the history of film in relation to American life by a leading American Studies scholar.

Films in Context (400c)

Carnes, Mark, ed. *Past Imperfect: History According to the Movies.* New York: Holt, 1995.

Brief examinations of over sixty films for their historicity.

Landy, Marcia. *Cinematic Uses of the Past.* Minneapolis: U of Minnesota P, 1996.

Marsden, Michael, Jack Nachbar, and Sam Grogg, eds. *Movies as Artifacts: Cultural Criticism of Popular Film.* Chicago: Nelson-Hall, 1982.

Analyses of film audiences, stars, genres, movies, and the human condition.

Mast, Gerald, ed. *The Movies in Our Midst: Documents in the Cultural History of Film in America.* Chicago: U of Chicago P, 1983.

Rollins, Peter. *Hollywood as Historian: American Film in a Cultural Context.* Lexington: UP of Kentucky, 1983.

Contextual studies of fifteen films, 1914-1980. Balances aesthetic and cultural analysis. Bibliographical essay.

Rollins, Peter C., and John E. O'Connor. *Hollywood's World War I: Motion Picture Images.* Bowling Green, OH: Bowling Green State University Popular Press, 1997.

Films about the Great War placed within the contexts of their years in production. From the heroics of the 1920s to the horrors of the 1930s and then back to heroics in the years before World War II. Later reverberations on television. Major filmography.

Rosenstone, Robert, ed. *Revisioning History: Film and the Construction of a New Past.* Princeton: Princeton UP, 1995.

Toplin, Robert B. *History by Hollywood: The Use and Abuse of the American Past.* U of Illinois P, 1996. A thorough study by a leading scholar.

Auteur Studies (400d)

Braudy, Leo, and Morris Dickstein, eds. *Great Film Directors.* New York: Oxford UP, 1978.
Major critics examine, among others, Frank Capra, Charles Chaplin, Robert Flaherty, John Ford, D. W. Griffith, Howard Hawks, Alfred Hitchcock, Buster Keaton, Orson Welles.

Chown, Jeffrey. *Hollywood Auteur: Francis Coppola.* New York: Praeger, 1988.
Both an auteur and a contextual study.

Kolker, Robert P. *A Cinema of Loneliness: Penn, Kubrick, Coppola, Scorsese, Altman.* New York: Oxford UP, 1980.
A thematic approach to major figures.

Maland, Charles. *American Visions: The Films of Chaplin, Ford, Capra, and Welles, 1936-1941.* New York: Arno, 1977.
The studio era's auteurs in a cultural context.

——. *Chaplin and American Culture: The Evolution of a Star Image.* Princeton: Princeton UP, 1989.

Von Gunden, Kenneth. *Postmodern Auteurs: Coppola, Lucas, DePalma, Spielberg and Scorsese.* Jefferson: McFarland, 1991.
The independent era's auteurs.

Decade Studies (400e)

1930s

Bergman, Andrew. *We're in the Money: Depression America and Its Films.* 2nd ed. New York: Elephant Paper, 1992.

1950s

Biskind, Peter. *Seeing Is Believing: How Hollywood Taught Us to Stop Worrying and Love the Fifties.* New York: Pantheon, 1983.

Dowdy, Andrew. *Films of the Fifties: The American State of Mind.* New York: Morrow, 1975.

1960s

James, David. *Allegories in Cinema: American Film in the Sixties.* Princeton: Princeton UP, 1989.

1970s

Monaco, James. *American Film Now.* New York: Oxford UP, 1979.
  A look at film as the 1970s came to a close.

1980s

Brodie, Douglas. *The Films of the Eighties.* New York: Citadel, 1990.

Palmer, William. *The Films of the Eighties.* Carbondale: Illinois UP, 1993.

Genre Studies **(400f)**

Altman, Rick. *The American Film Musical.* Bloomington: Indiana UP, 1987.

Basinger, Jeanine. *The World War II Combat Film: Anatomy of a Genre.* New York: Columbia UP, 1986.
  Best book on the subject and a good text for classes.

Cawelti, John. *The Six-Gun Mystique.* Bowling Green, OH: Bowling Green State UP, 1971.
  The first major statement about the western and about the formula/genre approach to film by an author in this collection.

——. *Adventure, Mystery, and Romance: Formula Stories as Art and Popular Culture.* Chicago: U of Chicago P, 1977.
  Further exploration of the formulaic aspects of popular culture genre in literature and film. A step beyond the previous discussion.

Doherty, Thomas. *Teenagers and Teenpics: The Juvenilization of American Movies in the 1950s.* Boston: Unwin, 1988.
  A fascinating study of some influential films ignored by critics who consider film strictly an art form.

Everson, William K. *The Detective in Film.* Secaucus: Citadel, 1972.

Wes D. Gehring, *Handbook of American Film Genres.* Westport: Greenwood Press, 1988.

A substantive overview of the following genres by major scholars in the field of film studies: Action/Adventure—western, gangster, film noir, World War II combat; Comedy—screwball, populist, parody, black humor, clown; Fantastic—horror, science fiction, fantasy; Songs and soaps—musical, melodrama; Nontraditional—social problem, biographical, art.

Each genre overview ends with a bibliographical checklist of books and articles plus a selected filmography in chronological order.

Grant, Barry. *Film Genre: Theory and Criticism.* Metuchen: Scarecrow, 1977.

Considers six genres. Contains a bibliography.

——. *Film Genre Reader II.* Austin: U of Texas P, 1995.

Eleven genres considered, with some essays repeated from his previous volume.

Kaminsky, Stuart. *American Film Genres: Approaches to a Critical Theory of Popular Film.* New York: Dell, 1977.

Leyda, Jay. *Film Begets Film.* New York: Hill and Wang, 1964.

A short book with lots of insight into an important genre, the compilation documentary.

Lopez, Daniel. *Films by Genre: 775 Categories, Styles, Trends, and Movements Defined with a Filmography for Each.* Jefferson, NC: McFarland, 1993.

More information than you can stand—but useful as a reference tool.

Mast, Gerald. *The Comic Mind: Comedy and the Movies.* Chicago: U of Chicago P, 1979.

A very comprehensive study.

McCarthy, Todd, ed. *Kings of the Bs: Working within the Hollywood System.* New York: Dutton, 1975.

Profiles of the journeymen of the film industry.

Nachbar, Jack. *Focus on the Western.* Englewood Cliffs: Prentice-Hall, 1974.

The best, short collection on the genre. Limited to the essence of the subject. Little jargon.

Rollins, Peter, and John E. O'Connor. *Hollywood's Indian: Portrayal of the Native American in Film.* U of Kentucky P, 1997.

Particular films examined for their stereotypes—or their attempts to go beyond the stereotypes—of the Native American experience. From the *Vanishing American* (1926) to *Pocahontas* (1995).

Schatz, Thomas. *Hollywood Genres: Formulas, Filmmaking, and the Studio System*. New York: Random House, 1981.

Solomon, Stanley. *Beyond Formula: American Film Genres*. New York: Harcourt, 1976.
An excellent classroom text written in nontechnical language. Basic characteristics of the Hollywood genre are described and then explored with a few examples.

Sickov, Ed. *Screwball: Hollywood's Madcap Romantic Comedies*. New York: Crown, 1989.

Silver, Alain. *Film Noir: An Encyclopedic Reference to the American Style*. Woodstock: Overlook, 1979.

Sobchack, Vivian. *Screening Space: The American Science Fiction Film*. 2nd ed. New York: Ungar, 1987.
A major genre examined by a major scholar. Cable TV now has a special channel for science fiction.

Telotte, J. P. *Voices in the Dark: The Narrative Patterns of Film Noir*. Chicago: U of Illinois P, 1989.
Telotte is a discerning scholar of film and this is one of many books on noir.

Institutional Approaches (500)

Gabler, Neal. *An Empire of Their Own: How the Jews Invented Hollywood*. New York: Anchor, 1988.

Gomery, Douglas. *The Hollywood Studio System*. New York: St. Martin's, 1986.
Inner-workings of the studios and their impact on product.

——. *Shared Pleasures: A History of Movie Presentation in the United States*. Madison: U of Wisconsin P, 1992.

Izod, John. *Hollywood and the Box Office, 1895-1986*. New York: Columbia UP, 1988.

Schatz, Thomas. *The Genius of the System: Hollywood Filmmaking in the Studio Era.* New York: Pantheon, 1988.
    Studio archives and inter-office memos provide a paper trail for the study of motion picture content and style.

Specific Jobs and Roles in Filmmaking (600)

T. L. Wright, and Alexandra Bouwer. *Working in Hollywood.* New York: Crown, 1990.
    Interviews with the various people who contribute to a film effort with first-person reports about the stresses, strains, and creative opportunities. Producers, directors, cameramen, casting directors, transportation coordinators, editors, sound mixers, etc. Informative and personal.

Documentaries (700)

Barnouw, Erik. *Documentary: A History of the Non-Fiction Film.* 2nd rev. ed. New York: Oxford, 1993.
    A broad-brush approach by a pioneer in film scholarship.

Barsam, Richard M. *Nonfiction Film: A Critical History, Revised.* New York: Dutton, 1992.
    Still the best overview of documentary as a genre. Strong on the classic films.

——. *Nonfiction Film: Theory of Criticism.* New York: Dutton, 1976.
    Statements by filmmakers and critics about the documentary art from the earliest days to recent times.

MacCann, Richard Dyer. *The People's Films: A Political History of U.S. Government Motion Pictures.* New York: Hastings, 1973.
    The best short survey of the pioneers in "public information" in England and the United States, beginning with the 1930s and working up to the era of television. Unusual for its interest in USIA productions.

Rosenthal, Alan, ed. *New Challenges for Documentary.* Berkeley: U of California P, 1971.
    Picks up where Barsam leaves off with emphasis on theory, criticism, history, *cinema vérité,* and ethnography.

Social Problem Films (800)

Roffman, Peter. *The Hollywood Social Problem Film: Madness, Despair, and Politics from the Depression to the Fifties*. Bloomington: Indiana UP, 1981.
Good library acquisition and a good starter volume.

Alexander, William. *Film on the Left: American Documentary Film from 1931 to 1942*. Princeton: Princeton UP, 1981.
An excellent exploration of the aesthetics and politics of a counter-Hollywood movement often very far to the Left.

Censorship (900)

Carman, Ira H. *Movies, Censorship, and the Law*. Ann Arbor: U of Michigan P, 1966.
An early survey, but very strong in the area of legislative and judicial aspects.

Leff, Leonard, and Jerold J. Simmons. *The Dame in the Kimono: Hollywood, Censorship, and the Production Code from the 1920s to the 1960s*. New York: Anchor, 1990.
Delightfully written survey based on files of the Production Code Administration and other archival sources.

Vizzard, Jack. *See No Evil: Life Inside a Hollywood Censor*. New York: Simon and Schuster, 1970.
Hilarious series of incidents from the experience of an "enforcer" of the Motion Picture Production Code.

Female and Minority Images (1000)

Cripps, Tom. *Slow-Fade to Black: The Negro in American Film, 1900-1942*. New York: Oxford, 1977.
A classic study of the black image based on scholarship that digs below the image.

Friedman, Lester. *The Jewish Image in American Film*. Secaucus: Citadel, 1987.
Historical overview: screen representations of a minority closely linked to the film industry.

Haskell, Molly. *From Reverence to Rape: The Treatment of Women in the Movies*. 2nd ed. Chicago: U of Chicago P, 1987.
A comprehensive survey, colorfully written.

242   In the Eye of the Beholder

Basinger, Jeanine. *A Woman's View: How Hollywood Spoke to Women, 1930-1960.* New York: Knopf, 1993.
   A solid approach to reception studies of film.

Fregoso, Rosa Linda. *Chicana and Chicano Film Culture.* Minneapolis: U of Minneopolis P, 1993.
   The best overview of the subject.

Devereaux, Leslie, and Rogers Hillman, eds. *Fields of Vision: Essays in Film Studies, Visual Anthropology, and Photography.* Berkeley: U of California P, 1995.
   A very focused text on representing different cultures and differences in visual meaning among cultures.

Norden, Martin. *The Cinema of Isolation: A History of Physical Disability in the Movies.* New Brunswick: Rutgers UP, 1994.
   An excellent study whose peculiar approach to film yields fascinating insights.

***Vietnam* (1001)**

Malo, Jean-Jacques. *Vietnam War Films.* Jefferson, NC: McFarland, 1994.
   An encyclopedia of Vietnam films from the U.S. and elsewhere, including the major films. Credits, synopses, and commentary for each film.

Rollins, Peter C. "Using Popular to Study the Vietnam War: Perils and Possibilities." *Popular Culture in the United States.* Ed. Peter Freese and Michael Porsche. Essen: Die Blau Eule, 1994: 221-31.
   Contains warnings about the high degree of subjectivity in Vietnam books and films.

Lanning, Michael Lee. *Vietnam at the Movies.* New York: Fawcett-Columbine, 1994.
   A Vietnam veteran assesses the cinematic heritage—with emphasis on the misinformation, stereotypes, etc. perpetuated by the Vietnam films.

Walker, Mark. *The Vietnam Veteran Films.* Metuchen: Scarecrow, 1991.
   Does not shy away from biker films, vigilante films, gangster films, horror films that construct their genre plots around the Vietnam veteran's dilemma.

Screenwriting **(1002)**

Engel, Joel. *Screenwriters on Screenwriting: The Best in the Business Discuss Their Craft.* New York: Hyperion, 1995.
 Recent reflections by scriptwriters on their work.

Hamilton, Ian. *The Writer in Hollywood, 1915-1951.* New York: Harper, 1990.
 Historical perspective on the writer's place in the system.

Journals and Periodicals (2000)

Cinema Journal. A quarterly journal that does not follow any single theoretical or political stance. Contact: U of Texas P, Journals Division, Austin, TX 78722-2250. $25/yr. in U.S.

Film & History. A quarterly, interdisciplinary journal aimed at humanists who wish to use film for research and teaching. Reviews, course descriptions, articles. Contact: Peter C. Rollins, Popular Culture Center, Rt. 3, Box 80, Cleveland, OK 74020 or http://h-net2.msu.edu/~filmhis $20/yr. in U.S.

Literature/Film Quarterly. Focuses on film adaptations of literary originals. Contact: Jim Welsh, English Dept, Salisbury St. U., Salisbury, MD 21801 or jxwelsh@ssu.edu $16/yr. in U.S.

Journal of Popular Film and Television. A pioneer journal that takes seriously the work of Hollywood with emphasis on genre, impact, and aesthetics. Contact: Heldref Publications, 1319 18th St. NW, Washington, DC 20036. $34/yr. in U.S.

Journal of Film and Video. Often carries special issues of interest to Americanists. Contact: Department of Communication, Georgia State U, Atlanta, GA 30303 or http://www.rtvf.nwu.edu/UFVA $15/yr. in U.S.

16

Selective Bibliography for Researching Television: Sources and Strategies

Robert J. Thompson

Like studies of the movies, but unlike those of Old English poetry, writing about television has two large and distinct audiences: those who read it for a living as scholars, teachers, and students, and those who read it because they love the subject. Not surprisingly, then, this writing falls into two separate categories. For the first audience, there are academic books and serious articles in scholarly journals; for the second, there are fan books and profiles in *People* magazine. While this bibliography will tend to focus on the former, the latter shouldn't be dismissed out of hand. Serious students of television should avail themselves of any useful data, and the literature of fandom often supplies a lot of valuable ideas and information between all the pictures and trivia tests.

As for the more scholarly research on television, most of it has appeared in the last twenty years. During that time, television studies has emerged as a healthy, independent academic discipline. But unlike disciplines such as literature, music, and the nonelectronic visual arts, which have produced centuries of old-fashioned historic/biographic/bibliographic studies on their subjects before turning to the text- and context-based approaches of contemporary theory, television studies jumped right in with the specialized language and approach of poststructuralist and postmoderninst theory. While there are a number of excellent books on how audiences make meaning out of the TV they watch, for example, there are surprising few historical and biographical studies about the television tradition and the people who created that tradition. This brings us to the first part of the bibliography.

Part 1: The Popular Tradition

Authorship

For most of its history, television has been an anonymous medium. Most people know the names of authors they have never read much better than the names of creators of TV shows that they watch every week. Even television scholarship has to a great extent eschewed the careful study of the people who make programs. By the time TV studies began to thrive in the late 1970s and early 1980s, the auteur theory had fallen from grace in the academy as a hopelessly romantic and old-fashioned way of looking at texts. To date, the field has offered no counterpart to the hundreds of monographs on individual artists that cinema studies has produced.

There is, however, a small tradition of TV auteurism. Two of the earliest books,

Ravage, John. *Television: The Director's Viewpoint.* Boulder: Westview, 1978.
Wicking, Christopher, and Tise Vahimagi. *The American Vein: Directors and Directions in Television.* New York: Dutton, 1979

tried to graft the director-centered notion of film auteurism onto the medium of television. The title of the book by Wicking et al. even paid homage to Andrew Sarris's seminal auteurist volume, *The American Cinema: Directors and Directions, 1929-1968.* While not deliberately, these two books managed to prove that series television was not a director's medium.

For the few who were doing television authorship studies, attention soon shifted to the producer. Muriel Cantor's book,

Cantor, Muriel. *The Hollywood TV Producer: His Work and His Audience.* New York: Basic, 1971.

had already acknowledged that TV was a "producer's medium," but her study was more concerned with the sociology of production, rather than with the shows themselves. One of the earliest auteurist pieces that took the producer as the principal creative entity was

Marc, David. "TV Auteurism." *American Film* Nov. 1981: 52-81.

Marc followed this with two books that included extended chapters on the works of individual producers:

——. *Comic Visions: Television Comedy and American Culture.* Boston: Unwin, 1989.
——. *Demographic Vistas.* Philadelphia: U of Pennsylvania P, 1984.

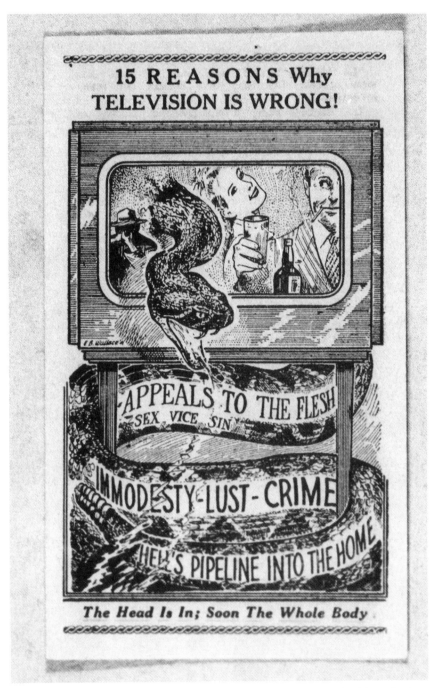

Frontispiece to an early 1950s polemic distributed by the Pilgrim Tract Society of Randleman, North Carolina. (Courtesy of the Winconsin Center for Film and Theater Research)

The first important book to announce the new approach, however, was

Newcomb, Horace, and Robert S. Alley. *The Producer's Medium: Conversations with the Creators of American TV.* New York: Oxford UP, 1983.

Newcomb and Alley offered a thoughtful theoretical essay positioning the producer within the complex TV production process as an introduction to a collection of interviews with eleven important television artists. A few years later, two of the producers Newcomb and Alley had interviewed, Richard Levinson and William Link, the prolific team that created a number of acclaimed series and TV-movies, released a similar collection of interviews:

Levinson, Richard, and William Link. *Off Camera: Conversations with the Makers of Prime-time Television.* New York: Plume/New American Library, 1986.

Individual studies dedicated to specific producers and writers are still few and far between, but there are some, including:

Clum, John M. *Paddy Chayefsky.* Boston: Twayne, 1976.
Considine, Shaun. *Mad as Hell: The Life and Work of Paddy Chayefsky.* New York: Random House, 1994.
Davis, Donald M. "Auteur Film Criticism as a Vehicle for Television Criticism." *Feedback* 26.1 (1984).
Engel, Joel. *Rod Serling: The Dreams and Nightmares of Life in The Twilight Zone.* Chicago: Contemporary Books,1989.
Marc, David, and Robert Thompson. *Prime Time, Prime Movers: America's Greatest TV Shows and the People Who Created Them.* Boston: Little, Brown, 1992.
Sander, Gordon F. *Serling: The Rise and Twilight of Television's Last Angry Man.* New York: Dutton, 1992.
Stempel, Tom. *Storytellers to the Nation: A History of American Television Writing.* New York: Continuum, 1992.
Thompson, Robert J., and Gary Burns, eds. *Adventures on Prime Time: The Television Shows of Stephen J. Cannell.* New York: Praeger, 1990.
——. *Making Television: Authorship and the Production Process.* New York: Praeger, 1990.
Wakefield, Dan. *All Her Children: The Real Life Story of America's Favorite Soap Opera.* Garden City: Doubleday, 1976.

More common than research about individual TV artists is work on institutional "authors," principally networks, studios, and production companies. These studies serve to remind us that television artist-producers work within a complex creative environment and that many forces are at work shaping what finally makes it to the screen.

Anderson, Chris. *Hollywood TV: The Studio System in the Fifties.* Austin: U of Texas P, 1994.

Bedell, Sally. *Up the Tube: Prime-Time TV in the Silverman Years.* New York: Viking, 1981.

Block, Alex Ben. *Outfoxed: Marvin Davis, Barry Diller, Rupert Murdoch, Joan Rivers and the Inside Story of America's Fourth Television Network.* NewYork: St. Martin's, 1990.

Ettema, James, and D. Charles Whitney, eds. *Individuals in Mass Media Institutions: Creativity and Constraint.* Beverly Hills: Sage, 1982.

Feuer, Jane, Paul Kerr, and Tise Vahimagi, eds. *MTM: "Quality Television."* London: British Film Institute, 1984.

Perry, Jeb H. *Universal Television: The Studio and Its Programs, 1950-1980.* Metuchen: Scarecrow, 1983.

Quinlan, Sterling. *Inside ABC.* New York: Hastings, 1979.

Smith, Sally Bedell. *In All His Glory: The Life of William S. Paley.* New York: Simon and Schuster, 1990.

Woolley, Lynn, Robert W. Malsbary, and Robert G. Strange, Jr. *Warner Brothers Television.* Jefferson: McFarland, 1985.

Anderson's book is especially good in describing how major film studios like Disney and Warner Brothers brought and adapted their styles to early television; Bedell's demonstrates how extensively a strong network executive can influence programming; and the Feuer et al. anthology goes a long way in identifying the corporate aesthetic of an independent production company.

Several producers and executives have written memoirs that include valuable inside information about the television they oversaw. The reader must, of course, take care when evaluating any memoir. The life of William Paley as told by William Paley in *As It Happened,* for example, sounded a lot different when it was told by Sally Bedell Smith in *In All His Glory.*

Barris, Chuck. *Confessions of a Dangerous Mind.* New York: St. Martin's, 1984.

Goldenson, Leonard H., with Marvin J. Wolf. *Beating the Odds: The Untold Story behind the Rise of ABC.* New York: Scribner, 1991.

Levinson, Richard, and William Link. *Stay Tuned.* New York: Ace, 1981.

Marshall, Garry, with Lori Marshall. *Wake Me When It's Funny: How to Break into Show Business and Stay There.* Holbrook, MA: Adams, 1995.

Oppenheimer, Jess, and Gregg Oppenheimer. *Laughs, Luck and Lucy: How I Came to Create the Most Popular Sitcom of All Time.* Syracuse: Syracuse UP, 1996.

Paley, William S. *As It Happened.* Garden City: Doubleday,1979.

Schwartz, Sherwood. *Inside Gilligan's Island: From Creation to Syndication.* Jefferson: McFarland, 1988.

Spelling, Aaron, with Jefferson Graham. *Aaron Spelling: A Prime-Time Life.* New York: St. Martin's, 1996.

Tartikoff, Brandon, and Charles Leerhsen. *The Last Great Ride.* New York: Turtle Bay, 1992.

Tinker, Grant, and Bud Rukeyser. *Tinker in Television: From General Electric to General Sarnoff.* New York: Simon and Schuster, 1994.

Weaver, Pat, with Thomas M. Coffey. *The Best Seat in the House: The Golden Years of Radio and Television.* New York: Knopf, 1994.

Whitfield, Stephen E., and Gene Roddenberry. *The Making of Star Trek.* New York: Ballantine, 1968.

Text

The discipline's most obvious unit of study is the television program itself. Several important works have generated theory as to how we go about seriously watching TV.

Theory

A good place to start is an examination of the viewing experience. Raymond Williams warns, in

Williams, Raymond. *Television: Technology and Cultural Form.* New York: Schocken, 1974,

that the viewing experience consists not so much in watching discrete programs as an ongoing "flow" of televised material, which includes a substantial amount of interstitial programming. While written before the wireless remote became standard equipment in the American living room, Williams's ideas take on even more importance in the age of channel-surfing. Some especially good ideas about how the differences between the medium of TV and that of film impact on the way in which audiences consume programming can be found in

Ellis, John. *Visible Fictions: Cinema, Television, Video.* London: Routledge, 1982.

Strategies for examining televisual texts include the early and influential

Fiske, John, and John Hartley. *Reading Television.* London: Methuen, 1978.

which applied the methods of semiotics to TV. A similar approach can be
found in

Silverstone, Roger. *The Message of Television: Myth and Narrative in Contemporary Culture.* London: Heinemann, 1981.

Other important theoretical works include:

Caldwell, John Thorton. *Televisuality: Style, Crisis, and Authority in American
Television.* New Brunswick: Rutgers UP, 1995.
Conrad, Peter. *The Medium and Its Manners.* Boston: Routledge, 1982.
Fiske, John. *Television Culture.* London: Methuen, 1987.
Hartley, John. *Teleology: Studies in Television.* New York: Routledge, 1992.
Inglis, Fred. *Media Theory: An Introduction.* Oxford, UK: Basil Blackwell,
1990.
Jhally, Sut. *The Codes of Advertising: Fetishism and the Political Economy of
Meaning in the Consumer Society.* New York: Routledge, 1990.

Some of the best television theory can be found in the collections
cited in the anthology section of part 2 of this bibliography.

History

Theory is best applied in tandem with some knowledge of the historical context of the material under consideration. The best general
sources for this context are the following two:

Barnouw, Erik. *Tube of Plenty: The Evolution of American Television* 2nd rev.
ed. New York: Oxford UP, 1990,
MacDonald, J. Fred. *One Nation under Television: The Rise and Decline of Network TV.* Chicago: Nelson-Hall, 1990.

The most detailed programming history is currently out of print and
stops at 1981:

Castleman, Harry, and Walter J. Podrazik. *Watching TV: Four Decades of American Television.* New York: McGraw Hill, 1982.

While its coffee table book appearance has caused many scholars to overlook it, this is truly an invaluable resource.

Several more histories have emerged over the past half-dozen years that, when taken together, begin to paint a more complete picture of the medium's development.

Boddy, William. *Fifties Television: The Industry and Its Critics.* Urbana: U of Illinois P, 1990.

Feuer, Jane. *Seeing through the Eighties: Television and Reaganism.* Durham: Duke UP, 1995.

Gripsrud, Jostein. *The Dynasty Years: Hollywood Television and Critical Media Studies.* London: Routledge, 1995.

Heldenfels, R.D. *Television's Greatest Year, 1954.* New York: Continuum, 1994.

Thompson, Robert J. *Television's Second Golden Age: From Hill Street Blues to ER.* New York: Continuum, 1996.

Watson, Mary Ann. *The Expanding Vista: American Television in the Kennedy Years.* New York: Oxford UP, 1990.

Wilk, Max. *The Golden Age of Television: Notes from the Survivors.* New York: Dell, 1976.

Individual Shows and Genres

This is the area where fan books tend to be more numerous than scholarly monographs. There are now six books each on *The Andy Griffith Show* and *Gilligan's Island,* for example, including a cook book for each series. A few of the better fan books are listed below, but researchers should remember that even the more trivial of this variety of "study" often includes useful episode guides, interview material, and discussions of the production process.

Adler, Richard, ed. *All in the Family: A Critical Appraisal.* New York: Praeger, 1979.

Alley, Robert S., and Irby B. Brown. *Love Is All Around: The Making of the Mary Tyler Moore Show.* New York: Dell, 1989.

——. *Murphy Brown: Anatomy of a Sitcom.* New York: Dell, 1990.

Daniel, Douglass K. *Lou Grant: Journalism as Television Drama.* Syracuse: Syracuse UP, 1996.

Dawidziak, Mark. *The Columbo Phile.* New York: Mysterious, 1988.

Fuller, Linda K. *The Cosby Show: Audiences, Impact, and Implications.* Westport: Greenwood, 1992.

Hill, Doug, and Jeff Weingrad. *Saturday Night: A Backstage History of Saturday Night Live.* New York: Morrow, 1986.

Lavery, David, ed. *Full of Secrets: Critical Approaches to Twin Peaks.* Detroit: Wayne State UP, 1995.

Lavery, David, Angela Hague, and Marla Cartwright, eds. *'Trust No One': Reading The X-Files.* Syracuse: Syracuse UP, 1996.

McCarty, John, and Brian Kelleher. *Alfred Hitchcock Presents.* New York: St. Martin's, 1985.

Tulloch, John, and Manuel Alvarado. *Doctor Who: The Unfolding Text.* New York: St. Martin's, 1983.

Waldrom, Vince. *The Official Dick Van Dyke Show Book.* New York: Hyperion, 1994.

Wolper David L., with Quincy Troupe. *The Inside Story of TV's "Roots."* New York: Warner, 1978.

Zicree, Marc Scott. *The Twilight Zone Companion.* New York: Bantam, 1982.

Related to these studies are the "making of" books that give a good sense of how the production process works. Two recent accounts,

Muse, Vance. *We Bombed In Burbank.* Reading: Addison-Wesley, 1994.

Paisner, Daniel. *Horizontal Hold: The Making and Breaking of a Network Television Pilot.* New York: Birch Lane, 1992.

give fascinating descriptions of the conception, selling, making, and failure of a contemporary TV pilot. Since many more pilots are rejected than are developed into series, these books offer a glimpse at what happens to most series ideas. The very best chronicle of a failed pilot, and one of the most rousing stories about the TV industry is still

Miller, Merle, and Evan Rhodes. *Only You, Dick Daring!* New York: Sloane, 1964.

Other examinations of the production process include

Alvarado, Manuel, and Edward Buscomb. *Hazell: The Making of a TV Series.* London: British Film Institute, 1978.

Elliott, Philip. *The Making of a Television Series.* London: Constable, 1972.

Silverstone, Roger. *Framing Science: The Making of a BBC Documentary.* London: British Film Institute, 1985.

Outdated but still filled with useful ideas, the classic genre study, is

Newcomb, Horace. *TV: The Most Popular Art.* New York: Anchor, 1974.

More recent studies of individual TV genres include

Bruce, Steve. *Pray TV: Televangelism in America.* New York: Routledge, 1990.

Himmelstein, Hal. *Television Myth and the American Mind.* New York: Praeger, 1984.

Kaminsky, Stuart, and Jeffrey H. Mahan. *American Television Genres.* Chicago: Nelson-Hall, 1985.

Kaplan, E. Ann. *Rockin' Around the Clock: Music Television, Postmodernism, and Consumer Culture.* New York: Methuen, 1987.

MacDonald, J. Fred. *Who Shot the Sheriff?: The Rise and Fall of the Television Western.* New York: Praeger, 1987.

Munson, Wayne. *All Talk: The Talkshow in Media Culture.* Philadelphia: Temple UP, 1996.

Rose, Brian, ed. *TV Genres: A Handbook and Reference Guide.* Westport: Greenwood, 1985.

Taylor, Ella. *Prime-Time Families.* Berkeley: U of California P, 1989.

Turow, Joseph. *Playing Doctor: Television, Storytelling, and Medical Power.* New York: Oxford UP, 1989.

Reception

A major thread of contemporary theory operates on the assumption that meaning is generated by the consumers of any given text. While a television show may have a "dominant reading," there are potentially as many interpretations as there are viewers. A pioneering work in this area was

Morley, David. *The "Nationwide" Audience.* London: British Film Institute, 1980.

but since *Nationwide* is unavailable to most viewers this side of the Atlantic, some of the following titles might prove more useful to American students of the television audience.

Allen Robert C. "Audience-Oriented Criticism and Television." *Channels of Discourse, Reassembled.* Ed. Robert C. Allen. Chapel Hill: U of North Carolina P, 1992. 101-37.

——. *Speaking of Soap Operas.* Chapel Hill: U of North Carolina P, 1985.

Ang, Ien. *Desperately Seeking the Audience.* New York: Routledge, 1991.

——. *Watching Dallas: Soap Opera and the Melodramatic Imagination.* London: Methuen, 1985.

Berman, Ronald. *How Television Sees Its Audience: A Look at the Looking Glass.* Newbury Park: Sage, 1987.

Buckingham, David. *Public Secrets: Eastenders and Its Audience.* London: British Film Institute, 1987.

Buzzard, Karen S. *Chains of Gold: Marketing the Ratings and Rating the Markets.* Metuchen: Scarecrow, 1990.

Drummond, Philip, and Richard Paterson, eds. *Television and Its Audience.* London: British Film Institute, 1988.

Fowles, Jib. *Why Viewers Watch: A Reappraisal of Television's Effects.* Newbury Park: Sage, 1992.

Harrington, C. Lee, and Denise D. Bielby. *Soap Fans: Pursuing Pleasure and Making Meaning in Everyday Life.* Philadelphia: Temple UP, 1995.

Jenkins, Henry. *Textual Poachers: Television Fans and Participatory Culture.* New York: Routledge, 1992.

Lewis, Justin. *The Ideological Octopus: An Exploration of Television and Its Audience.* New York: Routledge, 1991.

Livingstone, Sonia M. *Making Sense of Television: The Psychology of Audience Interpretation.* New York: Pergamon, 1990.

Morley, David. *Family Television: Cultural Power and Domestic Leisure.* London: Comedia, 1986.

Seiter, Ellen, Hans Borchers, Gabriele Kreutzner, and Eva-Maria Warth, eds. *Remote Control: Television Audiences and Cultural Power.* New York: Routledge, 1989.

Selnow, Gary W., and Richard R. Gilbert. *Society's Impact on Television: How the Viewing Public Shapes Television Programming.* New York: Praeger, 1993.

Tulloch, John. *Television Drama: Agency, Audience and Myth.* New York: Routledge, 1990.

Part 2: Assession the Contemporary Cultural Landscape

Television and Gender, Race, and Ethnicity

The representation of race and gender on television has been one of the field's major areas of concern. These issues tend to be found in many of the works cited throughout this bibliography as well as in many of the essays collected in the anthologies listed later. Some of the best books on the subject are:

Baehr, Helen, and Ann Gray. *Turning It On: A Reader in Women and the Media.* New York: St. Martin's, 1995.

Baehr, Helen, and Gillian Dyer, eds. *Boxed In: Women and Television.* New York: Pandora, 1987.

D'Acci, Julie. *Defining Women: Television and the Case of Cagney & Lacey.* Chapel Hill: U of North Carolina P, 1994.

Dates, Jannette, and William Barlow. *Split Image: African Americans in the Mass Media.* Washington, D.C.: Howard UP, 1990.

Fiske, John. *Media Matters: Race and Gender in U.S. Politics.* Rev. ed. Minneapolis: U of Minnesota P, 1996.

Gray, Herman. *Watching Race: Television and the Struggle for "Blackness."* Minneapolis: U of Minnesota P, 1995

Hamamoto, Darrell Y. *Monitored Peril: Asian Americans and the Politics of TV Representation.* Minneapolis: U of Minnesota P, 1994.

——. *Nervous Laughter: Television Situation Comedy and Liberal Democratic Ideology.* New York: Praeger, 1989.

Heide, Margaret J. *Television Culture and Women's Lives: Thirtysomething and the Contradictions of Gender.* Philadelphia: U of Pennsylvania P, 1995.

Kaplan, E. Ann. "Feminist Criticism and Television." *Channels of Discourse, Reassembled.* Ed. Robert C. Allen. Chapel Hill: U of North Carolina P, 1992. 247-83.

Lester, Paul M., ed. *Images That Injure: Pictorial Stereotypes in the Media.* New York: Praeger, 1996

Lewis, Lisa. *Gender, Politics, and MTV: Voicing the Difference.* Philadelphia: Temple UP, 1990

MacDonald, J. Fred. *Blacks and White TV: African-Americans in Television Since 1948.* 2nd ed. Chicago: Nelson-Hall, 1992.

Meehan, Diane M. *Ladies of the Evening: Women Characters of Prime-Time Television.* Metuchen: Scarecrow, 1983.

Montgomery, Kathryn C. *Target: Prime Time. Advocacy Groups and the Struggle Over Entertainment Television.* New York: Oxford UP, 1990.

Noble, Gil. *Black Is the Color of My TV Tube.* Secaucus: Stuart, 1981.

Noriega, Chon, and Ana M. Lopez. *The Ethnic Eye: Latino Media Arts.* Minneapolis: U of Minnesota P, 1996.

Pribram, E. Deidre, ed. *Female Spectators: Looking at Film and Television.* New York: Verso, 1988.

Shaheen, Jack. *The TV Arab.* Bowling Green, OH: Bowling Green State University Popular Press, 1984.

Spigel, Lynn. *Make Room for TV: Television and the Family Ideal in Postwar America.* Chicago: U of Chicago P, 1992.

Spigel, Lynn, and Denise Mann, eds. *Private Screenings: Television and the Female Consumer.* Minneapolis: U of Minnesota P, 1992.

Wilson, Clint, and Felix Gutierrez. *Race, Multiculturalism, and the Media: From Mass to Class Communication.* Thousand Oaks: Sage, 1995.

Television, Culture, and the Entertainment-Industrial Complex

The works listed in this catch-all category, by both scholars and journalists, attempt to position popular television and the television industries into a wider cultural context. Gitlin and Auletta, for example, describe the administrative workings of network TV with a degree of detail unavailable anywhere else, and Bianculli and Marc do the same for our own industry, the serious study of television.

Auletta, Ken. *Three Blind Mice: How the TV Networks Lost Their Way.* New York: Random House, 1991.

Bianculli, David. *Teleliteracy: Taking Television Seriously.* New York: Continuum, 1992.

Brown, Les. *Television: The Business Behind the Box.* New York: Harcourt, 1971.

Christensen, Mark, and Cameron Stauth. *The Sweeps: Behind the Scenes in Network TV.* New York: Morrow, 1984.

Cowan, Geoffrey. *See No Evil: The Backstage Battle Over Sex and Violence in Television.* New York: Simon & Schuster, 1979.

Gitlin, Todd. *Inside Prime Time.* New York: Pantheon, 1983.

Kellner, Douglas. *Television and the Crisis of Democracy.* Boulder: Westview, 1990.

Marc, David. *Bonfire of the Humanities: Television, Subliteracy, and Long-Term Memory Loss.* Syracuse: Syracuse UP, 1995.

Marling, Karal Ann. *As Seen on TV: The Visual Culture of Everyday Life in the 1950s.* Cambridge: Harvard UP, 1994.

Miller, Mark Crispin. *Boxed In: The Culture of TV.* Evanston: Northwestern UP, 1988.

Spitzer, Matthew L. *Seven Dirty Words and Six Other Stories: Controlling the Content of Print and Broadcast.* New Haven: Yale UP, 1986.

Tichi, Cecelia. *Electronic Hearth: Creating an American Television Culture.* New York: Oxford UP, 1989.

Anthologies of Critical Essays
As recently as fifteen or twenty years ago, there were few academic journals that would publish articles about television. To fill the void, the anthology emerged as one of the principal means by which scholarly pieces were distributed. Readers are directed to these for examples of a wide variety of critical approaches and methodologies. The pioneer,

Newcomb, Horace. *Television: The Critical View.* 5th ed. New York: Oxford UP, 1994.

was first published in 1976, and is now in its fifth edition. Older editions are worth investigating for valuable essays that didn't make it into the updated version.

Others anthologies include:

Adler, Richard, and Douglas Cater, eds. *Understanding Television: Essays on Television as a Social and Cultural Force.* New York: Praeger, 1981.

Allen, Robert C. *Channels of Discourse, Reassembled.* Chapel Hill: U of North Carolina P, 1992.

Batra, Narayan Dass, ed. *The Hour of Television: Critical Approaches.* Metuchen: Scarecrow, 1987.

Bennett, Tony, Susan Boyd-Bowman, Colin Mercer, and Janet Woollacott, eds. *Popular Television and Film.* London: British Film Institute, 1981.

D'Agostino, Peter, ed. *Transmission: Theory and Practice for a New Television Aesthetics.* New York: Tanham, 1985.

Drummond, Philip, and Richard Paterson, eds. *Television in Transition.* London: British Film Institute, 1985.

Gitlin, Todd, ed. *Watching Television.* New York: Pantheon, 1986.

Goodwin, Andrew, and Garry Whannel, eds. *Understanding Television.* New York: Routledge, 1990.

Hanhardt, John G., ed. *Video Culture: A Critical Investigation.* Layton, UT: Peregrine Smith, 1986.

Henderson, Katherine Usher, and Joseph Anthony Mazzeo, eds. *Meanings of the Medium: Perspectives on the Art of Television.* New York: Praeger, 1990.

Kaplan, E. Ann, ed. *Regarding Television.* Frederick, MD: University Publications of America, 1983.

MacCabe, Colin, ed. *High Theory/Low Culture: Analyzing Popular Television and Film.* Manchester, UK: Manchester UP, 1986.

Mellencamp, Patricia, ed. *Logics of Television: Essays in Cultural Criticism.* Bloomington: Indiana UP, 1990.

Modleski, Tania, ed. *Studies in Entertainment: Critical Approaches to Mass Culture.* Bloomington: Indiana UP, 1986.

Rowland, Willard D., Jr., and Bruce Watkins, eds. *Interpreting Television: Current Research Perspectives.* Beverly Hills, CA: Sage, 1984.

Vande Berg, Leah R., and Lawrence A. Wenner, eds. *Television Criticism: Approaches and Applications.* New York: Longman, 1991.

Part 3: Reference Books and Archives

The best general encyclopedias of American television are the following two. Both cover significant programs, people, and events that have shaped the television industry.

Bianculli, David. *Dictionary of Teleliteracy.* New York: Continuum, 1996.

Brown, Les. *Les Brown's Encyclopedia of Television.* 3rd ed. Detroit: Visible Ink, 1992.

Most of American TV's program history is reasonably well documented in a growing collection of reference works. The most indispensible single-volume guide is

Brooks, Tim, and Earle Marsh. *The Complete Directory to Prime Time Network and Cable TV Shows, 1946–Present.* 6th ed. New York: Ballantine, 1995.

Complete scheduling, casting, and series premise data is given for nearly every prime-time series, along with some interesting historical and critical factoids. The major limitation of this book is that it is restricted to prime-time series, thereby omitting soap operas, most game shows, and other series that aired during off-prime dayparts. For these, one must turn to

Alex McNeil. *Total Television: A Comprehensive Guide to Programming from 1948 to the Present.* 4th ed. New York: Penguin, 1996.

Besides including the entire TV schedule, McNeil often names the creators and producers of the series, which are conveniently indexed. Updated editions, unfortunately, are infrequent.

The following titles provide more detailed and specific programming information:

Bianculli, David. *The Dictionary of Teleliteracy.* New York: Continuum, 1996.
Castleman, Harry, and Walter J. Podrazik. *Harry and Wally's Favorite TV Shows.* New York: Prentice-Hall, 1989.
——. *The TV Schedule Book: Four Decades of Network Programming from Sign-On to Sign-Off.* New York: McGraw-Hill,1984.
Einstein, Daniel. *Special Edition: A Guide to Network Television Documentary Series and Special News Reports, 1955-1979.* Metuchen: Scarecrow, 1987.
Eisner, Joel, and David Krinsky. *Television Comedy Series: An Episode Guide to 153 TV Sitcoms in Syndication.* Jefferson: McFarland, 1984.
Erickson, Hal. *Syndicated Television: The First Forty Years, 1947-1987.* Jefferson: McFarland, 1989.
Gianakos, Larry James. *Television Drama Programming: A Comprehensive Chronicle.* 6 vols. Metuchen: Scarecrow, 1978, 1980, 1981, 1983, 1987, 1992.

Gianakos's monumental collection contains complete episode air-dates for most dramatic prime-time series. Some listings also include titles, writers, directors, and other production data. For all its irregularities, this is a very important, if comparatively unknown, resource.

Goldberg, Lee. *Unsold Television Pilots, 1955-1988.* Jefferson: McFarland, 1990.

Marill, Alvin H. *Movies Made for Television: The Telefeature and the Mini-Series, 1964-1986.* New York: Zoetrope, 1987.

Shapiro, M.E. *Television Network Daytime and Late-Night Programming, 1959-1989.* Jefferson: McFarland, 1990.

——. *Television Network Prime-Time Programming, 1948-1988.* Jefferson: McFarland, 1989.

Terrace, Vincent. *Encyclopedia of Television: Series, Pilots, and Specials.* 3 vols. New York: Zoetrope, 1986.

——. *Fifty Years of Television: A Guide to Series and Pilots, 1937-1988.* New York: Cornwall, 1991.

Woolery, George. *Children's Television: The First Thirty-Five Years, 1946-1981.* 2 vols. Metuchen: Scarecrow, 1983, 1985.

Listings of actors' credits can be found in:

Brooks, Tim. *The Complete Directory to Prime Time TV Stars, 1946-Present.* New York: Ballantine, 1987.

The Brooks guide is of limited use, however, because it only lists credits for ongoing roles in television series. Much more comprehensive listings are included in:

Parish, James Robert. *Actors' Television Credits 1950-1972.* Metuchen: Scarecrow, 1973.

—— *Actors' Television Credits, Supplement I, 1973-1976.* Metuchen: Scarecrow, 1978.

Parish, James Robert, and Vincent Terrace. *Actors' Television Credits, Supplement II, 1977-1981.* Metuchen: Scarecrow, 1982.

As for obtaining copies of television shows, the best bet is still a solid cable package, a VCR, a subscription to *TV Guide,* and a lot of patience. While most good libraries hold a copy of *MTM: "Quality Television,"* for example, very few offer videotaped episodes of *The Mary Tyler Moore Show.* For that you must depend on services like *Nick at Nite.*

An increasingly large body of television material is now available on home video. The best distributor is Movies Unlimited in Philadelphia. The current catalog (obtainable by calling 1-800-4MOVIES) has 47 densely packed four-column pages of TV offerings from *The Texaco Star Theater* to *The X-Files.*

Several excellent archives do exist across the country, most notably the Museum of Television and Radio in New York, but in most cases tapes must be viewed on the premises. A review of these archives can be found in the following:

Culbert, David. "Television Archives." *Critical Studies in Mass Communication* Mar. 1984: 88-92.

Godfrey, D. G. *A Directory of Broadcast Archives.* Washington, D.C.: Broadcast Education Association, 1983.

Slide, A., P. K. Hanson, and S. L. Hanson. *Sourcebook for the Performing Arts: A Directory of Collections, Resources, Scholars, and Critics in Theatre, Film, and Television.* Westport: Greenwood, 1988.

Contributors

Carolyn Anderson is associate professor and director of graduate studies in the Department of Communication at the University of Massachusetts at Amherst. She is coauthor, with Thomas W. Benson, of two books on the documentary films of Frederick Wiseman.

Bruce A. Austin is a research consultant based in Pittsford, New York.

William J. Brown is professor and dean of the College of Communication Arts at Regent University. His teaching and research interests focus on the international and intercultural dimensions of social influence and the use of entertainment-education strategies for social change.

Rod Carveth is chair of the Department of Mass Communication at the University of Bridgeport. He is author of over 30 articles and book chapters, and coeditor of *Media Economics: Theory and Practice*.

John G. Cawelti is professor of English at the University of Kentucky and author of *Adventure, Mystery, and Romance; The Six-Gun Mystique; The Spy Story;* and other books and essays on popular culture and American literature.

Gary R. Edgerton is professor and chair of the Communication and Theatre Arts Department at Old Dominion University. He is senior associate editor of the *Journal of Popular Film and Television*, and has more than fifty publications on film, television, and culture topics in a variety of books and journals.

Kathryn H. Fuller is assistant professor in the History Department at Virginia Commonwealth University. She is the author of *At the Picture Show: Small-Town Audiences and the Creation of Movie Fan Culture* and coauthor of *Children and the Movies: Media Influence and the Payne Fund Controversy* (with Garth Jowett and Ian Jarvie). She is currently working on a study of itinerant film exhibition in upstate New York.

263

Michael T. Marsden is dean of the College of Arts and Sciences and professor of English at Northern Michigan University. He is the coordinator of the Northern Michigan University Press, continues to coedit the *Journal of Popular Film and Television,* and has coedited eight books, including *Movies as Artifacts: Cultural Criticism of Popular Film; Directory of Popular Culture Collections;* and *The Culture of Celebrations,* and authored more than sixty scholarly articles.

Jack Nachbar is emeritus professor of Popular Culture at Bowling Green State University and coeditor of the *Journal of Popular Film and Television.* His publications include three books and numerous articles on western movies.

Martin F. Norden teaches film as a professor of Communication at the University of Massachusetts at Amherst. Portions of his essay were adapted from his book *The Cinema of Isolation: A History of Physical Disability in the Movies.* His most recent book is *John Barrymore: A Bio-Bibliography.*

Laurie Ouellette is a doctoral candidate in Communication at the University of Massachusetts at Amherst. She has published essays in *Transmission: Toward a Post-Television Culture* and *The Velvet Light Trap.*

George Plasketes is associate professor of Radio-Television-Film at Auburn University. He regularly publishes in the *Journal of Popular Culture; Studies in Popular Culture;* and *Popular Music and Society.* His latest book is *Images of Elvis Presley in American Culture, 1977-1997: The Mystery Terrain.*

Peter C. Rollins is regents professor of English and American/Film Studies at Oklahoma State University, where he teaches classes in film and society, and film aesthetics. He has made a number of historical films and edits *Film & History.* Readers can visit Film & History's Web site at http://h-net2.msu.edu/~filmhis/

Arvind Singhal is associate professor in the School of Interpersonal Communication at Ohio University. His teaching and research interests focus on the diffusion of innovations, communication and national development, and the educational uses of entertainment media.

Gaylyn Studlar is professor of Film Studies and English at the University of Michigan, Ann Arbor, where she also directs the Program in Film and Video Studies. Her books include *This Mad Masquerade: Stardom and Masculinity in the Jazz Age* and *Visions of the East: Orientalism in Film.*

J. P. Telotte is professor in the Literature, Communication, and Culture program at Georgia Institute of Technology. He is the editor of *The Cult Film Experience,* and author of *Dreams of Darkness: Fantasy and the Films of Val Lewton; Voices in the Dark: The Narrative Patterns of Film Noir;* and *Replications: A Robotic History of the Science Fiction Film.*

Robert J. Thompson is professor and director of the Center for the Study of Popular Television in the S. I. Newhouse School of Public Communication at Syracuse University. He is the author or editor of five books on prime-time TV, including, most recently, *Television's Second Golden Age: From Hill Street Blues to ER.* He is also general editor of an ongoing book series about television for Syracuse University Press.

Gregory A. Waller is professor at the University of Kentucky where he teaches film and popular culture. His most recent book, *Main Street Amusements: Movies and Commercial Entertainment in a Southern City, 1896-1930,* was awarded the Theatre Library Association's prize as best book in film studies for 1995.

Index

General Index

Film/TV Index